# the
# LIFE
# to
# COME

## Re-Creating Retirement

## STEVEN M. TIPTON

### Foreword by Martin E. Marty

## The Life to Come: Re-Creating Retirement

The General Board of Higher Education and Ministry leads and serves The United Methodist Church in the recruitment, preparation, nurture, education, and support of Christian leaders—lay and clergy—for the work of making disciples of Jesus Christ for the transformation of the world. Its vision is that a new generation of Christian leaders will commit boldly to Jesus Christ and be characterized by intellectual excellence, moral integrity, spiritual courage, and holiness of heart and life. The General Board of Higher Education and Ministry of The United Methodist Church serves as an advocate for the intellectual life of the church. The Board's mission embodies the Wesleyan tradition of commitment to the education of laypersons and ordained persons by providing access to higher education for all persons.

Wesley's Foundery Books is named for the abandoned foundery that early followers of John Wesley transformed into a church, which became the cradle of London's Methodist movement.

## The Life to Come: Re-Creating Retirement

**HIGHER EDUCATION & MINISTRY**
General Board of Higher Education and Ministry
THE UNITED METHODIST CHURCH

As a story of the life to come re-created
across generations, this book is dedicated
to Ann, Louise, Elaine, and Mark,
my companions all along the way,
to Evan and all our children, and to theirs.

# CONTENTS

CONTENTS

# FOREWORD

*he Life to Come: Re-Creating Retirement* is sure to engage anyone who reads it. Anyone? Should younger generations read it and join those poised to retire, whether they are age sixty-four or sixty-nine, seventy-four or seventy-nine, or more? They do have reason to read it, for the same reason they read books on the financing of retirement, whether they do so in the panic of immediacy or the leisure that long-range planners can enjoy. That would itself provide a sufficient market to make the effort worthwhile to a publisher or to anyone who has an eye on the millions who annually face existential, spiritual, and dream-worthy personal looks ahead. The multitude of caregivers to people of age or those who have in mind and on conscience someone approaching retirement, and those who anticipate needing care for age-appropriate concerns, are targets of this text. This includes people in health care, housing, entertainment, counseling, and pastoral care, among other fields. Of course, *anyone* in the prime of life might welcome this book as a guide to mapping out post-prime adventurous living.

How, you may ask, can an author of a single book reach such a complex potential audience? Read on and you will see why. Professor Tipton, to all who have read his work, studied with him, or, more casually, experienced his speaking, teaching, and friendship, is known as one who offers others gifts gained from extensive reading, searching, and research. That being the case, Tipton includes the counsel of experienced and expert professionals and scholars as well as everyday people to bring substance to the book. Tipton is a dialogically minded scholar, which means that he first listens. His format and style help lift this book above so many works of counsel and advice, because it follows the pattern described in Martin Buber's great *I and Thou*, that philosopher's personal and personalizing counterpart to works that Buber himself would see as full of citations and concepts but lacking awareness of and engagement with "the other," whoever he or she may be, or however many belong to this company.

We are all aware of experts who contribute to the genre of books whose titles begin "How to . . .". Let me hasten to insert in anticipation of criticism: the how-to genre, often panned and satirized when its output is superficial or directed to those who seek quick solutions to problems that have long nagged them, can offer many assets. There are good reasons to speak well of any program or book that helps people learn how to cope, plan, deal with grief, have a good time, and more. But to plunder a cliché, easy come, easy go. When a stranger, even a published billionaire, issues impersonal advice of a practical nature, an audience or a readership may be drawn emotionally to an assurance of quick-fixes and one-size-fits-all answers to complex personal questions that do not deliver. By contrast, Tipton is an author who listens, who notices. Think of this book as a guide to *avoiding* impersonal quick-fixes.

How can a book offer how-to lessons without falling into the superficiality trap? One answer: read this book and see how carefully Tipton avoids the impersonal and cliché versions of advice giving. Those who read this book will be introduced, or reintroduced, to experts whose work bears on reflecting on the life to come, including how to address and master many of the arts of living in retirement.

When I first began to read this book, I thought it was heavily academic in the conventional sense; as a friend of mine likes to say, "Even the footnotes have footnotes." But as I read on and kept following the notes, I soon found that here was the Tipton who knows the literature of aging, sociology of religion, and relevant angles on the culture in which the life to come unfolds. I must suggest why this feature is so obvious. The culture of academe, to which I happily belong, invites abstraction. Naturally, what I began to do when anticipating the life to come was to build on reading and research from decades encountered before, and then to deal with philosophically rich depictions and counsels about aging.

On my night table is a copy of Cicero's *De Senectute*, helpfully translated on the title page as *On Old Age*. The reason I have kept the book and given it an accessible place is that it was a final gift from a best friend to my wife, a singer, and to me, a nonsinger, from a friend and his wife, a singer. One of the two Ciceronian books bound with it is *De Amicitia* (*On Friendship*). My late friend, with that gift, helped link forever in my mind both aging and friendship. The friend's inscription reads: "Remembering our long walk and conversation through the years, made into song by Harriet and Joan." I go on at such length, because it typifies the address to events, experiences, communication, and implied counsel, which Steven Tipton's book so well captures.

In my mind, the inscription in that gift book matches the thesis of Tipton's book: how friendship and other gifts of company and congregation on the "long walk and conversation through the years" play their part in dealing with the life to come. How crammed, yet easily walked with, are concepts in Tipton's titles: dreams, doubts, money, selves, souls, and, for me, one of the most helpful chapters, congregating—in this case, across generations. Many people I know who counsel the very aged do all they can to bring together children and the aged, whether in their natural families or in formal caregiving locales and situations, including the sacred.

Did I intrude on and confuse the plot by introducing that personal note? Does doing so potentially violate the "ethos and promise" of retirement? If doing so is out of bounds, then Professor Tipton is living out of bounds. He could and sometimes does write condensed formal pieces dependent on some abstraction. But this book is of a different genre.

I am writing this in the five hundredth October since the beginning of Martin Luther's Reformation, and I am reminded of his awareness of genre. I will paraphrase something he confessed about his central teaching, which was the Pauline justification by faith. Although he wrote volumes on it, he confessed he did not like to preach on it. Why? Because in its formal way and with its abstractions, he lost the congregation. Some of the congregants, he complained, fell asleep, others chatted, still others wandered out. So what did the legendary theologian of justification by faith do to reach the congregation? He knew the people, and "so [he] told stories." Readers will find many engrossing, involving, and informing stories on Tipton's pages. They will stay awake and stay engaged with the chapters.

A theologian-mentor of mine, the late Joseph Sittler, allowed me to publish an interview he gave to a young theologian-pastor. Sittler called the topic something like "the peculiar loneliness of the very aged." When he spoke his words in the recorded dialogue, he was virtually blind; his ill wife was not capable of conversing; and many of his friends had died. We learned what relating to him meant, to him and to us. An organist and his singer-wife and my wife and I would visit the Sittlers and sing hymns and songs that helped "Joe" come freshly alert, even though his wife, a few feet away, could not converse or sing anymore. After the songs, the professor would tell what he had been reading lately—theology, *Moby Dick*, Henry Adams, or works of humor— although he was not quite "reading." The authors of the recorded books that he listened to had become his companions. He regarded them as conversation partners, more than we could have imagined.

This book is not about the care of the very aged but about facing and growing into retirement. But, given Tipton's ability to summon sources and include "the other" in narrative and counsel, I picture that readers will be better prepared for the book's final subject: "Waking Up to Tomorrow," which means living that life worth living.

Martin E. Marty

# PREFACE

*ON THE SEVENTH DAY*
*RETIREMENT AS ETHOS AND PROMISE*

On the seventh day God rested. What about us? Some 80 million Americans born between 1946 and 1964—a third of the nation's workers—are now retiring at the rate of ten thousand every day. They will keep coming for two decades. They will live at least eighteen years on average beyond the age of sixty-five, closer to a quarter of a lifetime than a sabbatical seventh. Will they have the time of their life? What will they make of it? Over the next twenty years, they will double the number of those on Medicare and Social Security, and thin by a third the ranks of payroll taxpayers per retiree. This seismic shift will drive national debates over public provision and public debt, taxes and spending, for the future we foresee.[1] Closer to home, this tidal wave of retirement will alter the moral rhythm and flow of American life and its social arrangement. It will offer extraordinary opportunities and challenges to congregational communities in particular to engage the aspirations of a legion of newly active volunteers and channel commitments of the faithful to serve the commonweal. It will open church doors wider to a generation of Americans remarkable for their selective, shifting participation in religious institutions, both in their organizational involvement and their giving, no less than their spiritual enthusiasm.[2] What will we make of it?

What must we do to make our dreams
come true? What can we do together to
keep the promise of the American dream?

Now is the time to think twice about retirement. Not only about its public policy and planning in the face of contested crisis, but about its ethos, woven into our own dreams and doubts of retirement, what we imagine and yearn for, what we fear and worry about. What must we do for ourselves to make our dreams come true? What can we only do together to keep the promise of the American dream?

Each of us can compose an intimate story of our own retirement only because we share a cultural constellation of images and ideals to stage its action, plot its drama, and judge its value, as we seek to live it out. Ideals and stories of retirement multiply and divide in our culture. They stretch across the social landscape of our institutions, from iconic advertising through financial planning strategies to retirement communities made in utopian images of endless play, romance, and civic harmony that counterpoint public debates over retirement rights and responsibilities, interests and obligations. So our snapshots and stories of hard workers, warm lovers, caring parents, and good citizens also affirm or question the virtues of free markets, strong families, good schools, and lawful government. By probing and parsing our stories and ideals of retirement as moral dramas and arguments in line or in tension with one another, we can come to think more consciously and critically about the institutions that these ideals charter. Making moral sense of retirement more clearly can help us come to reach it more fairly and realize it more fully.

This is a moral and social inquiry into re-creating retirement that probes its practical meaning in the everyday experience and shared imagination of Americans born in the postwar baby boom with a feel for its saving promise of true self-renewal and graceful fulfillment in this world, however shining or unsure salvation seems in the next.[3] It listens

xii

to stories of work, rest, prayer, and play told by a high-tech billionaire in Silicon Valley and a cleaning woman in Atlanta, by professionals and public servants. It explores the vivid landscape and quicksilver selfhood of an emerging ethos of retirement that urges us to get in shape, get healthy, and stay young; feel free to express ourselves, give something back, and fall in love again. It asks the advice of financial planners, psychotherapists, and ministers on the care of money, selves, and souls. It charts the changing pathways and public profile of retirement so upheld, for example, turned toward youthful "wellness," lifelong romance, and encore careers as glowing goods to inspire our golden years and turn back the hour of our death.[4] It digs deep into the contrasting moral traditions Americans share and contest in thinking through what makes life worth living, and a society worth living in and working for.[5] What does a life well lived in retirement look like? What sort of social arrangements help or hinder us in leading it?

Retirement is a time to rest and
relax but also to re-create our lives
and rekindle our love of life.

Retirement not only offers a time to rest from our labors and relax with family and friends—to travel, play, and have fun—but to re-create our lives and rekindle our love of life. It beckons us to find our true calling in action, and peace of mind in reflection; to seek the Spirit moving in the moment of each day, to seek the grace of God in prayer and love of neighbor. Retirement also marks a milestone of social progress we are now struggling to sustain, a victory for personal freedom and the pursuit of happiness won by a surging postwar economy, a prospering society, and a more just and generous government of and for the people, who now mistrust it so for faltering. What's fair and who's responsible? more and more of us ask, as the closer we come to retirement, the further away it seems. What should we do differently, when so many of us have saved so little? Can we do anything at all to close the canyon gaping between haves and have-nots along the lines of color and class, gender and generation?

There is enough good work that needs to be done for all of us to share in its doing for our common good and the good of creation. There is enough wealth in a land where one in three families own nothing for all of us to share in the fruit of our labors through living wages, like those who labor in the vineyard, like those who hear the prophet promise that they will build houses and dwell in them, and not lose them to another.[6] So it is written. And so we can wonder what will happen next. Many of us will be needy in retirement, since it has grown harder to reach and realize, even as it has grown larger in our eyes and hearts. Many of us will be able to respond to our neighbors' needs. Will we? Will we have to?

Through these currents of conviction and doubt we can discover the ways we imagine and intuit retirement, justify our judgments, and question our common sense. We can probe our peculiarly proactive and expressive sense of selfhood, capable of ongoing transformation and reinvention, that animates the can-do imagery of re-creating retirement, not just settling into it. Instead of rejecting this world for the next, such visions embrace a multiplex monism that accepts the protean possibility of this world, neither bound by original sin nor perfected by progress, as we cherish our freedom to choose our own path.[7] Everyone is born for something different, as Epictetus supposedly said, and MMPI-style aptitude testing certified for a generation of Americans better educated than ever before across a broader middle class. In retirement they can seek the sort of renewal and fulfillment that spring from the classical and religious roots of *genus vitae* and sacred callings, carried from cloisters into worldly work, lifted up in romantic self-expression at one with soul mates and nature, and committed to peace and justice in a beloved community beyond parochial walls.[8] Can such seeking serve us all, or only an elect?

What must we do to be saved? Every world religion answers that question with a whole way of life.[9] How does the moral drama of re-tirement today yield living answers to this question? From what familiar forms of suffering and difficulty does it promise to deliver us? How does it redeem work from its discontents, not only reward its achievements? How does it celebrate vibrant wellness, not only foster health, in the face of our finitude? How does it hold out hope and lift up love, not only stir passion and spark fun?

How we imagine and enact retirement in practice re-creates its meaning in redemptive visions of who we are and where we are headed. Can they keep the promise of our progress as a people of plenty? Can they prove equal to bearing the globalized burden of our prosperity, its ecological impact, and its fair sharing across generations as well as races, classes, and nations? The rising risks and costs we face in reaching retirement run through the moral predicaments of the social world we share, as we wrestle with paying fair taxes and fair wages, helping the needy, and seeking liberty and justice for all, given the urgency and con-tingency we feel in the course of our own lives. Is it true that "the only thing worse than death is outliving your money," as one mutual-fund company warns? What should we do about it? We'll find out, in the life to come.

# ACKNOWLEDGMENTS

Fellowships from the John Simon Guggenheim Memorial Foundation and the Louisville Institute enabled me to begin this project, and research grants from the Lilly Endowment enabled me to complete it. I am grateful for the generous support of these institutions and the good counsel of their leaders, particularly Craig Dykstra, Chris Coble, and Jessicah Duckworth at the Endowment. In conceiving this inquiry I am indebted to the exemplary work of Robert Bellah, Charles Taylor, and Martin Marty. In pursuing it I am thankful for the research assistance of Justin Latterell and the community of my colleagues at Emory University and its Candler School of Theology, led by Dean Jan Love. Robert Bellah, Ann Swidler, William Sullivan, Richard Madsen, and Brooks Holifield read successive drafts of the manuscript. Their critical insight and encouragement have made this book much better. So have its apt editing and crisp production by Kathryn Armistead and Jennifer M. Rogers at Wesley's Foundery Books.

Conversations with well over two hundred persons shape this story, including eighty who took part in recorded interviews, fifty quoted in its pages, and uncounted members of congregations in Silicon Valley and metropolitan Atlanta. For their wisdom and honesty, convictions and doubts, I am grateful, especially to Gene Tucker, Rex Kaney, Timothy Mc-Donald, Helen Hill, and Silas Hoadley; Michelle and Richard Casey, Mary Lou and Jack Gilbert, Halimah and Elia Van Tuyl; Marguerite and Bob

Fletcher; Nicholas Zirpolo, Paul Perko, Frank VanderZwan, John Ortberg, and John Liotti; Susan Allen Grady, Susan Pinson, Jon Gunnemann, Rod Hunter; and, first and last, Kristin Mann.

All the names of informants and interviewees in this book are pseudonyms. Any similarities are purely coincidental. Specific descriptive details have been excised or changed to preclude personal identification, while remaining consistent in socially and institutionally representative terms, for example, in identifying a source as a seniors' minister, youth minister, lay leader, CEO, municipal employee, financial planner, or psychotherapist. All interviewees were asked for and granted recorded oral and/or written waivers before interviews, and all interviews were coded and keyed to actual names on lists held in confidence and stored separately from the interview tapes and transcripts, according to standards for such ethnographic research overseen by Emory University's IRB review board, which approved this project.

# DREAMS AND DOUBTS OF RETIREMENT

## WHAT WE HOPE FOR, WHY WE WORRY

Can we retire securely and freely after working long and hard? Over the past generation Americans have come to doubt the truth of that prospect in fact, even if they believe it should be flourishing in all fairness. Once it was. The dream of a secure and comfortable retirement came true for more and more Americans after World War II. The average age of retirement fell from sixty-eight in 1950 to sixty-three by 1975, and the proportion of retirees to workers rose five-fold from six in one hundred in 1950 to thirty in 1985. Now the dream is receding. Americans working today face more insecurity in retirement than their parents did, the first such reversal in modern U.S. history.[1]

No one story can do justice to this generational sea change. But it is a profoundly personal story we can engage with a wide social reach through following three first-person accounts at the center of this chapter, told by a Silicon Valley CEO sailing smoothly into retirement, a cleaning woman in Atlanta working on without rest, and a public servant struggling to make ends meet in a city near bankruptcy.

After retiring early from bearing the burdens of heading a major scientific corporation, Bill Hanson started up a small research firm he devotes two days a week to chairing in a close circle of colleagues he

1

admires and enjoys. He continues his calling to lead and mentor others in business, serve the community, and share more fully in the everyday lives of his family and friends, with time of his own set free to study and play. By contrast, after decades of cleaning the homes of others, who paid her in cash without paying taxes for Social Security, Ella Mills works on because she must. She deserves to rest, she knows, and she longs for the freedom to take care of her own grandchildren and great-grandchildren, and really get to know them. God will provide, she prays, and rest will come at last. Kelsey Tyler is not so sure that the city she serves will avoid bankruptcy and keep its promises on pensions and health insurance in retirement. Working longer hours for flat pay and straining to cover the home front in the face of her husband's shift work, Kelsey struggles to pay the mortgage and save to send the kids to college. There must be fairer ways to share wages, work, and rest to take better care of our families and cities, she argues, if only we join together with the public spirit and political will we need to govern ourselves wisely. Let's see how these three stories, and our own, have emerged through striking economic, social, and political changes in America over the past generation.

Has this generational reversal since World War II changed how we think about retirement and make moral sense of it, or simply how we feel about reaching it? Over the past decade fewer of us have come to feel very confident about retiring comfortably. As some ten thousand Americans retire every day now, only one in five nearing that day feels sure about it, and only one in two has saved or invested $25,000 toward it.[2] A generation ago just one in nine workers expected to delay retirement beyond the age of sixty-five, and just one in twelve actually did so. Today a third of baby boomers aged fifty-five to sixty-four now report pushing back their plans to retire, and a third of those aged sixty-five to sixty-nine are still working.[3] Flat wages, ebbing pensions, lost savings, more debt, costlier health care, and lower household wealth than the prewar generation inform their decisions to work longer, especially since 2008. But so do better health, longer life spans, and significantly shifting values in favor of continuing an active, engaged, and productive life at work. More women as well as men are working longer and later now because they enjoy it. They identify with what they do on the job and get fulfillment from it, not just income.[4] These "generative" virtues of adulthood, in the Aristotelian usage of Erik Erikson's popularized life cycle psychology, figure crucially in re-creating retirement in a less linear, leisured, and either-or relationship to the world of less onerous work.[5] Featured in national media stories, policy studies, and personal advice books, such ideals inspire "dream job" second careers, "encore performances" in civic ventures, returning to school to pursue the arts, or volunteering to tutor the needy.[6]

Higher levels of educational attainment, tied to more fulfilling occupations, go along with higher expectations of baby boomers to work past sixty-five. This holds true for both women and men, as their career paths converge, particularly along professional tracks. Sixty is the new fifty, testify advocates of a new stage in the midcourse of life for a new generation. Sixty is the new seventeen, counter critics, at least for this generation's disadvantaged members who lose or leave their career jobs and reenter the labor force in lower-wage sales or service jobs at Wal-Mart or McDonald's to make ends meet. Barely half of baby-boomer households are on track to maintain their earlier standard of living in retirement, while at least a quarter will fall far short. Most at risk to wind up with retirement income at or near the poverty level are those without higher education or advanced job skills, good health, union cards, or employer pensions, particularly people of color and women heading households on their own.[7]

Diverging odds of poverty and hardship in retirement, tied to economic inequality and social difference, cue a tale of two cities resegregating over generations. In 1950 almost half of all men aged sixty-five or older were still at work in the United States. That fraction fell to only one-sixth by 1993, but it has since rebounded to almost a quarter of all men, and one-third of all workers aged sixty-five to sixty-nine.[8] Why keep working? Reasons vary, but they are usually twofold: because many older Americans love to work, and because many cannot afford to retire. Half of older Americans continuing to work say they do so to stay active and involved, while half say they do so for added income.[9] Working longer because you need the money to meet your basic living expenses is the reason that comes first for more than two-thirds of those who earn the median wage or less. Working longer because you want to stay active or you love what you do is the reason that comes first for more than two-thirds of those who earn more than twice the median wage.[10] These twofold reasons begin to tell a tale of two cities we can follow out and interpret. But can we revise it? Can we bring these two cities closer together in one nation, as we pledge, with liberty and justice for all?

The dilemmas of retirement are not only financial. Greater longevity and better health have left almost two-thirds of baby boomers feeling younger than their chronological age by nine years or so, and feeling convinced that "old age" doesn't begin until age seventy-two. Americans with college degrees now live into their 80s on average, some twenty years longer than their elders did when Social Security set retirement age at sixty-five in 1935. But living longer can open the door to fearful contingency as well as inspiring possibility. "I'll tell you exactly how much money you need to retire securely," proposes a financial planner wryly, "if you tell me exactly when you're going to die and whether you'll get really sick before then."[11]

Because we know not the day or hour of a final year far in the future, we trust, we can embrace retirement in the activist, protean spirit of its emerging ethos. But we can also fear the uncertain danger of "living too long" as well as not long enough.[12] Falling ill or starting to fade in vigor may clearly point the way to retiring sooner from an unloved job if not a beloved calling, in order to spend more time with family and friends, and maybe spend more resources sooner too. But the prospect of living on for decades with nothing to do but have fun and get bored can be terrifying. That threat looms even if you have enough money to reach to age one hundred, and you do not outlive those you love along the way. It looms if you find no encore career or commitment compelling enough to take the place of work in staying active and in touch with others in the wider social circles we inhabit as community members and contributors. What if you like your job, in fact, and want to stay on full-time in the college philosophy department or the local police department, the corporate law firm or the corner store, but you are obliged by contract or prompted by carrot and stick to go? What then?

More deeply, we can see the shifting shape of these dreams, doubts, and dilemmas of retirement in terms of a recast soteriology, a new answer to the old question, "What must we do to be saved?" Divided and diminished if not denied, the dream is now turning away from the more generous, graceful Arminian assurance of a secure retirement shared by everyone who works long and hard, grounded in Social Security, defined-benefit corporate pensions and low-cost health insurance since World War II. It is now turning toward a much more uncertain and unequal ordeal. You're on your own and up in the air, caught in a riskier predicament, with echoes of Augustine and Calvin In its widening divide between a small elect of the saved and growing crowds of those in peril, still striving, and falling short. Defined-benefit (DB) company pension plans and retiree health benefits guaranteed on top of Social Security payments rising with the cost of living in the postwar era have given way to defined-contribution (DC), do-it-yourself 401(k)s, IRAs, and multiple-choice Medicare supplement plans since 1980. "This isn't your daddy's retirement," cautions a mutual-fund company. "And it's not for the faint of heart."[13]

Reaching retirement is much more demanding and challenging now than a generation ago. Now you are on your own in a "yo-yo society," which has shifted more risk from employers and government onto individuals and families since 1980.[14] "Retirement needs a new plan" in response, declared Prudential Insurance in advertising its guaranteed annuities in 2012. "If not now, when?" it asked. "In the aftermath of the financial crisis, the U.S. retirement system hangs in the balance.

Something has to change," Prudential argued. "Not just a commitment to save more. But a fundamental shift from 'savings' to 'lifetime income planning.' Why? Because we're living longer. Retirement costs are rising. And fewer of us can rely on a pension to provide income in retirement."[15]

We face a harder lifelong regimen of saving and investing that requires not only more proactive willpower but a set of financial skills that even educated Americans gain only gradually if at all, as they grow older and make mistakes along the way. Start planning early in your twenties, and recognize that "financial literacy needs to be a lifelong pursuit," urge financial advisers in behalf of regular contributions made to diversified investments in 401(k) and IRA mutual funds. "When is a dollar worth more than a dollar?" they ask. "Right now. And your retirement depends on it," they answer, warning that procrastination doesn't pay.[16] Even so, diligent saving habits and sharper investing skills offer no guarantee of financial security in times of low interest rates and volatile stock markets, like those of "the lost decade" since 2001, when baby boomers on the threshold of retirement wound up with little or no gain in savings. Grant the problems of investment losses, low interest rates, inflation or stagflation, and spiraling medical costs that threaten estimates of how much savings, times compounded interest, it will take to retire at some movable future date, concede financial experts. Then, they add, face up to the certain alternative: "Save nothing now, and that's exactly how much you'll have when you retire."[17]

## RETIREMENT RISING AND RECEDING

However striking these changes in outlook and odds, they compose only the latest chapter in a longer story of retirement rising to meet ever more Americans after World War II, then receding before us. The middle class doubled in size and real household income between 1948 and 1973, as hourly pay kept pace with rising productivity, and income grew more quickly at the bottom than at the top of society. Since then, pay has fallen far behind productivity, and income has grown more quickly at the top than at the bottom, while it has sagged in the middle. This has pinched the middle class and made our prosperity much less equally shared, although the economy has continued to grow. As middle-class wages have stagnated and pensions ebbed, retirement has receded. "The closer I come to retirement, the further away it seems." By ringing true to such experience, images of retirement as a mirage, posed by pundits and advertisers alike, have sprung up and spread.[18] They convey a sense of disappointment and frustration at working long and hard yet failing to achieve the freedom and security to retire. They imply the indignation many feel at the unfairness of a broken covenant and breached social compact on work and its rewards, and their anger at the promise betrayed of an honest wage paid for an honest day's work and rest well-earned at the end of the day.

Between dreams and doubts of retirement lie dilemmas that are at once personal and social. Even before the Great Recession, few Americans were saving enough for retirement, and they were becoming more concentrated at the top of the income ladder. When the financial crisis hit home, many Americans were forced to draw down their savings to pay off pressing debts and make up for lost jobs and income. Hoping to double their money over the past decade by saving and investing, they saw their median net worth plummet from 2007 to 2010 by 40 percent on average and plunge by 33 percent for households aged fifty-five to sixty-four and nearing retirement. Instead of cushioning their retirement and securing their credit, the value of home equity dived by $6 trillion when the housing bubble burst and left 13 million Americans owing more on their mortgages than the worth of their homes.[19]

Recovery has come slowly and unevenly. Between 2009 and 2015, income for the top one in a hundred households rose by almost 40 percent, and a resurgent stock market restored the value of their investments. Families in the bottom 99 percent saw their incomes grow at one-fifth this rate, and by 2015 they had recovered only about two-thirds of their losses in the Great Recession. Job growth outpaced wage growth, so more people were working, but many still struggled to get by, including a third of all households surveyed by the Federal

Reserve in 2015. Almost half of all said they could not cover an emergency expense of $400 without borrowing or selling something. One in three U.S. workers has no retirement savings or pension, including a quarter of those aged sixty or older. Two in three of all working-age Americans have no employer-sponsored retirement plan, and millions of them face lives of poverty when they stop working.[20]

Why so? American jobs and wages once bounced back quickly after a recession, and middle-class jobs paid enough to save for retirement. But downturns over the past generation have bred "jobless recoveries," as output rebounds but good jobs and wages do not. Led by "superstar firms" that concentrate sales in major industries and minimize mid-level jobs, employers improve productivity and profits by investing in technology and cutting payrolls. Large-scale automation of routine handwork and headwork by robotics, computers, and information technology hollows out the middle of the job market. Only one in four Americans works in a routine job today, compared to one in three in 1985, and our factories now produce twice as much with one-third fewer workers. Recent losses of seven in eight manufacturing jobs stem mainly from greater productivity, not greater imports. Employment performing a limited set of repetitive tasks by rote and rule has dropped by a third since 1990, mostly within one-year windows in recessions. Firms fire but do not rehire, while consolidating and moving manufacturing jobs overseas in a global economy based on greater international trade, cheaper labor, and more mobile capital. Machines replace manpower to take on the routine administrative tasks of sorting, counting, and filing, once done by secretaries and bank tellers, as well as the routine manual tasks of making and growing things, done by factory machine operators and farm laborers. Jobs decline in both pink-collar clerical and administrative positions (two of three held by women), and in blue-collar production, craft, and operating occupations (five of six held by men) at the core of the middle class.[21]

Wages lag and participation in the labor force shrinks for the less educated, particularly blue-collar males displaced from manufacturing jobs into service occupations, such as janitorial and protective services.

Employment in these low-wage service occupations has grown since the 1980s, along with highly paid bright-collar professional, technical, and managerial occupations, especially "STEMpathy" jobs that require science, technology, engineering, and math skills along with empathic interpersonal communication. At the same time, contingent workers in outsourced, subcontracted jobs on call in the "on-demand economy" have mushroomed to nearly one in six U.S. jobs today, widening wage inequality and the ranks of the working poor while cutting down on pensions, unions, health insurance, and workplace regulations. This polarization of jobs at the top and bottom, with the hollowing out of routine jobs in the middle, has led to greater economic inequality in a "two-tiered society" that reflects not only structural changes in technology and global markets. It also reflects a weakening of the nation's equalizing institutions—strong unions, schools, public provision, trade regulation, progressive taxation, and public investment in infrastructure—backed by bipartisan lawmaking to check the most extreme market outcomes and ensure that citizens benefit fairly from economic growth through democratic self-government.[22]

The U.S. economy has more than doubled in size since 1980, lifting average wages by 60 percent to $64,500 in 2014 for the nation as a whole. But the top tenth of earners took $7 out of every $10 gained, leaving the bottom half of all earners flat for three decades at about $16,000 in average wages before taxes and transfers. The bottom half collapsed from earning 20 percent of all national income in 1980 to only 12 percent in 2014, while the top 1 percent shot up from earning 11 percent of the total in 1980 to 20 percent in 2014. They tripled their yearly income from $428,200 in 1980 to $1,307,800 in 2014, jumping from twenty-seven times as much take-home pay to eighty-one times as much as a typical earner on the bottom half of the income ladder. In the top half except for the top tenth, middle-class earners lost about 5.5 points in their share of all national income since 1980. In the top tenth except for the top 1 percent, upper-middle-class earners gained about 3 points in their share of the total since 1980.[23]

Over the last three decades, government taxes and transfers have done little to redistribute income overall or raise income for working-age Americans on the bottom half of the income ladder in the face of these massive shifts to the top in *pretax* income distribution. Since 1980 pretax income has risen only for the elderly among the bottom 50 percent, due to increases in their Social Security benefits and private pension distributions. Almost all the meager growth in *posttax* income for the bottom 50 percent since 1980 comes from Medicare and Medicaid, and almost all of that has gone to meet the rising cost of health care. Not by taxes and transfers alone can we guarantee the good of retirement or curb the economic inequality that threatens it, policy analysts conclude, without distributing more equally the primary assets of human capital, financial capital, and collective bargaining.[24]

In 2011 corporate profits after taxes jumped to a record eighty-year high of 10.3 percent of the overall size of the economy, and wages fell to a record eighty-year low of 43.7 percent of GDP. At the same time, corporate taxes fell to 21 percent of corporate profits, a new low since World War II and a third lower than the 1960–2010 average of 34 percent. Personal taxes dropped under 14 percent of total personal income, well below the fifty-year average of 15.5 percent. Why have wages lagged so far behind rising productivity and record corporate profits? Automation, information technology, and offshoring more routine jobs played parts in this wrenching turnabout since the 1970s. But much of the credit goes to corporations radically reallocating their earnings away from wages and reinvestment over the past twenty years to buy back their stock on the open market to pump up the price of shares and hike their dividends to maximize "shareholder value" and inflate executive compensation driven by stock-based pay. From 2003 through 2012, for example, S&P 500 companies used more than half of their earnings to buy back their own stock, and an additional third to pay dividends, leaving less than a tenth to raise wages or improve jobs for workers, while ballooning CEO compensation to $30.3 million on average.[25]

After years of flat wages and jobless recovery before the Great Recession and an uneven rebound from it, a more comprehensive new "supplemental" poverty measure in 2011 showed one in six Americans living below the poverty line, and more than one in four living in or near poverty. By 2015 this measure had improved to show one in seven Americans living below the poverty line, although that still exceeded the prerecession rate of one in eight in 2007. In 2015, moreover, nearly one in four Americans remained in or near poverty at less than 50 percent above the poverty line of $24,250 for a family of four by the official poverty measure, while almost one in three remained poor or near-poor by the supplemental measure.[26]

Among the world's thirty advanced national economies, the United States ranked last in equality of wages and other compensation in 2017, and twenty-ninth of thirty in the effect of taxes and transfers to reduce inequality of market income. It ranked twenty-fifth in social protection, and twenty-third on the "inclusive development index" used by the World Economic Forum to measure how well economic growth translates into social inclusion. Deepening inequality in the United States over the past generation clearly stems not only from technological change, market dynamics, and economic globalization but from political choices in making public policy and remaking public institutions. In particular it stems from "the retreat of institutions developed during the New Deal and World War II," concluded economist Emmanuel Saez, "such as progressive tax policies, powerful unions, corporate provision of health and retirement benefits, and changing social norms regarding pay inequality. We need to decide as a society whether this increase in income inequality is efficient and acceptable and, if not, what mix of institutional and tax reforms should be developed to counter it."[27]

## INEQUALITY AND THE GOOD OF RETIREMENT

Driven home by lagging wages, lost jobs and pensions, low mobility, and mounting debts across the middle class since the year 2000, have our doubts overtaken our dreams of retirement? Have deepening economic inequality and persisting poverty over the past generation opened new gaps among Americans not only in income and assets, but also in our felt freedom to retire happily and fairly? Today college graduates are much likelier than those without degrees to say they feel sure they will be financially prepared to retire. So are those with household incomes of $100,000 or more compared to those with less than $50,000.[28] But are these gaps evident in our values and visions of retirement, not only in our circumstances and resources for putting our common ideals into practice?

For all the complexity of economic causes and effects in this ongoing story of inequality and poverty, it is nonetheless important to understand it as a moral drama with unsettling civic implications for how we pose and answer questions of what's fair, who deserves what, and who is responsible for making things right at what cost. This is particularly true as our society grows more segregated by income into different neighborhoods, suburbs, schools, and places of work and play. Only 40 percent of Americans live today in middle-income neighborhoods, compared to 65 percent in 1970. Over a third of American families now live in areas of either affluence or poverty, up from just one-sixth in 1970, with the affluent rising from 7 percent to 16 percent of all families.[29] Has this narrowed the everyday interaction of affluent Americans with those worse off, and deepened differences between their ways of life? Has it shrunk their reservoir of mutual empathy, and blurred the vision of their mutual understanding when it comes to common concerns, for example, over fair wages and taxes, or adequate provision for pensions and health care, education, and employment?

Far fewer children escape poverty or move onward and upward through school and work in metro areas of America more segregated by income and race, with lower local taxes and weaker public schools, fewer married parents, looser social networks, and spottier involvement in congregations and civic groups. By the time she turns three, a child born into a low-income home has heard 30 million fewer words than a child from a well-off family, a deficit that usually compounds over time in unequal schools.[30] Job polarization is carving out larger-scale inequalities between cities and regions themselves, particularly between thriving coastal cities and heartland plains strapped by Rustbelts with the largest losses of college graduates as well as industrial jobs. Yet even as 2016 voting patterns retraced the Rustbelt epidemic of "deaths of despair" among less educated white Americans suffering economic hardship, African Americans could still expect to live four years less on average than their white counterparts, face jobless rates twice as high, and endure wage gaps a third wider than a generation ago.[31]

High inequality and low mobility threaten "middle-class America's basic bargain—that if you work hard, you have a chance to get ahead" and leave poverty behind, declared President Barack Obama a year after his reelection. The defining challenge of our time is making sure "our economy works for every working American." Failing to meet it not only puts retirement at risk. It poses "a fundamental threat to the American Dream, our way of life, and what we stand for around the globe," Obama warned, by diverting progress, fraying families, and undermining faith in the good of government and free enterprise alike. On the contrary, charged the Tea Party movement, the Club for Growth, and GOP fiscal conservatives, the welfare socialism of tax-and-spend big government reduces half of Americans to dependency. It unfairly entitles them to take what workers earn by vainly trying to do good with other people's money. It strangles job creation with red tape, and handcuffs free enterprise with needless taxes, rules, and health insurance subsidies.[32]

Americans can argue over changes in law and public policy that follow from such critiques, or dismiss their logic. Recent polls show us doing both. Two of three Americans agree that the gap between the rich and everyone else has grown over the past decade, and they likewise agree that government should act to reduce this gap, although this majority includes 90 percent of Democrats but only 45 percent of Republicans. Four of five Americans agree that the government should act to reduce poverty. How? Three of four Democrats favor raising taxes on the wealthy and corporations to help the poor, since most Democrats believe that government aid does more good than harm, because people can't get out of poverty until their basic needs are met. Six of ten Republicans favor cutting taxes to encourage investment and economic growth, since most Republicans believe that government aid to the poor does more harm than good by making people too dependent on government. Only a third of Americans remain convinced that some people are rich because they worked harder, and some are poor because they did not work hard enough. By contrast, half believe that the rich have had more advantages than others, and the poor have been held back by circumstances beyond their control. Predictable differences in income and party identification bear on these views. Yet across both these dividing lines six in ten Americans in 2014 believed that the economic system in this country unfairly favors the wealthy, *and* they also believed that most people who want to get ahead can make it if they're willing to work hard. By election day in 2016, however, three in four voters agreed that "the American economy is rigged to advantage the rich and powerful," and that "America needs a strong leader to take the country back from the rich and powerful."[33]

In such shifting light from several social angles, we can surely see the good of enabling Americans to save more for retirement and protect their savings and homes from economic crises, to count on Social Security and Medicare, and take part in IRA accounts or pension plans with every employer. We can also ask how to reshape retirement planning away from the uneven, unreliable core of 401(k) investments. We can question how to tackle the larger challenge of a secure retirement and adequate health care for longer-lived seniors in an aging population without cheating generations to come of the education, health care, jobs, wages, and homes they need to prosper, pay taxes, and share responsibility for our future.[34]

The glare of the 2016 presidential election revealed the political impact of wider gaps in social experience and moral judgment between the educated upper middle class in the top fifth of American households and those in the middle, with the poor more isolated at the bottom and working families struggling to stay afloat. Driven by greater income inequality, these gaps further separate rungs of the social ladder defined by residence, marriage and household formation, schooling, occupation and pension, health and stress levels, tied together more tightly in turn as dimensions of social advantage.[35] The influx of more affluent, educated voters into the Democratic Party helped replace the white working-class voters who switched to the GOP over the past generation. But it also helped distract Democrats from responding to working-class concerns in tandem with organized labor.[36] Less affluent but well-educated, culturally liberal, and independent younger white voters in the 2016 Democratic primaries proved readiest to answer the call from Sen. Bernie Sanders to make a "political revolution" by hiking taxes on the rich and raising wages for workers, breaking up big banks, and spending much more on the social safety net, job creation, health care, and student aid. Older white voters with less education, income, and job prospects, meanwhile, proved readiest in the GOP primaries to answer Donald Trump's call to "make America great again" by bringing back manufacturing jobs and prosperity for deserving workers, protecting Social Security and Medicare for the middle class, pinching programs for the poor, cutting taxes for the rich, and fencing out immigrants and imports.

Economic populism and nationalism in response to desperate hardship and deepening division resounded across political parties and ideologies, however at odds their audiences and angles of approach, to decide the 2016 election. At the same time, this partisan combat reflected the gaping distance between those at the top and those at the bottom of the social ladder. It underscored the need for greater moral coherence and political cohesion to engage the problems of the poor, help struggling workers, and serve the good of the country as a whole.[37]

Citizens need not be equal in income and education to engage in self-government. But democratic citizens of different backgrounds, unequal resources, and diverse social positions must share a common life and decide in common how they want and need to live together, if government of and by the people is to endure. Otherwise it threatens to tilt toward the most powerful and divide the body politic through bitter protest, mistrust, and withdrawal driven by anger and despair, if ordinary citizens find themselves in a society so unequal that no matter how hard they work, they cannot make ends meet, buy a home, pay for college, or save for retirement. Democracy thrives only if it sees to the universal distribution of hope as well as rights, and gives to all its citizens a representative voice as well as a fair slice of the economic pie.[38]

Can we face these challenges when we think twice about retirement? Can we summon the moral imagination and judgment we need to resolve our gridlock of ideology and interest in order to rework the economy and re-create retirement? The best-off Americans may offer examples for moral insight and comparison when it comes to retirement, if they can help us think about the moral goods and practices of retirement that we actually share as ideals across lines of color, class, gender, and generation. Which aims and visions are worth enabling in practice and institutional arrangement for the good of everyone in our society, however favored or bypassed they may be in terms of economic success and social advantage? Let's see as we follow the story of one highly successful American sailing smoothly into retirement, then listen to another striving and struggling to catch up, and hear from a third faced with falling short and working on without rest.

## FREEDOM TO RETIRE AND UNRETIRE

"I actually attempted retirement when I was in my forties, and I failed," confesses Bill Hanson with a ready smile. Gifted with calm attention and articulate energy, he is a Silicon Valley high-tech "serial CEO," as his friends put it with genuine admiration. But the story of his early retirement has its serious side, he makes clear, tied to larger questions he continues to weigh along the arc of his life as he nears seventy. Coming from a large, close-knit family and a churchgoing Presbyterian childhood, Bill enjoyed "the cars and girls" of a gregarious adolescence before he discovered a passion for the humanities as a college undergraduate in a good public university near his hometown in the Northwest. Doubtful about becoming a scholar, doctor, or lawyer, he went on for an MBA almost by default, then came to work in Silicon Valley as a junior manager for an innovative, fast-growing scientific corporation. "Within weeks I fell in love with the work; I really did," he recalls. A remarkably careful listener, collaborative colleague, and deft strategist, he rose rapidly through the corporate ranks for more than a decade, then left to help start and run a scientific company of his own.

A few years later, when Bill's startup was sold to a much larger corporation, "I made all the money I would ever need," he realized. "There are lots of things I really want to do, I said, so I decided to retire at forty-five." But eager investors in a related startup soon lured him into heading it, despite his cautioning them that he would stay only for the near term. "That was failure number one," he laughs, repeated more than once, then followed by his chance-of-a-lifetime return as CEO to lead his original firm in a demanding second-generation reorganization. On the cusp of its turnaround, a multinational giant in the field made the firm an offer its board didn't refuse. "That was a moral challenge," Bill judges, "since I really thought it was the wrong thing to do." Outvoted, he joined an exodus of top executives and scientists who left the firm with severance packages that gave them more than enough time and money to decide what they really wanted to do next. It wasn't as easy as it looked. "I didn't know exactly what I was gonna do, but I told myself I was never going to be a CEO again."

Why not? "I'd like to think of myself as being a principle-driven manager. Principles start with strategy, they start with customers, they start with investors and workers, and you live that all the way through," Bill replies. That was easier to do when Bill was starting up and running smaller companies "Once you go someplace much bigger, with a longstanding culture and lots of political cross-currents," he learned, "it's far more difficult to put in place principles everyone can share and operate from. You cannot always escape conflict, and having to fire people. On the other hand, if you can come through that and band together, you can turn the battleship around, and we did. That was fulfilling." But it was also an arduous campaign that took years and took its toll, as Bill came to realize fully only afterward.

Soon after losing the helm of the corporation he had worked so hard to turn around, Bill visited his childhood home and went camping with old friends along a winding river valley in the wilderness nearby. Sitting around the campfire on their second night out, Bill closed his eyes for a moment and felt himself lifted up into the star-filled mountain sky. "Then I looked down, and I saw the campfire and the river in the canyon. I saw my attaché case floating on the river. Then it opened up, and all my business papers flew up out of it. Millions and millions of pages. I watched them swirl around and spread out on the river in the darkness. Then I watched them float away!" Whether it was the work of his imagination or some larger revelation, Bill took this experience as "a profound signal that I should not be carrying a briefcase anymore. I know that."

How did Bill act on that knowledge? "Things worked out slowly, but surprisingly," he answers, more than a dozen years after his liberating vision. "I'm surprised at what I'm doing today. It isn't what I would have predicted, but I actually love it. I've always enjoyed my work, my family, my friends, all that. But now I really have a grin on my face a lot." Why so? Bill found a way to follow out his vision by letting go the burdens of a corporate CEO, while continuing his calling to lead and mentor others in business, serve the community, and share more fully in the everyday lives of his family and friends, with time of his own set free to study, play, and reflect.

As board chairman of a small high-tech research firm for most of a decade, Bill Hanson devotes two days a week to working with its executives and scientists. They are engaged in specialized basic research with high costs and contingencies to match the scale of its potential medical impact and commercial promise if it unlocks the genetic codes at the core of a constellation of chronic diseases. "I really admire these people and I enjoy them. It's been rewarding to help them get started. As they progress, I'm adding less value now, and I'm working my way out of a job. That's great." Bill could capitalize on working as a corporate consultant or board member with other high-tech executives and investors well aware of his green thumb with startups. But he deflects such offers in favor of informal conversations with wider circles of former colleagues and collaborators. "People know I won't hire on, but I'm always willing to have a cup of coffee. I probably have one conversation a week, real low-key, that's kind of a mentoring relationship, even if I haven't seen someone for a year or two. It's kept me in touch with a wonderful group of people I've worked with in one place or another over the years. It keeps me in touch with the principles and values of how I think organizations should be run, and the actual difficulties of doing that on the ground."

At the same time, Bill is leading a campaign to raise funds for a new regional hospital complex. "It's a good cause, and it needs to be done, even if I can't say I always enjoy asking people for money." He feels warmer about a much smaller, more personal philanthropic effort. He began it with a circle of venture-capital colleagues to save a score of village clinics in the Andes, bankrolled by a friend who lost his fortune as a tech investor in the financial meltdown of the Great Recession. "He's a wonderful guy, and it makes your heart sing to be able to keep this good thing alive."

Rounding out each day for Bill and resting at its heart are hours free to spend with his spouse, children, and grandchildren, usually after a full morning's work, exercise, and lunch at home. "Our children have ended up living nearby and having kids of their own fairly early. So we've got a bunch of grandchildren just a few minutes away, and there's not a day goes by I don't see a grandchild," Bill says with a warm smile. "Children's literature is a longstanding hobby, and I love reading to the grandchildren. I redid my office at home to add a little library for them, with a secret door they think only they know about," he laughs, "where they like to come in and read."

With small circles of close friends reaching back for decades, Bill can talk seriously as well as play and relax together with trusted colleagues.

After reading a trio of books on cell biology, human consciousness, and personal identity, for example, he and several friends met for an early dinner at the home of one colleague on a hill overlooking San Francisco Bay. "We started talking at five in the afternoon, and finished at noon the next day. It was terrific fun, and it was really meaningful." Adventure travel and delight in water sports still draw Bill overseas on trips with friends, trekking the Andes and diving the South Pacific, and into the gym at home almost every day to stay in shape. For all the rich range of his activities and relationships, Bill lives quietly by the standards of his neighbors in a woodsy haven at the edge of Silicon Valley that features multimillion-dollar homes on multi-acre lots.

If Bill Hanson seems to be living an all-American dream of retirement, what does he see when he looks around at others? Are there ways to open up the possibility of his own freedom and fulfillment for others less blessed by his extraordinary talents, efforts, and good fortune to do their best nonetheless and enjoy the fruits of their labor in retirement? "I feel fortunate," Bill replies, "to come from a loving, solid family. To meet the right woman to marry. To get a good education and come to Silicon Valley and a great company at the right moment. I know I'm not always the smartest guy in the room full of superbright people around here. It's not false humility. I think I've got myself pretty well calibrated. Emotional maturity has helped me, and I've learned a lot of that from my wife. Early on, some great mentors had a profound influence on me. I'm still in touch with the pastor of the church I went to growing up, an amazing man, who gave me a summer job there as a youth director. I learned to respect people," he emphasizes. "If I'm with somebody I respect, I pay a lot of attention to what they're doing and how they're doing it," Bill says of the heedful practical wisdom that marks much of his daily work and his business leadership over decades.

Bill thinks of the economic struggles of friends and family members, some of them no less gifted or well schooled, who have traveled much rougher roads in life than he, whether by occupational choice, accident, or fate. Short of emergencies or dire need, Bill and his wife have not intervened with big financial gifts or loans to smooth their way. But he and his wife have helped educate more than a dozen children across several generations and branches of their large extended families, and they foresee a growing need to help others they love as they age and retire. "I empathize personally with what's going on," says Bill. More broadly, he reflects, "I know there are problems with globalization and the abuses of capitalism" that have grown over the past generation in the United States. "When I first became a CEO, I was making maybe twenty times what the janitor made," he recalls. "Now it's probably closer to two thousand times. It's seriously skewed, and that inequity is a serious problem."[39]

The challenges of work at living wages leading to secure retirement are more economic problems than political challenges, Bill believes, but resolving them responsibly will take both good government and good business "Too many people in our country today are vying for jobs that are portable. That has to change," he vows, however demanding the changes we have to make in investment, policy, and education turn out to be. We have enough to work with, he believes, and it is doable if we're willing to pull our own weight as well as share social responsibility. "A generation ago you could study whatever you liked and still find a viable career path. Today you need to be much more strategic in your school and career choices."

Individuals need to face up to their personal responsibility to study, work, and save steadily over a lifetime in order to retire securely, Bill urges, and their families, schools, and firms need to help them do so. "At the same time, we really have to work harder in this country to make sure things are fair for everyone," he recognizes. "That includes taxes. I'm all for inheritance taxes, and I think they should be higher. That gets me thrown out of a few cocktail parties," he notes with a smile, "but I think the deck should be reshuffled every generation." The intersection of Silicon Valley's global pool of educated talent and venture capital with academic research and high-tech industry offers Bill a meritocratic framework to weigh these questions. But his firsthand experience also gives him a keen sense of the uncertainties and limits of the high-tech marketplace, its deep dependence on huge public investments in science and education, and its tight ties to public regulation and evaluation, policy, and lawmaking. These ties run from Silicon Valley to the Congress, White House, and courts through every level of government and locus of public argument, including networks of advocacy and lobbying, for example, as they bear on FDA drug trials, Pentagon procurement, IRS rules for issuing and taxing public offerings, and bargain rates for local property taxes paid by high-tech industries.

> Retirement is an opportunity to open
> up and try something new, to be
> who you intended to become.

Navigating carefully through partisan political claims and ideologies, Bill Hanson stresses instead his passion for "doing business ethically, understanding how important it is to the way people live, the values they actually believe in." It is no less important in its own way among coworkers and colleagues, he notes, than how we live in our families, friendships, and communities of faith. "People derive real meaning from business," and its moral integrity or failure deeply influences their lives for good or ill, Bill judges, comparing the impact of specific Silicon Valley firms and industries such as Hewlett Packard across generations on their workers, neighbors, and the larger community. "With friends, family, colleagues, we are in community," he affirms, "yet knowing how to be a good friend, husband, CEO: it's not easy to do. That's where I try to put my effort, where I try to influence people when I get the chance, even if it's on a small scale."

Growing up in a large, ecumenically open Presbyterian congregation, Bill read Tillich and Bonhoeffer in his college years, and he has followed the search for the historical Jesus. He sustains an ongoing dialogue with siblings who remain deeply engaged Christian churchgoers, even as he has explored other religious paths and practices. "I'm not sure about efforts to reconcile logic and religion, but I'm not simply a humanist," he says. "I concluded that I was going to live my life as if there really is a Jesus and he's watching my every single move. Believe me, I don't do that well, but I think that's how we ought to live. We'd be better as a society, we'd be better as individuals, if we do. Every day I fail, but every day I try, and every day it's on my mind." That commitment carries over into Bill's sense of the future and his own finitude. "I'm not particularly concerned about dying. Every now and then it kind of crosses my mind," he allows. "But it's not a big driver. I'm not particularly interested in my 'legacy,' if you will. I don't feel as if I need to do something important to leave a monument. I've sort of taken the challenges as they've come. I've fallen into some things I didn't expect, like helping the clinics in the Andes, because I believe in them, although I don't particularly enjoy fund-raising. So I hope in five years I'm not asking anybody for money."

Transition into retirement should not be abrupt, as Bill Harison sees it now. "It should be more a gradual shifting, where there's some continuity of aim or intent, even if the way you do it changes and the actual form of it changes. Before, I was running a company. Now I'm chairing it, helping the CEO come along, mentoring colleagues. That's age-appropriate," Bill judges. "At the same time," he adds more sharply, "with some of the issues the company is dealing with now, I feel like I'm using every bit of the experience and wisdom I've gained. I've been through proxy fights. I've gone up against corporate raiders. I'm glad I can draw on that." Will such involvement go on as long as Bill can keep it up? "The grooves run deep, and I do feel it," he acknowledges, "I obviously have a need to be needed. We all do. But I hope in five years I get far fewer phone calls, and when I get them, that I don't feel quite the same need to respond. I'd like to have a shorter to-do list when I wake up in the morning."

Moving toward retirement has begun to open up time and space for Bill. He's eager for more room to embrace what he now finds most important, and what is still to come. "Right now I do have a fair amount of free time, because I manage my time well. But I don't want to always have to manage my time so well. I shouldn't have to still be doing that"—Bill shakes his head—"and still be asking my wife to take up the slack for me to do it. Our relationship is better when I'm more in her tempo." That also holds true for the social spacing of work and life at home, as Bill learned once he was freer to work from home, and his work washed over the house. "I had to change that. Now the work phone rings only in the office. I don't wander around the house on the phone. I rarely take a call after six, and people know not to call."

Does retirement beckon Bill to do much more, much less, or something entirely different? "It surprises me," he answers after a pause. "What I yearn for, what I enjoy most has changed. I still do some interesting travel, but if I never traveled again, I would be just fine. Golf is OK with me, but it's not a passion. Some people spend a ton of time playing golf or managing their money. You can do that if you have enough time or money. But why would you want to? Sometimes I'd much rather be just sitting with my wife at home in the evening, watching a good foreign movie on cable, than going out someplace fancy. Or go out to watch the kids play in a basketball game, seeing them light up and yell, 'Grandpa!' That's more fun than going to the opera." What about doing less? "I still hold on to doing, maybe too much so. I'd like to create more free time over the next few years, and see what happens when I have an afternoon with nothing to do."

Bill Hanson's story of work and retirement is worth thinking over in terms of freedom, success and failure, fairness and justice. Its account of happiness and fulfillment is worth weighing in terms of what makes up a good way of life, the kinds of practical activities and relationships that make life truly worth living. It is certainly a success story in the usual sense, but we can think twice about what makes it so. There is freedom *from* want, from not having enough to live in the present, to be sure, and from worrying about having enough to provide for the future. There is freedom *to* retire or do something different that comes to Bill early in middle age, remarkably, as great good fortune and reward for being in the right place at the right time with the right stuff. But this freedom is not without its own sort of problem or question, Bill suggests, even if it's the kind of problem most Americans would love to have. What would you do if you had all the money you need for the rest of your life, and you had half of your life still in front of you? Bill first "failed at retirement," he says with a smile. Then he went on to serve again as a high-tech CEO, not because he needed the money, but because he loved the work and wanted the chance and challenge of continuing to take part in it.

"Needing to be needed" has played a key role in Bill Hanson's deciding to stay actively engaged in work then and now, he acknowledges, along with his recognition of just how intrinsically fulfilling the work has proved in its principled collaboration and mentoring, shared teamwork and achievement, not only its commercial profits and what money buys. What It buys is ongoing participation, contribution, connection, and membership in community.[40] In fact, Bill has given money, time, and effort to continuing to work as a board chairman in ways that make the most of the collaborative and mentoring dimensions of work he prizes, while handing off to others the bulging briefcase of a CEO's administrative burdens he tired of bearing. He was free to do so, even if he was not so free simply to retire and do something entirely different, because he did not find an alternative calling—golf, travel, art, study, investing, or philanthropy—that he loved as fully as the work he was already doing. Bill tried out alternatives in good measure, within the ambit of his ongoing relationships and responsibilities to family, colleagues, and community. He faced a real dilemma to retire early or march on as a CEO, and he transformed the terms of its resolution fruitfully even if he did not resolve its tensions completely. Indeed, he looks forward to the possibility of more time opening up with nothing to do, and so perhaps freeing up the way he holds on to "doing," even if it leads him to doing nothing radically new in the form of an alternative calling.

With age has come greater freedom of choice for Bill to share more of his attention and activity with his family, to redeem the sacrifices they, too, have made to enable him to respond to the demands of a corporate career, and to reset more equally the balance of mutuality with his spouse. Norms of reciprocity and mutual regard inform these choices, for example, to stop taking evening business calls at home. But these norms enter into a larger picture of a good way of life drawn by practical virtues enacted in specific social relationships and institutional arrangements, including spouses talking over dinner without being interrupted by business. So, for example, happiness inheres in the mutual enjoyment and shared attention of Bill watching films at home together with his wife, reading stories to a grandchild, and discussing books with friends, no less than collaborating with corporate colleagues to chart a company's strategy or save a score of clinics in the Andes.

Bill Hanson's sense of calling as a colleague and mentor at work reaches into his leisure, play, and life at home with family and friends. It also reaches into his civic efforts, fund-raising and all, in seeking to be a good friend of the city, even as he aims to steer clear of partisan politics and set a good example by "doing business ethically." His sense of freedom from needing to bolster his legacy or leave a monument may reflect his rare accomplishment in starting up one company after another, tempered by the lucrative loss of the company he turned around, and his continuing commitment to a cutting-edge scientific venture that could fail to achieve a real scientific breakthrough or turn a real profit, or could succeed dramatically in doing both. Whatever the final accounting of profit and loss, Aristotelian ideals of good friends and citizens echo through Bill's moral account, particularly in the cardinal virtue of heedful practical wisdom he admires in others and seeks to nurture in himself, in tandem with the temperance and prudence of "emotional maturity" bred by experience.[41] He invokes the central moral example of Jesus, significantly enough, with a stress on the unselfish love of neighbor and conscientious self-judgment that would make for a better society, not only better persons, marked by the mutual aid of Good Samaritans like those in the case of the Andes clinics.

When it comes to justice and fairness across a wider range of social relations and orders, Bill Hanson joins ideals of principled leadership and social good with a vision of personal virtue and example grounded in following Christ and reaching out to help the needy. Justice is also a virtue of institutions and their arrangement, as he describes it, for example, in profits more or less fairly shared by Bill as CEO with the janitor and line employees at work, no less than the tempo of family life more or less fully shared by Bill with his wife at home. He acknowledges his own good fortune in relation to the justice of living wages and a secure retirement that everyone deserves, as long as they do their part to study, save, and work hard. Individual responsibility for Bill extends to being "much more strategic in your school and career choices" to meet the meritocratic demands of today's job market. But he also sees the moral need for institutional responses by business and government together to resolve "the problems with globalization and the abuses of capitalism" that deprive hardworking Americans of viable jobs, living wages, and a fair share in our commonwealth. Bill favors meritocracy at school and work, but he also acknowledges its limits and requisites, for example, in calling for higher inheritance taxes and fairer provision for public schools and public welfare.

How far do Bill Hanson's ideals of virtue and responsibility, of happiness and the freedom to pursue it within a good way of life, reach through the whole of American society, including those with far fewer resources than he? Do they share his moral vision and logic, even if they lack his advantages, for example, in putting their children first even if they cannot afford to send them through college debt-free, buy them a house nearby, or welcome them into a library of their very own? Let's look first near the other economic end of the world of work and retirement in America, then turn back toward the middle class defined by what Americans earn and own, while looking all along the way at both what holds us together and what divides us as persons and citizens.

# REST FOR THE WEARY

"I'd retire right now, if I could," vows Ella Mills, "if I had the money. I'm tired. My legs are tired, my back is bad," she explains, after standing up, kneeling down, and stooping over for almost fifty years of cleaning other people's houses and caring for their children. A forceful, resilient woman still in her sixties but feeling the wear of doing domestic labor since her teens, Ella not only needs to retire, she testifies, she deserves to retire. "If you work hard all your life, you should get to rest and enjoy your life. Do the things you never did in life, never had time for. Go on a trip, go on a vacation. Get a chance to really spend time with your grandchildren, your great-grandchildren; when you're working, you didn't have time to do that. Get to know them. Take a trip somewhere you've never been. That's what I'd do." Yet even if she had all the money she needed never to work again, she would still look for something to do once or twice a week, like looking after a toddler, "because I want to be doing something. I wouldn't want to just sit at home, looking at the four walls, watching TV."

As it is, Ella works every day she can except on Sunday, if she can get it off to attend a neighborhood Baptist church led by an eloquent, insightful pastor who knows her well. Her grown children are struggling to care for their own families, including a dozen grandchildren and more than a dozen great-grandchildren. The small Social Security check she receives as the widow of a day laborer barely begins to pay her household bills, bus fare, and the mortgage she must meet to hold on to her modest home. With peeling paint, barred windows, and a double-locked metal door, it sits in a run-down in-town suburb a block back from the bus stop, at a corner crowded by a pawnshop and liquor store next to an auto body shop behind a cyclone fence topped by razor wire. Ella can dream of retirement, but for now even a vacation is out of the question. "Go on vacation? I got to stay at home. Pay all that money to go stay in a hotel, when I got a bed at home? Uh-uh."

If financial need keeps Ella Mills at work, financial risk runs through retirement itself for her and others who have worked long years serving households who often paid them in cash without reporting their wages or providing for their payroll taxes. "With Social Security it depends how much you put in," she points out. "For a long time, until things changed with Martin Luther King and all, but even now, you work cleaning someone's house and they don't put in anything for Social Security, you don't get anything. Nothing from nothing leaves nothing. That what you get. My mother cleaned houses too. She never retired because she never had anything to retire on." Could things have been different for Ella? Could she have taken a different working path than her mother did? "When I was younger," she says, "I had a chance to keep working behind a cash register at Rich's, the department store. I did it for a while, but I didn't want to stay there. I didn't want to have to be nice all the time. Whatever attitude people bring in there, you can't just tell them to behave. So I went back to cleaning houses." Had she stayed, she sometimes thinks now, "I'd have my retirement money from them, and all those years of Social Security paid in. But I did what was right for me."

Even so, what is not right are employers who break their promises to pay a living wage and provide a fair pension to those who have worked hard over a lifetime to hold up their end of the bargain. Ella Mills knows "a heap of people that lost their retirement money because they wanted to still work, and then when it came down, the people they worked for filed chapter 13, so they couldn't have no money." Public jobs and pensions have grown less and less secure. "Lots of people I know working for the county for so many years, got laid off before they could retire," Ella says, "because the money was short. Some of them lost their houses, their cars, everything, because there's no jobs out there now. It's not fair. It's really not." Even the safety net of Social Security disability has grown harder to reach, Ella knows well from cases of family members and friends. "People wait for five to seven years sometimes, still trying to get on disability," she says. "Lots of them still waiting when they die."

## Work and rest. Take part and share. Ask, What's fair?

Is there any real rest or reward in this world, before we die? "Some people live like there's no heaven or hell. But there is," Ella Mills says with conviction. "They need to get in the Word and read the Bible." Only heaven can offer heavenly rest and true peace of mind, but people can make a kind of hell on earth by the evil they do. This gives moral confusion and difficulty room to rule the world. "Bible says you can't tell winter from summer sometimes, summer from winter," Ella notes. "Only sign is the bird in the tree." Of the many children she has cared for over the years, only a few call or write to stay in touch and thank her for all the help and love she has given them. "They're my babies," she says. "They always be my babies." Of one, struggling through college, she says, "I'm proud of him. He's gonna make it. I tell him, being in school, you feel like you can't figure out what the answer to the problem is, tell Jesus, and he'll give you the answer, and you'll get it right. Pray and tell God, and he'll do it." God will provide, Ella prays, and faith in God's providence will avail.

At the same time, for the school-age children she cares for, including her own grandchildren and great-grandchildren, Ella Mills also sees there is little she can do to help them with their homework. "This day and age, I'm like a newborn," she admits. "I don't know their lessons; I don't know nothing. I tell them, 'Get your mother help you do it.'" Schooling is different now, she realizes, than when she left high school for steady work. It's harder and costlier now to pursue higher education far enough to carry over into a steady job with living wages to raise a family and save for retirement. "Disability, insurance, hospital, old-age plan: that's a good job. I'd work on a garbage truck for that," Ella vows, "but you can't hardly find that anymore."

Can the rules and decisions that govern work and retirement be more just, even if life can never be entirely fair? Ella Mills thinks first of

Social Security and all of those she knows receiving it but nonetheless unable to retire. "Lots of people on Social Security, but they still have to work to pay their bills, mainly because there's not enough in there to make ends meet." It should be enough, Ella believes, if you work hard all your life and do an honest day's work for an honest day's pay. "It's law. It's on the books," she says of Social Security. "But that don't help if you're working off the books." Then Ella thinks back to the small, close-knit neighborhood of country cabins and shotgun shacks where she was raised in a section of wooded bottomland at the southern edge of Atlanta. "We didn't have running water. We had outside toilets. Just like in the country. No streets paved, no streetlights. Bears and deer come into the neighborhood. We had ice man, coal man, wood man, rat man. We didn't have no garbage man. We played in the tin cans. Bury the cans, everything else give to the hogs and chickens to eat. But we had three meals a day. Good food. No Burger King, McDonald's. You could eat off the land back then. Peach trees, pecan trees. Go pick blackberries, greens. You can't do that now."

Ella thinks about what has changed since then, for better and worse. "We were poor, but country poor," she sums up, with enough food to eat, a house to live in, and others to look out for. "Parents raising their children then, not children raising themselves like now. Parents not raising their children, even little kids, like the eight-year-old child just got pregnant and have a baby down at Grady Hospital." The neighborhood watched everybody's children. "When we were coming up, your momma come home, you got a neighbor telling her what you did. Looking out for you." Neighbors looking out for each other and the good of a community "where everyone knew you, and they knew your family," points back to a bygone time and place. But it points forward, too, to the possibility of citizens caring for one another and holding government accountable to serve everyone. It points out the challenge of finding feasible ways to keep this promise of justice and mutual care when it comes to work, rest, and retirement across American society today.

Ella Mills sees no prospect of freedom *from* the labor she must carry on, ailing or not, as long as she can in order to make ends meet. She cannot foresee when she will be free *to* retire, only when she will be forced to stop working because she is no longer physically able to keep cleaning houses. Yet she can certainly imagine retirement as the chance "to rest and enjoy your life." She needs and deserves to retire, she makes clear, since she has worked long and hard. Rest for the weary is itself a great good, Ella affirms. But so is active enjoyment of life's gifts, first of all, the mutual love and care she shares with the children, grandchildren, and great-grandchildren with whom domestic labor for others has left her so little time. That inherent good is a common good that Ella Mills shares with Bill Hanson and most all Americans across all sorts of family arrangements and household assets, however much or little help they can give those they love in the way of money, expertise, or social advantage. Ella cannot tutor her grandchildren in junior high or pay their way through college, but she has taught them to love, learn, and pray.

Ella Mills has worked long and hard enough to deserve enough from Social Security to retire on. That moral truth is inscribed in law on the books. But it is undercut in practice by the fact that many of her employers have paid no payroll taxes for her domestic labor off the books, and she can count on scant benefits from Social Security. "Nothing from nothing leaves nothing." She could have chosen the then-reliable Social Security and pension plan of another job as a department-store cashier, she recognizes, but that job demanded more diplomacy and deference than her sense of honesty and dignity would let her give. And when she returned to domestic labor after deciding what was right for her decades ago, who could have foreseen so many victories of the civil rights era hollowed out for working families by the flat wages, job layoffs, pension cuts, and slashed safety net of the past generation? Ella acknowledges the role of choices she has made in shaping her difficult road to retirement. She also sees the social landscape shifting to make that road narrower and harder for her to climb, along with her family and friends.[42]

This struggle has not shaken the faith of Ella Mills in God's providence or saving grace. But it has tempered her belief in America's progress, and the willingness of good-hearted people to carry their personal gratitude for her labor to care for their children and homes into the responsibility of citizens to care for one another and to give back to those who have worked so hard for the good of the city. Against the great glass skyscrapers and historic church spires of Atlanta's downtown skyline today, and the foreclosed bungalows and shuttered storefronts of its downscale neighborhoods, the image of Ella's childhood community of shotgun shacks in the bottoms offers a double-edged benchmark, of country-poor neighbors with so little of their own and so much to share.

## STRIVING AND STRUGGLING FOR SECURITY

"I wanted some security for the future. That's why I took a pay cut to leave private industry and come to work for the city ten years ago," explains Kelsey Tyler briskly, waving toward the sleek grandeur of Silicon Valley's biggest city hall across the street from her small office in an older municipal building. "I was making good money for a middle manager, but I got tired of playing musical chairs in tech. The startup company stops, and you don't have a job anymore. You're an independent contractor-consultant-adviser they don't owe a thing. I wanted to be able to plan for the kids, get health insurance and a pension we could count on." Decisive and direct in demeanor, Kelsey was nonetheless past forty when she made the move, with a school-age son and daughter she and her husband, Walt, put first after waiting years to start a family. Laid off from a better-paid technical job, Walt was working overtime to push up his pay as a delivery truck driver for a company without much health insurance or pension benefits.

"You vest in the city pension system after five years, get bumped up at ten, and get health insurance coverage for life after fifteen years," says Kelsey, ticking off on her fingers the benefits of going to work for the city. She closes her hand into a fist. "That's the way it was. Now they want to change the contract. It's all at risk since the financial meltdown. Our pension fund lost a ton of money. The city's been running budget deficits for years, but now they're off the deep end. It's really scary." She grimaces. "It's like we're on a sinking ship. You've got to get off, but you don't know if there's a lifeboat, or you have to jump." Should she try to hold out for another five years, if she can weather the risk of layoffs and an indefinite salary freeze, in order to lock in the lifetime health insurance? Or should she jump now? After all, it's likely that benefits will continue to thin and the time required to earn them will continue to lengthen, backed by the mayor's threat to declare bankruptcy to resolve the city's pension crisis. It's a pressing dilemma, and Kelsey isn't sure what to do.[43]

"Life is out of balance," Kelsey Tyler can say for sure, in the course of working longer hours for flat pay and straining to cover the home front in the face of Walt's overtime shift work. They struggle to pay the mortgage in a no-frills subdivision of Silicon Valley, yet save enough to send two children to college in just a few years. "I have to be up at six every morning and out of the house by seven. I don't usually get home till after six at night. Time to rest on the weekend? Time for a little leisure? No way! There's barely time to get things done at home that I don't have time to do during the week." It's a familiar theme for a generation of dual-earner American families straining to stay in the middle class, Kelsey knows, and she knows how much worse it can be for single mothers trying to do it all alone.[44] But she doesn't believe it has to be this way. It wasn't this way when she was growing up with her two older sisters in the Bay Area in a nicer suburban house than her own. It was bought with a VA loan and paid for by the steady salary her father earned as an electrical engineer. Her mother stayed home to take care of the girls until Kelsey started fourth grade, when she went back to work as a secretary to help the girls through college at campuses of the University of California then charging less than a fifth of what they charge for in-state tuition today. "Let everybody work from 9 to 3, four days a week. Then you'd have full employment," Kelsey proposes. "You'd have time at home, and you'd have time for people to get together and work for social change too. They wouldn't be so tired that all they can do when they get home is flop on the couch and turn on the TV."

The need to change how Americans work, rest, and retire is clear to Kelsey from her own experience. It also resounds through the skewed politics she hears swirling around the problems of pensions, health care, and public provision. "The conversation is all wrong," she is convinced. "It shouldn't be taxpayers complaining that public servants have all these benefits that should be taken away from them, because we can't afford to pay for them and we don't have them ourselves," she argues. "It should be that everybody needs them, and we need to create the kind of economy and government that give them to everybody." Is that possible? "You bet," she answers crisply. "Look at how much Silicon Valley companies pay their CEOs, and how little they pay in taxes. They've turned the companies into piggy banks for big investors and executives. They get to keep all their carried interest and capital gains while they cut pay and benefits for everyone else. It didn't used to be that way. It doesn't actually need to be that way for them to compete and create jobs. Don't believe it."[45]

Retirement is a chance to
rediscover, recalculate, and redefine
yourself and our world.

Kelsey's own work for the city in behalf of "community services" with local civic and neighborhood groups anchors her judgment that overworked, underpaid Americans have too little time to be good citizens with their neighbors as well as good parents with their families. When she thinks about retirement and forgets for a moment whether she can ever reach it, she feels relief. "Retirement means relief from the stress," she explains, "especially now, with all the budget pressure on city offices." But it also holds out the promise of relief from restraint on her own moral agency, and release to live out her ideals. "It would be a relief to be proactive and get to figure out what you really ought to do with yourself, and what you just don't have time to do when you're working," Kelsey declares. Is that such a hard problem for her to figure out right now? "Not really," she laughs. "I know the house would be cleaner. I'd spend more time with my kids. I'd see more of my husband and have more fun together. Get more exercise." She raises her voice. "Make the world a better place. Look around and see what needs to be done. Write to your congressperson. Agitate! That's what I'd like to do."

In fact, Kelsey has done a fair share of civic volunteering and neighborhood activism, well above and beyond her paid job for the city. "I try, but it's hard to keep it up," she admits of her civic efforts, for example, in behalf of "Transition Towns," a social network of groups in local communities dedicated to reducing their reliance on carbon fuels and building alternative energy systems with short supply chains, ranging from community gardens to light-rail public transit systems.[46] "It takes time, even meeting once every two weeks, like we're doing now, to get the word out and build membership. It takes pushing to keep it moving, especially when you've got a day job and a family. I just get tired."[47]

Tired or inspired, however, Kelsey insists she doesn't feel like a world-saver. Raised Catholic and still committed to making sure her children get to Sunday Mass and graduate from the parish grammar school, Kelsey balances between her faith in this "world without end" created by God's grace, and her fears of ecocatastrophe bred by human ignorance and greed. "I don't think I have to change the world all by myself," she attests. "But I know that there are enough people to do it, and that we all need to be doing our part." She pauses for emphasis before judging: "We may not be doing enough. That's the truth. I live close enough to the freeway, so I can wake up every morning and hear all the cars whizzing by. I can smell the smog. I can see the graphs with the lines just going up and up, with all the carbon we're pouring out. Then I listen to the news: Drill, baby, drill! Get everything we can from tar sands and oil shale, while China says they're not cutting back on coal if we don't go first. I hear it, and I think maybe we're toast already.

Maybe we are! We just don't know it yet, but we're already past the tipping point." Kelsey frowns. "Take it too seriously, and you wonder if maybe it was a bad idea to have kids."

Short of the apocalypse, Kelsey can recognize the good of her cause, and the good fortune and vocational choices that enable her to work for that cause, whatever the ultimate success or failure of her efforts. "I'm lucky I get to work on the things I work on," she allows. Still, she worries about the future in both the short run and long term. "Will we have enough to pay the bills, send the kids to college, and retire?" she asks. Unlike the much-publicized largesse of the big salaries, benefits, and retirement packages enjoyed by the city's top officials, she points out, "most people at City Hall are making $50,000 or less. Right now the pension plan gives you two-thirds of that, so you need to save more. But that's hard to do. If we get less, it will get even harder. We're struggling now. Will we have to keep struggling to retire, and then just squeeze by on subsistence?" The answer is yes, Kelsey fears, especially if she and Walt refuse to saddle their children with college debt.

Kelsey's long-term concerns spring from her conviction that we cannot sustain the future if Americans keep living the way we do now, and the rest of the world keeps following our lead. "We produce too much, we consume too much, and we burn too much carbon doing it," she sums up. Why? "Greed drives us, and it comes from fear that we don't have enough. We actually do, but only if we change the way we live now. If we don't, then the greediest guys are actually right. It will keep taking more and more money to live in a nice, safe neighborhood with good schools and good jobs, with a nice retirement ahead, and fewer and fewer of us will be able to do that." It doesn't have to be this way, she insists. "Look at the planning and zoning decisions, the spending on public transit and freeways. That's what makes people have to drive in from Stockton to get to their jobs in Santa Clara County, because they can't afford to live closer or drive an electric car you can plug in to the solar panels on your roof. They can't take a train, because there isn't one."

Many Americans want real change to resolve these problems, Kelsey believes, but they fear that it will take away their livelihood and disrupt their daily lives, already under mounting financial strain. So they dream of returning to the normalcy of a long-gone past of cheap energy and housing set in wide-open spaces under clear blue skies. In fact, to reach the future and sustain it, Kelsey stresses, "we have to change how we live, how we power ourselves. We have to change our relationship to energy and shrink our carbon footprint. Maybe we have to move lower down on the food chain." Who is willing to do that? "I don't know," Kelsey replies. "But I am."

Kelsey's vision of a sustainable way of life frames her hopes of retirement freeing her to live her own life truly. "We can buy less. Buy local, so the money stays in your community, and the community stays self-supporting. We can make it so the food comes from nearby instead of thousands of miles away on a truck or plane. Silicon Valley used to be full of orchards. Just like Wales in the "Transition Town" film, where now they fly in apples from South Africa, and they pay for the oil to do it at $100 a barrel. They're trying to replant the orchards, so they can eat their own apples, and so can the people in South Africa. Then we can all save on the oil, and maybe after a while even the people in China can get paid enough to buy what they make, too."[48]

In the meantime, though, can't Kelsey make her way safely to retirement, however hard the path and steep the climb? "Maybe, but I don't know," she replies. "Maybe our generation will make it, but I'm worried about my kids. Things have gotten so bad in the economy, in the environment, just in our lifetime. Are we going to come out of it? Is there a boom coming around the corner, or is it just another jobless recovery? Is cold fusion or solar power going to save us? Are we going to come up with some great carbon sequestration system we can put in tomorrow to turn around global warming? I sure hope so, but I doubt it. So I am worried. I look ahead, and I see uncertainty big and small when it comes to the environment, the financial situation, the health insurance situation. It doesn't have to be that way, but it is that way, and I feel it."

In low moments, Kelsey feels the unfairness of working hard and playing by the rules over decades of adulthood, yet now in her fifties facing the peril of broken promises instead of the assurance of just rewards earned by her efforts. "I feel very uncertain about the future, despite having done all the things I thought I was supposed to do. You do your part, and you find out you're getting screwed by people far, far away from you, who only care about their own bottom line. It's disheartening." What can be done? More than one thing in more than one way, Kelsey is convinced, when she looks up again more hopefully. It can be done by citizens joining together in social movements, by more responsive economic initiatives, by more responsible government. "People are waiting for government to fix it, and it's not happening," Kelsey says of the skewed ways we order how we work and retire, and we hold on to our unsustainable way of life. "People need to start doing it on their own. They can, even if it's only starting their own garden and eating lower down on the food chain. Buying hybrid or electric cars, if they can afford to, and putting solar panels on their house. Expand the market, cut the costs." Kelsey has not given up on the power of personal example and shared experiment to inspire others to make small but real changes in their own lives. It can reassure them, too, through their own experience that their hopes can overcome their fears, that they can take responsibility for their own communities, and they can work together to bring government back to providing for the people and preparing for the future.

Struggling and striving to secure the future for her family and children as well as get through each week, Kelsey is painfully aware of how little freedom she has *from* the daily demands of worthwhile but underpaid work and overloaded parenting. She stresses how little freedom she has to live out the balance she prizes in her everyday activity at work, home, and a civic calling that spans her family and community. She has a sharp sense of how powerfully she is caught and constrained within a larger social order. It demands longer hours at lower pay of both Walt and herself. It withholds the promise of a secure middle-class future, even to hardworking, college-educated dual-earner families like theirs. It promotes the polluting overproduction and overconsumption of an environmentally unsustainable way of life, while it holds hostage the time and energy Kelsey needs to carry out her commitment to transform the way we live.

Kelsey conceives retirement as a calling, at once personal and political, centered on sustainable civic ideals of household economy that reach from backyard apple orchards and rooftop solar panels to global energy policy for a public household that embraces a worldwide *oikos*. Less a prophet of ecotopia than a grass-roots organizer for "transition towns," Kelsey sees herself seeking to live out the small steps and balanced daily round she advocates to open up the path toward a larger future we can all share and sustain.[49] To advance such social change, she trusts voluntary association to build exemplary moral movements instead of partisan political lobbies—along the lines of Tocqueville's distinction between America's "intellectual and moral associations" and its "political and industrial associations"—to win over the hearts, minds, and votes of citizens to take the lead from private industry blinded by short-term profit and government cowed by short-term debt.[50]

The injustice Kelsey discerns is also personal and political. In leaving private industry to work for the city, she sacrificed salary for security, only to have the city threaten to renege and "change the contract" after more than a decade of service. Kelsey also points out the injustice of working longer hours for flat pay—a decades-old staple of salaried managers and white-collar workers pressed to get more done with less—as one symptom of an unfair political economy rather than a necessary means to gaining greater productivity in a more competitive global era. Don't believe it has to be this way, she counters, if earnings, taxes, and benefits were fairly shared and regulated. Agitate! Not only for a bigger slice of the economic pie to reclaim a middle-class future for working families, but for alternative public policies and practices that can reorder our political economy and energy use to reverse global warming. Willingness to change how we power and feed ourselves requires environmental education, Kelsey argues, but it also calls for moral conversion from greed and fear of not having enough. That in turn means changing the way we live so that all citizens can be assured of living wages and pensions as well as health care, schooling, and safe streets. Is that too much to ask of America today? Not if you "do your part, work hard, and play by the rules," Kelsey answers, and join with other citizens to practice democratic self-government instead of giving up on it.

## FAIRNESS AND CARE ACROSS GENERATIONS

As the dream of a secure retirement recedes in America, it raises questions of justice and mutual responsibility that run along lines of color, class, and gender. It also raises questions of fairness and care across generations. Americans born since 1950 have become less and less likely to outearn their parents and enjoy higher living standards. Between baby boomers and their parents, widely rising postwar household incomes, living standards, and education levels have given way since the 1970s to deepening divides between those more or less well schooled, well-off, and well married, as routine administrative and manufacturing jobs have ebbed, wages lagged, unions shrunk, and public provision thinned for all but a fortunate few. Between baby boomers and their children, and for generations to follow, even deeper divides and differences will challenge us to give everyone their fair share and give each her due, while we treat equals equally and care for those in need.[51]

Social Security, Medicare, and Medicaid for the elderly consumed nearly half of the federal government's spending in 2016. Spending on Social Security and Medicare alone will increase by a third over the next decade, as the ranks of Americans sixty-five and older grow by a third, ten times faster than those aged twenty to sixty-four. This increase will amount to a massive transfer of public funds from poor children and families to better-off seniors, since mandatory retirement spending will squeeze out discretionary spending budgeted for most poverty programs, unless retirement benefits are cut or taxes are raised.[52] As

Congress continues to debate these alternatives, where will we stand, if not in the predictable play of age-graded interests, and how will we vote?

Unequal opportunities and outcomes in education and employment across generations continue to run along familiar lines of color and class in America today. High school dropouts were three times likelier to be out of work than college graduates in 2016, and educational gaps are now widening across generations. Only one in ten of those now seventeen to twenty-four years old earns a college degree, while one in three remains jobless, underemployed, or no longer seeking work. Despite steady job growth to cut the official jobless rate to a postrecession low under 5 percent by 2016, wages still lagged for most American workers, including many recent college graduates, while wages among the top tenth of earners with college degrees jumped more than 6 percent since 2014, three times the average raise for all workers.[53] In the longer run, social differences growing between generations may make it harder for them to pull together responsibly when it comes to equalizing opportunities to study, work, and retire. Minorities account for almost all U.S. population growth since 2000. By mid-2012 white births no longer made up a majority in the United States for the first time in the country's history. Non-Hispanic whites still number some two-thirds of the U.S. population, but most are now older than forty and bearing fewer children. Hispanics, with a median age under thirty, now make up more than a quarter of all births, Blacks nearly one in six, and Asians almost one in twenty.[54]

As the United States passes these demographic milestones on the road from a predominantly white European populace to a more globalized, multiethnic country, we can ask whether older Americans will prove willing to provide for a much more diverse younger generation that looks and sounds less like they do. Will they be willing to reach across deepening divides of schooling and employment, as the children of more and less affluent families are raised in more segregated settings and face more unequal outcomes? Affluent college-educated parents have invested much more money and time in their children over the past generation. Less-educated parents have increased only slightly the time they spend caring for their children and the money they spend enriching their education, since they are more often stressed financially, strapped for time, and parenting without a partner. As richer kids have grown more active in school and after school, poorer kids have grown more detached and doubtful, less successful in school, less hopeful about their future, and less trusting toward their society and its institutions.[55]

Will Americans be willing to pay to educate and employ the next generation of youth from minorities and poorer families fairly enough to enable them to compete in a global economy, and to care for the surging number of baby boomers as they age into retirement? Compared to other developed nations, with lower immigration and fertility rates, the United States enjoys the demographic advantage of a younger population sizable enough to support the rising ranks of its aging members. But if older Americans do not provide for the next generation, they will not be able to provide for them in turn. However powerful the prudence of such reciprocity, Americans in recent decades continue to wrestle over the practical implications of civil rights, equal opportunity, and nondiscrimination when it comes to unequal schooling, jobs, wages, health care, and public provision. Charged by controversy over immigration flaring along ethnic and partisan lines between generations, these conflicts over public provision, schooling, and job creation have burned most fiercely in states with the biggest differences in racial and ethnic makeup between old and young, including Texas, Florida, Arizona, Nevada, and California.[56]

Nine of ten American voters from 1948 to 1970 were white. But whites added up to fewer than three in four voters in the 2008 election, and they will likely number fewer than two in three by 2020.[57] As the Republican Party becomes more identified with older, married "conservative Evangelical" white Protestants and "traditional" white Catholics, and the Democratic Party with younger Americans marked by greater religious, ethnic, and racial diversity, will Americans narrow or deepen their divisions over what's fair, for example, when it comes to good schools, living wages, and affordable health care and housing? Will they come together or apart over what's caring when it comes to the compatibility of capitalism and faithful values in helping the neediest?[58] Partisan interests and ideologies forged in the heat of electoral battles will figure in any answer to such questions, as the 2016 presidential campaign made explosively clear. But so will the inspiration and integrity of Americans' moral convictions across generations as they work and retire together or apart, and as they argue and reflect together in public or in smaller, more segregated circles of opinion and interest.

## FREEDOM, JUSTICE, AND THE PURSUIT OF HAPPINESS

Freedom *from* work to rest or play as you please still dances through our dreams of retirement today. But callings that compel, connect, and inspire us come to the fore, as we find in the stories told by Bill, Ella, and Kelsey. These callings emerge as we seek freedom *to* fulfill our highest hopes for what we can do with the rest of our lengthening lives, and we seek to answer our deepest desires for what we can experience and express in doing it. Freedom to do and feel and take part with others in the pursuit of happiness does not leave behind win-or-lose competition and success-or-failure comparison. But it angles away from their frustrations and burdens toward doing our best at some endeavor, art, sport, or study for its own sake, and for the sake of sharing it with family, friends, or colleagues over a good meal, game, or book, a sweet song or a heartfelt hymn.

For a generation born into two decades of spreading prosperity and progress after World War II, then facing economic downturns and divisions, an unsettling sense of doubt has set in about equal-opportunity ideals of freedom to compete, win, and do better than before, much better than our parents if not our peers. A rising tide lifts all boats. But the success of an outstanding or fortunate few now seems to come more and more at the expense of others who have also worked hard and done their part, but gotten a smaller slice of a growing pie. They find themselves becalmed at low tide, stuck in a stalled waiting line, as privileged ones cut in up ahead. Fewer of us outearn our parents, and most of us have not had a real raise in take-home pay since 1980. Mobility has remained alarmingly low and turned more uneven, except near the very top, while the challenge of getting to the top has grown more strenuous and anxious, and the fear of falling has grown closer and more real. As the gap in life spans between rich and poor grows wider in America, progressive principles built into the design of Social Security are gradually turning more regressive in practice, since more benefits accrue to the more affluent over longer life spans, and fewer go to the poor who live little longer.[59]

In response to this deepening material need and moral difficulty, encore careers and volunteering in retirement have expanded to help the neediest and do good for others, to give back to the community and make the world a better place. Such response has spread not only among the most fortunate, such as Bill Hanson, but among millions of middle Americans in churches, charities, neighborhoods, and civic groups across the country. Criticism has mounted, too, that philanthropy, charity, and do-gooding by good-hearted volunteers, however sincerely done and freely given, are not enough to remedy what ails us.

We need justice too. We need more equally shared economic growth, backed by better health care and education for needy children that lead to better jobs with living wages secured by collective bargaining. That means not only slicing the economic pie more evenly, but reforming our public household more fairly and wisely, as Kelsey Tyler puts it, to devise different ways to power and feed ourselves, to share work and retirement with dignity. That is what we must do to support and enable good ways of life for everyone, as Ella Mills asks. Justice not only sets fair rules and procedures for distributing goods, defining rights, punishing wrongs, and balancing exchanges. It patterns practical virtues that come together in the fabric of our everyday activities and relationships woven into ways of life, framed and fostered by the institutional arrangements that structure our society.[60] How we form families, play games, go to school, do business, lend money, pay wages and taxes, offer or deny public provision, cast votes and make laws: all these practices go into shaping the society that shapes ourselves in turn, and sustains or shifts the moral visions we live by and the virtues we live out. Let's do good and do right.

Easier said than done? Of course, given the enormous economic costs and benefits at stake, and the powerful political interests in play. But moral visions and judgments of retirement can make a world of lawful difference, too, in the ways we think and feel about the good of retirement, and the fairness of how we reach and realize it. To appreciate the layers of language and imagery that define the moral drama of retirement, and the institutional angles and frameworks of its staging, let's turn to those who advise and influence us, from advertisers stirring our dreams of retirement through financial planners sharpening our strategies to reach it, to therapists clarifying our self-awareness and pastors caring for our souls in light of the life to come.

# GOOD ADVICE ON THE CARE OF MONEY, SELVES, AND SOULS

## FROM FINANCIAL PLANNERS, THERAPISTS, AND PASTORS

### FOLLOW YOUR DREAMS

White sand beaches and windswept waves that stretch forever along the golden shore, silvered streams that flow through mountains and rivers without end, water lights dancing across the lake as the sun sets ever so slowly: we've seen and felt it with the ones we love, given by grace and fortune, and we've seen it again in our dreams. There's nothing quite like it in the moment, and that moment echoes endlessly in images and stories advertising where to go and what to do with the rest of our lives in retirement as an endless vacation. Paradise on earth takes many forms and settings—hunting or fishing in the high country, sailing islands in the stream, driving emerald green fairways through the pines, following seasons at the symphony, ballpark, racetrack, slopes, or shore. Travel to Vienna or Verona for the opera, Paris or Florence for high art, Nashville or New Orleans for down-home music. Take a big bite of the Big Apple, and leave your heart in San Francisco. Trek Yellowstone, Yosemite, or Nepal. Ride the waves in Hawaii and Bali. Ski the powder in Vail or Chamonix. See the wonders of the world, climb its peaks, swim its shimmering seas.

Can we do all this with the ones we love? Can we fall in love again? Yes, we can, promise our hosts at romantic resorts in the islands. Can we renew our bodies and revive our spirits to experience anew all that life has to offer? Yes, we can, promise our doctors, with the medicines and regimens we need to keep the promise of lifelong romance, play, and athletic adventure to express and fulfill our innermost selves. Depicting silver-haired surfers aglow on shining shores, a leading hospital advertises the medical care needed to stay at one with the wind and the waves. "Joints aren't designed to last a lifetime," an expert orthopedic surgeon notes, but they can be replaced for a generation of those, unlike their parents, who "are unwilling to give up their active life-styles as they age."[1]

## Plan for retirement and get good, sound advice.

Entering into the moment, enjoying its fullness in harmony with nature, and embracing its rhythm with the one you love hold out a promise made by centuries of Romantic celebration of selfhood aglow with passionate feeling and flowing in poetic time to the whole of life in all its poignant beauty yet fleeting transiency too.[2] From the contemplative heights of Cambridge Platonism and the intimacy of Jane Austen's novels to the romantic castles of modern entertainment and consumerist daydreaming, "beauty is momentary in the mind—the fitful tracing of a portal; but in the flesh it is immortal."[3] Can we stretch these moments into an endless summer? Can we extend these seasons into immortality or at least lengthen them through all the years of our lives to come? Answering yes accepts the bright promise and open invitation of advertising for retirement as vacation. It poses the predictable problem of retirement saving and spending, to be solved by sound financial advice and prudent planning. It can present an interpersonal challenge to be met by therapeutic insight. It can also reveal a spiritual journey to be lit by prayer, meditation, and reflection on the grace of God and the truth of human existence.

In cultural and creedal terms, advertising, financial planning, therapeutic counsel, and the care of souls suggest the growing importance of "health," enhanced into vibrant "wellness," as a moral and social good at the center of reflecting on retirement as a personal way of life and state of grace, no less than debating in public why we should cut or extend social spending to cover Medicare, Medicaid, and Obamacare.[4] This vision of good exerts wider practical influence on faithful Americans across more or less orthodox soteriologies in weighing what they must do to be saved from suffering and seek salvation in this world if not the next. It focuses our heartfelt moral intuitions in turn, for example, in putting self-actualization alongside neighbor-love or before it, since "you have to love yourself before you can love anyone else," or in grounding self-acceptance in disciplines of moral perfection or religious devotion that range from traditional spiritual exercises through aerobics to vegan diets and hot yoga.

## THE FIRST DAY OF THE REST OF YOUR LIFE

Golden sunset years? Instead imagine retirement as the dawn breaking bright on thousands of mornings to come, each one the first day of the rest of your life, and all of them together stretching out for years and years after you retire. So suggest the snapshots on the opening page of a series of "Day One Stories" told by Prudential Insurance.[5] They show the sun rising over shimmering scenes of a wooded lake, green hills, breezy seashore, and pastel desert, seen from a beckoning porch, patio, pier, or the window of a warm kitchen and greeted with a cup of coffee, a morning walk, or a yoga workout. A tote board set among the snapshots counts the numbers of Americans who have retired since the beginning of 2011, reaching 5 million by 2012 and rising as you watch. Click on a larger panel in the middle of the page, and learn that "the biggest generation in American history is retiring. 10,000 people every day."

Then listen to a soft-spoken, engaging gentleman in his sixties talk of having had enough of selling menswear for decades, and deciding firmly, "I'm done. As soon as I could access the retirement plan, I'm outta here." And here he is now, playing sweetly with his beautiful young grandchildren, gently embracing his lovely wife on the sofa in the living room of their snug home, fishing on a nearby lake in the morning, and later on preparing the catch for dinner. "It is truly the first sunrise of the next phase of your life, you know," he proclaims. "So far, so good!"

A second story begins with a woman sipping coffee on the porch of a woodsy lakeside home, as she says, "Happiness comes and goes. But I think contentment is always there, even underneath when you're having a problem. I mean, to be content, you have to want what you've got." Widowed after thirty-five years of fruitful marriage, she recalls how her husband reached up and touched her face just before he died, and how she has found the strength to go on, getting up and hugging her dog and her children each day, and looking ahead to what's to come.

## Be prepared: financial advising and planning for retirement raise moral questions.

Other vignettes follow: a silver-haired father waters the front lawn of his suburban ranch home and works expertly in his garage woodshop, as he testifies that he has taken care of his kids and family for decades, and "now it's my time." He has put in 168,000 hours over thirty-seven years in the stagehands' union, designing and building television stage sets. He can feel his body breaking down—his back, shoulder, knees. Now he's ready to leave Los Angeles and build a dream house of his own in the country.

"Jobs come and go," confides an African-American businesswoman. "In the end the only things that really matter are just your family and friends." She's glad to wake up on her own, without the alarm clock buzzing at 5 a.m., and to find she doesn't miss the office schedule at all. She's officially classified as a senior citizen, but she doesn't feel like one. "Baby boomers believe we never die," she laughs, and she has her grandchildren to keep her busy and young. However much money she has, she says, "that's what I'm gonna live within," free at last to get back to who she really is. "Most people today live to work. But it shouldn't be like that. We should work to live." And now she can. "Today is my day, open. Just take it as it unfolds."

The AARP likewise invites Americans planning to retire to let the Association guide them to fulfilling the dreams that wind through their working lives yet reach beyond the workaday world. It can help them answer the question, "What's Next in Your Life?" as they follow out their reveries and voice their inner desires.[6] A greying diner turns to his companion over the table of an elegant restaurant to promise, "You know, when I grow up, I'm gonna own my own restaurant." A father roasting marshmallows with his children over a campfire in the woods, pledges, "I want to be a volunteer firefighter." A librarian shelving books whispers, "When I grow up, I want to write a novel." The hard-hatted driver of a paint truck spraying the centerline of a gritty city street shouts, "I wanna go on a road trip." A lovely woman in a wheelchair, gazing at a picture postcard of the Taj Mahal, vows, "When I grow up, I'm going to go there." A laborer leans on his shovel in the rubble of a demolished office building, and declares, "I want to fix up old houses." An announcer intones, "At AARP we believe you're never done growing." At last a handsome silver-haired woman in a commercial bakery looks up from putting the final flourishes of flowered frosting on a tiered white wedding cake to nod fondly with a smile, "*I want to fall in love again.*" Amen! "Discover what's next in your life," concludes the voice-over to a closing picture of a bright red travel bag. "It's yours free when you join today."

# LIFE WELL PLANNED

Retirement is just around the corner, financial advisors remind baby boomers now advancing from their midfifties to early seventies.[7] "It's the place we all want to get to," attests one such financial firm in its online advertising, not only "a long and lively retirement" as a matter of fact, but "the comfort of knowing you'll be able to enjoy the lifestyle you want, for as long as you live." That comforting promise holds out no certainty of salvation in the world to come, but it offers the certainty of security in this world, freed from its fateful contingencies and disappointments. It calls for a rational and effective program of "lifetime planning," because "getting there starts with a plan" that is moral as well as practical. "Take a daily dose of practical wisdom and timely tips. Find inspiration in animated tales of planning happily ever after. Get some good advice and give a little of your own," invites the firm's website. This advice includes strategic instruction, for example, "The surest way to financial happiness is to spend less than you bring in." But it also urges, "Enjoy the good times and plan for the hard times," and it declares, "Wealth is not meaningful until it is shared."

Such advice on the opening pages of today's "Planner's Almanac" harks back to 1732 with the first annual edition of *Poor Richard's Almanack*, distilled in its preface, "The Way to Wealth," which Ben Franklin first mapped out in 1757. However apocryphal in some cases, his leading maxims still echo today:[8] "Time is money . . . A stitch in time saves nine . . . Early to bed and early to rise makes a man healthy, wealthy and wise . . . God helps those who help themselves." Franklin's advice is essentially prudent and pragmatic, down-to-earth and often materialistic. But its prudence is a moral virtue nonetheless, not just a strategy, and its common sense relies on a larger vision of the world and life's purpose. The way to wealth is straightforward: "Increase your means or decrease your wants. The best is to do both at the same time." But wealth does not by itself lead to happiness, as Franklin makes clear. "Money has never made man happy yet, nor will it; there is nothing in its nature to produce happiness. The more of it one has, the more one wants." Instead the purpose of money is "to purchase one's freedom to pursue that which is useful and interesting," measured by standards of social benefit as well as personal satisfaction that imply democratic equality and progress, on one hand, and individual autonomy and accomplishment, on the other.

Getting ahead by dint of one's own industry and frugality propels part of Franklin's story, to be sure: "Human felicity is produced not as much by great pieces of good fortune that seldom happen as by little advantages that occur every day." So, too, come social recognition and status, with a biblical ring that echoes Franklin's strict Calvinist upbringing as well as expressing his opportune deism: "Seest thou a man diligent in his business? he shall stand before kings" (Proverbs 22:29 AKJV). Honesty is indeed the best policy, Franklin thought. It is good because it is useful in assuring credit. Were it not, it would be no virtue at all. But the utility of virtue, embodied in the creditworthiness of persons and enacted in their diligent labor and saving, is grounded in an inherently good way of life that transforms the meaning of happiness itself.[9]

Ben Franklin concluded "The Way to Wealth" with an emphatic maxim: "Get what you can, and what you get hold; 'tis the stone that will turn all your lead to gold."[10] Yet for all the reason and wisdom of this philosopher's stone, its alchemical magic works through a kind of deist miracle. Its success relies upon divine providence in a free market full of contingencies that can ruin the upstanding and reward the unworthy. Advised Franklin, "After all, do not depend too much upon your own industry and frugality and prudence, though excellent things, for they may all be blasted without the blessing of Heaven; and therefore ask that blessing humbly, and be not uncharitable to those that at present seem to want it, but comfort and help them. Remember Job suffered, and was afterwards prosperous."[11]

So he was, but only after a rewarding rewrite of the biblical text to yield this happy ending. Franklin elsewhere counsels a Stoic sort of self-reliance in the face of fickle fate, since "happiness depends more on the inward Disposition of Mind than on outward Circumstances," and he holds the world's injustice against its Creator: "I believe in one God,

Creator of the Universe in that He ought to be whipped from pilar to post and back again for His shameful actions toward Humanity."[12]

Today the way to wealth mapped by financial planners leads more directly to "financial happiness," but the prudential logic of Franklin's double-entry bookkeeping remains in force. Lay a foundation to create "a sustainable plan in which you spend less than you earn and direct savings toward important goals," begins the "lifetime planning" advice of a leading firm of financial advisors with a broad swath of upper-middle class clients across the United States.[13] Manage and eliminate debts, they advise, while starting an emergency fund with three to six months of living expenses and planning for near-term goals, such as starting a family or buying a car. "Managing your competing needs and goals" comes next, via a strategy to "prioritize your goals and plan accordingly, while always being thoughtful about your current lifestyle choices versus future wants." Make retirement your first priority by making the most of tax-advantaged retirement accounts and employer benefits. Plan ahead for the college education of your children. Choose "investments suited to your needs, constraints, obligations, and goals." Manage risks by working to "mitigate volatility in your portfolio, identify risks, and find appropriate insurance where needed (renters/homeowners, health, life, disability, etc.)."

At the center of this sequence of challenges lies "making the transition" to retirement, met by strategies of "keeping your retirement plan on track" through maximizing contributions, considering rollover strategies, and planning distribution schedules. Then estimate expected time of retirement and map out an "exit strategy" well in advance. Maximize government benefits such as Social Security and Medicare. Plan to care for an aging parent, if need be, and "ensure you can help your children without hurting yourself . . . determine what you can do without adversely impacting your own plans." In retirement, streamline your finances to better manage cash flow; deal with health care issues such as long-term care; maximize income from pensions. Start to plan a legacy through estate distribution and charitable giving. Finally, counsels this leading firm of financial planners, protect your wealth. Ensure it ends up where you want it to, and it leaves a lasting impact, by working to "identify the causes you care about most and create a generous, tax-advantageous giving strategy."

Such advice for a life well planned sounds sensible and straightforward. It also sounds detailed and demanding enough to call for professional help to get started right away. Since "ought" implies "can," its prudent strategies and stress on making goal-directed choices and setting priorities to maximize the benefits of wealth and minimize the risks of debt imply the steady earnings of educated professionals and successful business managers. Can it be heeded by Americans further down the economic ladder, most of them nearing retirement with no more than $25,000–$50,000 in savings and no more than Social Security payments in income? "We can't help you," answers an advisor for one of the country's largest financial planners, off the record. "I'm sorry about that, but $50,000 is just too little too late. Put your money in a savings account at 1 or 2 percent, and keep your fingers crossed. Try not to get sick, and stay at your job as long as you can. That's about all you can do."[14]

For those who can do more, setting priorities and "managing your competing needs and goals," let alone distinguishing needs and wants, is not always so easy or so rational an exercise. "I love it when clients have a dream," declares Eric Olson, a veteran financial advisor who specializes in working with state employees as well as high-tech managers in Silicon Valley.[15] "That gets me up in the morning. Don't tell me you want to be a multimillionaire when you retire." He frowns. "Tell me how you want to live and tell me why. That lets me work with the usual problem of champagne tastes and a beer budget when it comes to realizing those dreams. Tell me your goals. Then let's look at your resources and responsibilities, and see how we can achieve those goals even if we can't do it exactly the way you've been thinking."

The most common problem that financial planners face, according to Eric, stems from weakness of the will, not fuzzy fiscal calculations.

"People tell you their goals for retirement, but they live for today. They're not willing to change what they do and spend every day, whether it's that new pair of shoes or going to Starbucks twice a day for a latte. It's those day-to-day habits. They can be making $200,000 a year, and when I ask about discretionary income, they say, 'What?' When I press, they say, 'I think we can start with $100 a month.' That just kills me!" He shakes his head.

Then comes the task of setting priorities. "We can work little by little toward the big dreams at the end of the rainbow in retirement," emphasizes Eric. "But we need to save for emergencies and maybe add disability insurance here and now, and make sure we can pay for college for the kids. Stocks are not a good investment if you have to pull out cash when the market's down to pay tuition bills or pay your mortgage if you lose your job, or pay the hospital if you get sick," cautions Eric. "You need cash for the short term, stocks for long term, and bonds for in between."

Long-term investment strategies are easy to work out, once clients can set realistic priorities and commit to following them. That's the hard part. "Get your ducks in a row; then you can blow your spending money however you like," allows Eric. "I try to start with behavioral advice to people, based on what their goals and values are. But sometimes you have to question their goals or their commitments, if they can't make security number one," he warns. "Let's be realistic. You can't buy happiness. You can only give yourself the chance to live it out. That's the point of planning."

Moral judgment and evaluation underlie this advising process, and enter into it explicitly when clients struggle with "realistic" self-understanding and commitments. "I actually spend a lot of time with clients sorting out what they want," notes Eric. "They want it all." He smiles. "But they also want what they don't need, and they don't always want what they do need, at least they don't want it very much." That creates problems of moral discernment, not only financial budgeting, Eric reflects, which stem from "disordered desires." As a financial advisor, he can't solve such problems, he admits, but he can recognize and flag them. "I'm not a priest or a psychiatrist." Eric holds up his hand and laughs. "But I was raised a Lutheran, and I studied Maslow's hierarchy of needs in college. So I know what's going on, and I can say so. I can ask clients what they're going to do about it, because they don't have enough to do everything. You have to put safety and security first," he stresses, "before you get to buying the ski chalet in Aspen or the villa in Tuscany."

Is it possible to achieve freedom from fear of financial insecurity? "Not entirely," answers Eric, "but you can minimize it. You can insure against it and transfer the risk to an insurance company. Work out a good plan that moves more of your money from equities into fixed-return assets the closer you get to retirement. Don't get out of the market at sixty-five and let inflation eat up your savings. But make sure you have the first ten years of money you'll need in retirement invested in safe positions. You can diminish the fear about the worst that can happen. You don't have to worry about being old and needy." On the other hand, he adds, "When the stock market is hot, and you're making 20 percent a year, or you see your next-door neighbor in Silicon Valley flipping houses and making a million a pop, it's hard not to be greedy. Take the risk, win the fast money. Spend it now. There's more coming in." Since the one-two punch of the Great Recession beginning in 2008, a decade after the dot.com boom went bust, he observes, "it's easier for clients close to retirement to hear us when we tell them, 'You're looking good. You have enough. You don't need to risk it all and mess up.'"

Here strategic thinking and minimax logics of risk and return give way to the vices of greed and fear, envy and resentment, or they rely on the virtues of wisdom and temperance as well as prudence. "You can't get away from judgments about how people live," Eric attests. "But in this business you find out everyone's like a child, and the first thing you gotta do is not tell them no," he adds. Instead, he explains, "I'll ask clients early on, 'What does money mean to you?' Sooner or later, they'll usually say something about happiness, so I'll ask, 'Well, then, what does happiness mean to you?' If they say it's a vacation house on the beach or the ski slopes, then I'll ask why. Usually it's about feeling good, feeling peace and serenity, they say, and having a good time with their family. We can work with that, maybe renting a place for a week or a month every year instead of trying to buy it for millions you don't have or you can't get without putting your security at risk or gambling with college for your kids. Why buy the beach house if it costs you peace of mind?" Eric asks. "Answer that question, and you'll feel better. You'll do better, before you retire and after you retire," he promises. "But sometimes we never get that far," he admits. "They want it now, however they justify it."

In response, acknowledges Eric, "I can say, 'Better not,' but I can't say no. I'm in a service position, and they're the boss. It's their money and they can spend it down, until it dies before they do." Who wants to think about dying or outliving your money? "No one," replies Eric. "A good life and a good feeling about it for the rest of your life: that's what I'm selling, what I hope I'm selling. But I can't force them to buy it." Nor can he change the widening canyons of economic inequality he sees lifting up wealthy Americans, pinching the middle class, and pressing down on the poor. "The haves are doing fine, and the have-nots are up against it," Eric sums up. "Income is flat all around, except at the top. But income is not the problem, from where I stand," he stresses. "Outgo is the problem, and the only way to solve that is to control your spending, save more, and save smarter."

Calls for economic justice or redistribution may sound fine in principle, Eric concedes, but they are politically implausible and probably infeasible in practice, "because even if we can take money away from the people who earned it, we can't tell the people we give it to how to spend it." Instead he urges, "We need to love our neighbor, and help them help themselves." We need to realize that "love is critical to happiness," he concludes by invoking the Good Samaritan and Buddhist ideals of compassion. "What's the use of more money if you suffer more, if you don't take care of yourself and the people you love every day? That's not success or progress."[16] What is real happiness, then? Can a financial advisor answer this question for his clients? "Well, that, I think, is defined by each individual," Eric parries. "I can't tell them, but I can talk with them about it. That's the real conversation. Everything in life is making choices."

Do financial advisors play the part of moral guides if not priests and psychiatrists? Another veteran advisor to educated professionals in the Bay Area weighs the question and nods.[17] "I was a social worker for years before I started doing this, and there's a lot of cross-over," reflects Carol Stein, "even before the bottom dropped out in 2008, and more people began asking, 'Am I still alive?' Not just 'Do I have enough money? Do I have enough health insurance?'" Questions of retirement as fulfilling activity and aspiration lie at the center of such moral guidance and inquiry, but so do fears and worries about the future's uncertainty:

I ask them, "What are you going to do?" And people have all kinds of ideas, even people who have been sitting in a cubicle for the last thirty years and haven't had a chance to do anything. They want to play music, learn Spanish, ride a motorcycle all around Europe. I ask, "Do you want to volunteer?" Almost all of them say, "Yes! I like kids, I'm gonna tutor at the school or help out at the church."

But even if they're not worried about having enough money, they can be worried about letting go of the job. "You're one of the lucky ones," I'll say. "You can be free. You can reinvent yourself." But that can be scary, too, and you want something to hold on to.

So, you look for continuity by taking it step-by-step. One tech-writer client has been writing romance novels on the side for years, and getting them published, and now she's retiring to do it full-time. Another one, a big corporate marketing executive, is starting a small business on the side, a lunch counter in an office building downtown. That's more of a stretch, but she's got the tiger by the tail, she's got the money, and she's got a partner behind the counter who's done it before. So I'm telling her to go for it.

Moral responsibilities and social loyalties often bear on questions of financial provision and constraint that advisors weigh with their clients. For example, notes Carol, "Adult children borrowing from their parents or leaning on them instead of working harder or living within their means, that gets harder to handle once you retire. The client has to decide. But we'll run the numbers to show them they can't stick to their plan if they keep handing out $10,000 to their kids every few months. If they can't say no, then send the kids to us, and we will."

Is that so different from what a therapist or minister might do in similar circumstances? "It's a lot like it," answers Carol. "It involves the same kind of interpersonal dynamics, the same skill set. You really have to listen to people, understand their feelings and relationships, and help them face the reality of things that can be painful," not always but often. She nods. "You care about them too. You get to know their family, their hopes and dreams. You're not just handling their money. People call me every day about work, job hunting, buying a new house, going into the hospital, all kinds of things."

In fact, even though legal contracts and fiduciary rules define these fee-for-services relationships between financial advisors and their clients, "they have to trust you, and they have to like you," Carol sums up. "They have to overcome their doubts or suspicions about Bernie Madoff, and you have to convince them that won't happen here. There has to be a kind of conversion, even a 'Come to Jesus' experience, where they give you their trust, before you can act as their financial doctor, make a diagnosis, and expect them to follow your prescriptions." On the other hand, she adds, "We need to keep a degree of measured distance in order to do our job. We need to stand back far enough to see things clearly and help them, especially if they don't have enough money, or they have just enough to retire. Like a lot of our clients, they can't afford to stop short or take a big hit, because they don't have enough time to get their money back, and they don't have enough capital to get by with less."

Some prospective clients can't face the facts of such financial necessity, and others continue to wrestle with them, Carol suspects, because "they have always gotten by in the past, with a little help from their friends, or their parents. They keep hoping that somehow things will go back to the way they were. Maybe not when they were kids and the pie always kept getting bigger, but at least back to the eighties or late nineties, when you could get 10 percent fixed on your money, and the market kept going up and up." So the struggle goes on, at least for those still striving to retire in a generation that grew up in postwar prosperity before facing a leaner adulthood in the decades since 1970. "If I have to, I remind them it could be worse," adds Carol. "They could be out of a job and going through their savings to pay the rent. They could be part of the 47 percent. They could be so screwed!"[18] Indeed most fee-based financial advisors know their "comfortable but not really rich" clients well enough to admit the conspicuous absence among them of Americans with scant assets to invest in stocks, bonds, or annuities. They sense the anger of those on the bottom half of the income ladder, struggling to get by without a raise in decades, and they concede the predicament of the poor they feel powerless to help.

The Great Recession and its "great correction" in the stock market and home equity, let alone its great impact on economic hardship and inequality in America, make life grittier and riskier for almost everyone, as financial advisors recognize. "Burglaries are up by a third all around the Bay Area," noted one in 2010. "If you have nothing, you have nothing to lose. You'll risk your life and threaten somebody else's to grab their wallet." But many financial advisors also hold up the moral lessons that the Great Recession teaches. "Wants have outrun needs for a long time," Carol reflects. "Now we have to face the truth that life is not all about wants. It's about taking care of what you need, about being a good steward of what you have, in order to take care of your family, your future, your kids and their education. Having to tighten our belts and default to safety means having to figure out what's really important," she has come to realize in her own family. "Christmas or Hanukkah is about giving. It's not about how much stuff you get. The house you're in is about making it a home. It's not about owning it forever, because you can't. You're just borrowing it for a while."

A financial advisor who calls himself "tough-minded" and works primarily with successful entrepreneurs and small businessmen in the Atlanta area laughs at the thought of doing social work on the job, but he nonetheless acknowledges the "values dimension" of his work. "It's not just arithmetic, calculating what they have to put in and what they can get out over time," Bruce Jelen says.[19] "Call it financial security, but what I'm really selling is freedom. Freedom from fear of not having enough. Freedom to choose how you want to live." That's what money buys, as he explains it. "You're scaling dreams to reality. You're dealing with what people really want to do with their lives and their money, even if you don't agree with what they want. You can tell them that," he growls with a grin and a hint of his Chicago roots. "But your job is finding out what they really want, given their own values, and then seeing if they can do that with what they've got, and seeing how they can do it. If it doesn't add up, you tell them that, and you lay out options." That process shifts in specific detail, but it remains a balancing act and an exercise in proportion. "In the nineties everyone was telling you they wanted to buy high-tech and make at least 20 percent every year, and you're telling them they need to stay balanced to be safe. Now everyone wants to be safe, and you have to tell them, 'You need to accept some risk and volatility to get 4–5 percent and stay ahead of inflation.'"

Financial planning also turns on stories of family relationships, loyalties, and conflicts that span generations. "I probably know more about the intimate relationships in the family of some of my clients than any members of their family will ever know," Bruce Jelen judges. "I hear more of their frustrations and venting about getting old and useless, not just investment losses and medical costs, but being demobilized financially and demoralized personally." How does he respond? "If you feel let down," he asks in turn, "are you letting yourself down? Can you do more with less? Can you do something tomorrow? Go out and volunteer at church, take a friend to lunch, take a walk with a neighbor. Don't just sit around and watch TV and eat chips."

Each case is individual, and no one prescription fits all. It's easy to start planning early on for smart people with solid pensions, good health, and many interests, he observes. "It's hard to do it for people who are already retired, on fixed incomes, watching their assets melt down and their stockbrokers burn them to the ground."

In such difficult cases, explains Bruce, it makes sense to cut investment losses, disillusion "blind faith in stockbrokers," refinance mortgages, and turn to affordable annuities to guarantee a minimum income. "Most of the despair I find is driven by finances and health, people losing their money or their health or both," he reports. "When I need to, I'll go through all their credit-card statements with them, and all their medical prescriptions. I'll send them back to talk with their docs. I'll talk to Visa with them. Start there, take it one step at a time over a few months, and you can cure a lot of the depression I see. Think about selling the big house that's tying you down and tying up your capital. Put more choices on the table," Bruce insists. "That's the only real value money has while we're alive. Expand your means to make for more choices, if you can. If you can't, choose within your means, experience more security, and find out you can enjoy life more when you're not depressed about money."

Granting this diagnosis of despair in individual cases, argues Bruce, a broader challenge in retirement, even for those who are healthy and financially secure, stems from withdrawal from social activity and relationships woven into the fabric of working life. "People retire and they want to be free to expand their lives. What happens instead? They find their lives shrinking. They get out less. They feel less a part of the community around them," he observes. "What they want and need is more sense of connection and engagement, like they had at work. They don't want to go down to the senior center and sit around. They want to go do something that matters out in the world, that's satisfying and enjoyable."

What can retirees do that matters? Where can they find it, and how can we better provide for it? Volunteering activities abound in religious and civic groups, Bruce replies. But why not seek more public opportunities and provision for community service, beginning at the local level? "Instead of giving all the money away to Goldman Sachs and big corporations," he proposes, "government could budget just a little of it to help capable, energetic retired people to become more active in their own communities. Help them enhance the quality of life in their own communities and run them better, and that would lift up their own spirits in the process."

By way of example, Bruce points to affluent retirement communities, however privileged their citizens and deep their pockets, for model programs that could be fostered in other locales through state and federal funding. "Look at Hilton Head or La Quinta in California, and you see people who are retired, who have money and brains. They're looking for things to do besides golf, things that add to the quality of life in the community—parks and recreation, the arts, school enrichment programs, infrastructure. There's high involvement by people who can think and do. Yes, some of them are big shots trying to outdo each other." He shrugs. "But there's plenty of people talking and working together, getting real results everybody can see. They feel good about it, and it inspires them to do more." Bruce echoes Tocqueville in celebrating vibrant voluntary associations and town hall meetings at the heart of participatory democracy in America for enlightening self-interest and enlivening the common good. "Business, pleasure, and community service *can* go together. The less altruistic, the better!" he exclaims. "People will get more involved when it feels good, *and* they can see it benefiting themselves, too. It offers them places to go and things to do with other people. It gets them out of the house, and that solves a big problem for lots of retired people."

Beyond such prospects and proposals, allows Bruce, lie the facts of human aging, declining capacities, and spreading symptoms of chronic degenerative disease, as many Americans live longer, healthier lives. "Aging catches up to all of us," he says, "so you need to begin early on, way before you retire, in broadening the base of where you put your time, and what you learn to enjoy. If you used to climb mountains and now your knees are shot, you need to start fly-fishing, snorkeling, or painting mountain landscapes." Such activity and sociability go hand in hand, he observes, "Most women are better at retirement, because they're more sociable. They're better at supporting and enjoying relationships." So, he asks with a smile, "Why not put them in charge of making our communities and government more that way? That's one progressive idea I can support as a libertarian who hates big government almost as much as I hate big banks."

What of human finitude and fate, persisting beyond parables of active, sociable retirement that stretch from the present to eighty-something? "Not all of them, but many of my older retirees have grown up with faith in God," reflects Bruce. "They trust in some life after this life. They try to love their neighbor. They engage in small acts of kindness, they feel goodness in giving and receiving. In their eighties and up, that faith sustains them. Not so much in our age group, sixties and younger. Our mortality? Most of us haven't had to face it yet, and I don't know how well we will when the time comes. We can still boogie. We can still get an artificial hip and get back out there. Go in for a nip and tuck, and come out looking better or at least tighter. Go to church or temple? Not so much, unless you have to. Send your kids to a religious school? Sure, if it's the best one they can get into."

Is that a change for the better or worse? "I don't know if I can judge," replies Bruce, holding up a cautionary hand. "Going to church, I could say, goes along with having a stronger moral compass and a stronger community. For some folks, but not for everyone." Can he say the same about life and death? "The only people who want to live forever are people who fear death," he answers, "and I can say the ones who don't are the ones I've come to like best and admire most over the thirty years I've been doing this, and getting to know hundreds of people in the last years of their lives. In fact, sometimes I'm the last one there when they go." He pauses.

"There is a season to it all, and when it's your time, it's time to go," he concludes. "I do believe that, even if I don't know what comes next."

## PERSONAL PROSPECTS
## AND QUESTIONS IN COMMON

Financial advising and planning for retirement raise deeper moral questions that many advisors and their clients ignore, confesses Carol Stein as an investment advisor long committed to environmental and social justice. These questions have grown more urgent and harder to answer in her experience since the late 1990s:

> After thirty-plus years of doing this, as I come closer to retirement myself, I find myself feeling more and more disillusioned on behalf of my clients. For myself, too. Through all the ups and downs since 1980, I've tried to help people find their way to some measure of security without doing more harm than good in the world.
>
> But in the past few years the tide of greed driving the financial deception and political chicanery has risen so high at the top, with no respect for the common person down below, that it's left me feeling absolutely frustrated and angry. It's flattened out my clients' portfolios over the past ten years, so all we've worked for has lost the promise it once held. No matter what we do, no matter how hard we try, we have very little control over the outcome, because just a few people calling the shots have so much control.[20]

Where does that leave her and her clients? "You do what you can. What else can you do?" she asks in turn. "Fortunately, most of my clients have enough saved and enough smarts to trim their spending sails or work longer, and wait for the market to come back," she replied in 2012. "Some of them don't, and that's the hardest part, telling them they just can't retire anytime soon. Sometimes they won't hear that, and I have to cut them loose."

Most of Carol Stein's clients are "level-headed" professionals with progressive political views. "They're looking for enough, not just more and more so they can get and spend to the max," she says. "They're conscious of what they want to do, and conscientious enough to give up a little by not putting money in big oil or coal or tobacco, for example, or the weapons industry. They want to have enough money to make it to 95, if they stay healthy, and not have to worry about it. There's an emotional part to it," she explains, "so I'll ask them about money in their family, growing up. I'll factor that in when it comes to questions about planning to pay off the mortgage instead of keeping the mortgage-interest tax break, if it makes them feel really good to pay it off and not have to worry about it anymore." Freedom and responsibility figure in her work, she attests, especially "the counseling side you can't reduce to calculation and control," or surrender under the powerful pressures of economic adversity and political betrayal. Nor can she avoid moral difficulties and emotions in the present, as parents pass away and inheritance conflicts arise, she adds. She points to a box of tissues on a side table in her office. "When it's crying time, you need to cry, then dry your tears and make good decisions."

Nonetheless, as a financial planner dedicated to "socially responsible investment and social change," Carol grapples with the moral difficulty that seeking a better world has led her clients to bear undue financial burdens, indeed punishment in financial markets, instead of reaping their due rewards. "I'm fortunate to work with people committed to good causes and good charities. We screen to stay away from enterprises doing bad—global warming, child labor—and invest in enterprises doing good, for example, clean energy, microfinance. We try to change corporate behavior for the better, like employee health care and affordable housing, through shareholder activism and proxy voting. My clients really care about world hunger, world peace, peace in the Middle East. They want to do something to support these causes, not just look around the world at all the wars and famine, and look away."

Carol Stein's clients have not come to question their commitments to peace and justice, but they do question the powerful forces that frustrate their efforts to live them out. "They don't blame me, but they are disappointed that we haven't done better, while Exxon and Goldman are doing just fine." Carol frowns. "They blame them for rigging the global economy, and the politicians for letting them get away with it." Does this carry over into practical changes in her financial planning and advising? "We talk more politics now, but what I can actually do about it is just focus more on helping clients handle volatility and risk, easing off and dampening it down by going to different investment options and financial vehicles," Carol says quietly. "Even so, the loss of fortune I've seen since 2008, the stress and illness it's brought to my clients and friends, it's taken its toll on me. It's frustrating. It's disgusting!" she exclaims. "In 2012 I wanted to strangle Paul Ryan! I couldn't bear to watch any more of it on TV, because it's not fair and it's not true."

Such problems of investing for the public good as well as the good of your own retirement cannot be resolved within the institutional framework of American pension plans and politics today, cautions Noah Morris, a successful investment advisor in Silicon Valley trained in an elite business school.[21] Neither can moral principles be cut off from investment practices to earn reliable returns for retirement. "Good financial planning is half counseling and half calculating," as he sees it. "Most baby boomers who go to financial planners today want to do as well or better than their parents, who were professionals or business managers of some kind, and they're afraid they won't make it. They're afraid even if they have a million or so by the time they're 55 or 60, even if they own their own home, or most of it, and even if they don't suffer from 'affluenza.'" The exploding costs of Bay Area real estate help inspire such fear, he grants. But much of it is due to "the sense that you should do everything for your children, to help them make it to success and safety in an unsafe world" of rising competition and contingency in school and work.

Money doesn't buy happiness but
poverty can bring misery.

"Money doesn't buy happiness," Noah notes with a nod to recent research in behavioral economics, "once you get past misery in poverty. But people like to feel at least a little above average for their peer group. They want to do better than their parents, or at least a little better than their friends and siblings." Where does that leave us? "Playing a losing game," laughs Noah dryly. "Choose your peer group carefully, let's say, but by definition everyone cannot be above average, except maybe in Lake Woebegone or the Friends School." Professionals and managers in the top tenth of households by income will get by nonetheless, he observes, and most of them have "gotten the message to max their 401(k) and take deductions to minimize their taxes. But there's still half of America with almost nothing saved, almost no net worth, and it's not clear what's going to happen to them, except suffering."

The history of employer-funded retirement plans defies economic logic and justice alike, argues Noah, since such plans turn on a conflict of interest for executives and directors of companies trying to cut costs and increase earnings. "Do you really want your boss setting up your trust fund and doing your investing?" he asks. "I don't! Employers shouldn't be in this business at all. Most of the plans are poorly managed. I can outperform their investments 99 percent of the time." Is there a better way to provide for retirement for everyone? "Sure, why not set it up through a cabinet post and a full-scale agency for personal finance?" Noah answers forcefully. "Put Elizabeth Warren in charge. Redesign Social Security to go all the way up and down the income ladder, and go all the way out to cover everyone adequately. Then add a layer of voluntary contribution on top of it, like FDR wanted," he proposes. "Keep corporations out of the process, because they are *not* persons or citizens, and almost none of them actually operates for any higher public purpose," he argues.[22] "Corporations are fine for what they do—maximize productivity and profits. But don't let them mess up the tax code and retirement rules in order to cut their labor costs and inflate their share price."

There is actually a missing sector in America's political economy, as Noah Morris sees it, which spans conventional boundaries between consumers in a free market and citizens in a free republic. "Except for *Consumer Reports* for cars and toasters, there's nothing there. It's totally blanked out by advertising," he charges.

> It's where we have a right to get accurate information and reliable advice about making economic and social choices from someone who has no vested interest, because they're not selling something. We should change that. That's not socialism or big government! It's Econ 101! It's where supply meets demand through efficient competition given perfect information. It's making free markets work for free citizens by equalizing knowledge and agency among market actors trying to plan rationally for their own retirement, instead of rigging the system to keep them tied up and in the dark. You can even stick with a 401(k) model to supplement your real pension, but at least allow access for employees of every company to the best providers with the lowest expenses. Give them Vanguard index funds, not just Merrill Lynch. Give them an investment time-horizon of forty years and enable them to stick to it, even though that's much longer than they think, because historically you need a window of twenty to twenty-five years to make the stock market work reliably for you.

Short of such social changes, what are we to do? Ideally, everyone employed at living wages could retire securely, Noah muses, if only they saved and invested 10 percent of their income every year from their first year on the job. Let them follow the numbers of the retirement calculator available on the website of every mutual fund and insurance company. Granted that the cost and time of schooling have expanded over the past generation, jobs have grown less steady and careers less continuous, while housing and health care have grown more expensive. But still, Noah asks, "How much have you got now? How much will you have at retirement? Take 4 percent of that and see if you can live on it," he proposes. That exercise is straightforward, however iffy the market returns, but it points to a savings threshold beyond what many Americans find feasible to reach, he argues, "so they simply ignore it."

Even for those who can afford to retire on their pension, savings, and investments, reflects Noah, "retirement as some kind of withdrawal makes less sense to people now. Even if they want permission to get out of a job they hate, they want to be free to choose something else to get into, not just play golf or goof off. They want a second chance, a second start. Move to Costa Rica and build your dream house," he laughs, "or move to Sea Ranch and build a pottery studio." Dreams of self-renewal and self-expression, echoing in advertisements for retirement communities, annuities, and mutual funds, resonate with utopian communities, eco-sensitive "simple living," yoga retreats, and romantic visions of artist colonies by the sea and truly communist societies in college towns. There individuals are set free from workaday routines and the division of labor to renew their innermost selves together with like-minded friends, loving companions, and congenial neighbors as fellow citizens of a pure participatory democracy.[23]

"If you're a professional with a steady job, and you're a good saver and a prudent spender," concludes Noah, "you can retire and get free from your job sooner than you think. But then what are you free to do?" he asks quizzically. "That's actually scary for more people than you think. It may be harder than you think to find out, or it may take longer. Maybe there's no community to support it. Probably there's no market for it, if you want to do something and get paid for it." Moreover, he adds, "To find your path, you have to find someone to take it with you. Can your spouse come along? What about your kids, if you're still taking care of them, or your parents?" Here the distinction between "freedom from" and "freedom to" takes practical form and social substance in specific relationships and institutions that open up or cut down individual choices, which are themselves colored and constituted in cultural terms. Here, too, the prudential choices that financial advisors calculate rely in turn on moral values and visions that therapeutic thinking explores and spiritual insight reveals.

## THERAPEUTIC THINKING ABOUT AGING

Modern theories of the human life cycle and psychologies of moral development trace their cultural roots in the West, as we will see in chapter

3, to overarching visions of human origin and destiny in biblical terms of divine creation and redemption, and classical terms of the virtuous *polis* tuned to the lawful order of the soul and the universe. Such religious worldviews evolve "pervasive configurations of the course of life," as Erik Erikson puts it, whether as a spiral of rebirths or a crossroads to heaven or hell. Various ways of life harbor more or less explicit images of life's course, whether as a common journey or a competitive race. Knowledge, conviction, and experience combine in such conceptions of the life cycle, and they in turn embrace stories of individuals in the sequence of generations, the social order of institutions, and the history of cultures.[24]

Erikson depicts productive, creative, and caring "generativity" as the cardinal virtue of psychological and social adulthood, gradually ripening into the wisdom of old age in its moral integrity of experience and inclusive understanding. Parenthood is the social model and moral metaphor at the center of Erikson's picture of human dependency and maturity in reciprocal relationship. Mature humans need to be needed, to care for the needy, to teach and learn, institutionalize and reform. Where mutual care and enrichment fail, stagnation and boredom ensue in adulthood, and generations grow estranged from justice as a practical virtue, overcome by ambivalence between fixed obligation and narrow self-concern. The wisdom of old age responds to the need for an integrated heritage in each oncoming generation, yet it remains aware of the limits of knowledge gained in one lifetime and one historical moment. The integrity of old age stands ready to take leadership in the present yet eventually give it up on the way to joining the ancestors of the future. Where wisdom fails, despair takes hold in the face of death, masked by disgust and bitterness that time is too short to start over and fate too cruel to accept as life's finite frame. Old age evokes the ultimate concerns and paradoxes of one life to live in the sequence of generations, in all its loss and finitude as well as fullness. It brings near the mystery of religious and philosophical paths to seek transcendence through renunciation that affirms life's meaning and generosity that accepts life's end.[25]

Popular psychologies of retirement today commonly focus on the creative, dynamic aspects of generative adulthood. Less burdened by parental concerns to guide the next generation, or check the self-indulgence of adults acting as their own children, they celebrate the prospect of youthful self-renewal and self-discovery through a fresh start in life or a second career started afresh in midlife. Why not, for example, conceive of "the second half of life," beginning at age fifty or sixty, to set the stage for an "encore performance" in a new career of second-stage entrepreneurship and innovation.[26] "If the old golden years dream was the freedom *from* work, the dream of this new wave is the freedom *to* work—in new ways, on new terms, to new and even more important ends." So promises Marc Freedman in *Encore*, a guide to "finding work that matters in the second half of life" for members of the baby boom generation.[27]

"Demography turns out not to be destiny," by this account, tuned to the hopeful expectation of well-educated baby boomers for health and energy to spare well into their eighties and nineties, fueling the purpose-driven progress of their "Careers 2.0" and postponing conventional retirement through their seventies and beyond.[28] Retirement is being displaced by a new stage of life and work, declares *Encore*, that is now "opening up between the end of midlife and the arrival of true old age, a period that essentially amounts to the second half of life, at least adult life."[29] Greater longevity is now reordering the life cycle, in short, and a new stage of life is now enabling a new world of work. It stretches beyond bridge jobs at Wal-Mart for needy seniors to spur new dreams for the best and brightest of the baby-boom generation, and create new benefits for the society as a whole.

This hopeful prospect resonates with some psychotherapists in Silicon Valley, ringing true to their experience in counseling patients concerned with retirement and inspiring their own visions of a better future. "Freud thought the first few years of life structured your personality for life," notes one such visionary psychotherapist with clients drawn mainly from high-tech engineers and professionals.[30] "Then developmental psychology stretched this out through different stages of life. Now neuroscience is showing us how plastic the adult brain turns out to be. Things keep changing in our brains," sums up Frank Costa with an engaging smile. "That means we can change our minds by the different things we do, and the different ways we live. Learning can be lifelong." But does such capacity for change ensure adaptive learning on the road to truly valuable knowledge, let alone practical wisdom? "Sure, you can imagine maladaptive 'brave new worlds,' or look around at what's wrong with this world, from job stress to global warming," he concedes. "But neuroscience doesn't just appeal to engineers because it ties consciousness to productivity in ways you can measure. It opens a new door to wisdom traditions of forming conscience, developing mindfulness." He nods. "That gives us another way to think about 'progress' and pursue it besides trying to get more stuff."

Nothing could be more valuable, counsels Frank, since "becoming more self-aware frees you from needing more material stuff to feel satisfied and comfortable." That in turn will not resolve problems of global warming and dimming, resource depletion and population growth. But it will enable us to reconceive retirement as part of a larger effort to live more consciously in harmony with others and the environment. That is certainly no mean feat. But is it no more than a utopian hope and ideal of perfection for the privileged? "Let's be realistic and start from where Americans are now, when they ask what it will take for them to retire comfortably," Frank replies. "Whatever that is, they all have a right to it, since each one of us is an individual, and the individual is more important than the collective. That's what gives us our right to burn all the carbon fuel we want and we can pay for, no matter what it does to the planet," he observes with an ironic smile. "So we need to find a better way, utopian or not, that begins by enabling people to experience something different and change their minds about what they need and how they want to live." Many of Frank's clients prize their professional or technical work and enjoy the intrinsic value of its problem-solving practice and accomplishment. But they also say, "I'd like to slow down," he reports, and "feel freer to choose my own pace and priorities," if only they didn't have to do too much in such a hurry in order to make a living.

Such experience leads Frank's clients to recognize their own desire for different structures and processes to take better care of their lives. "They are already looking for different social schemes, let's say, or rituals and customs, even if they can't spell them out or live them out all at once." But they can think about them metaphorically and hypothetically, for example, in terms of shifting from hardware to software in computer and communications technology, minimizing physical scale and extending social networks, and thereby "changing our habits of administering the self to keep us in closer touch with others." How so? "Limbic urges to feed, fight, or flee are essential for physical survival," Frank answers. "But you need to sublimate your drives and enlighten your interests in order to get along in our more delicate world, let alone figure out our problems of how to find alternative energy or how to share the wealth." To the extent that material and social progress frees us from spending all our time on our own survival, "we have the luxury we need to attend to the planet's management," he promises. "But actually we need to do this personally, too, in how we interact with the people around us every day," he stresses. "That's something I try to teach people in therapy. Getting driven and angry with each other messes things up. Having fun, having sex, talking things through is much better for you, for them, and for your immune system."

How do such therapeutic ideals apply to retirement? "Most people experience some kind of yoke in their work, and they'd like to get out of it, if they only could," Frank replies. "Some have chosen that yoke for good reasons, to support their kids and family, even if their work doesn't much suit their gifts and predispositions, and they carry it out as their responsibility. They feel like they had little choice in the matter, given few resources and lots of pressure to make a living." By contrast, Frank points out, "Around here, in Silicon Valley, people with plenty of resources do a lot of what they want. Not all of them and not all the time, of course, and it's not so generalizable. Even so, I hear them saying they would like to get out of the 'have-tos' in their world. Even professors at Stanford want to get off committees, teach less, and have more time to do research. Even therapists in Palo Alto want fewer patient-contact hours, with less paperwork, and more time with interesting people they really like and can help." Frank smiles. But in almost every case, underscores this psychotherapist and consultant, "regular work structures a person's life; and when they stop working, they don't have a clue about how to create structure in their own life, because it's all been set up by others in the workplace. So they join volunteer groups, churches, clubs. Maybe they start golfing or fishing a lot more. That's all fine on a behavioral basis. But what is the underlying meaning of the structure they're trying to generate for themselves?" asks Frank. "Does it make their life whole, and connect it with others? Does it bring them together to take part in a bigger whole and make it better?" He leans in and raises his voice, "Does it really plug you in and light you up?"

As we age, we can find or form fulfilling roles, processes and situations, answers Frank, where "we can put together these kinds of larger meaning with the small things we do every day with other people. That's what feels satisfying, and it leads to harmony." His patients include many professionals in technical and managerial fields who have graduated from "aces and spaces" education, excelling in narrow specialties but remaining largely ignorant across the sweep of the arts, humanities, and comparative studies. They are particularly eager to "make life whole, not just fill in the gaps, but become more integrated with yourself and others and the world," he sums up. Seen as an ongoing experiment in social learning, retirement can open up to embrace the aims and attitude of this quest. "That's the virtue of it. It's not given on clay tablets from above. It's actually immanent in what's already present, in what people are after," says Frank, by contrast to the intellectual abstraction of perfectionist ideals or ethical arguments. "That superstructure can be useful for discussion," he grants. "But you need interactive modeling and practice to guide you in becoming more integrated between how you feel inside and what you do outside. That's how people catch on."

Americans living longer, healthier lives in retirement want to share them in harmony with friends and family, Frank affirms. They want to devote their time to enjoying life with their spouses, children, and aging parents, "not fighting over Grandma's silver and just waiting for her to go." Such good morale can be amplified and extended from familiar relationships and leisure activities, urges Frank, to include people in all sorts of living situations—persons living singly, in childless couples, with same-sex partners or friends—in diverse forms of group living and retirement communities. "Yes, Holland and Sweden have more socialism than we do, and closer extended families," Frank notes, "but they are developing new styles of elder communities with practical advantages we can learn from, like economies of consumption and space, co-ops for buying groceries and providing medical care." Likewise, we can learn from the voluntary-association model of senior residences and lifelong learning programs, based on common aims and interests, growing up around U.S. college campuses. "Most of them are ridiculously expensive, but not all of them," he points out. "Most of the people are highly educated, sophisticated, cosmopolitan types, who go to symphonies and lectures. But we can still learn from their good business models," and apply them to a broader base. For example, they can enable factory or office workers who want to "go fishing or gardening up at the lake, to go in together and buy property there, and put up prefab housing and a little clubhouse." In such settings, Frank adds, work can become optional, at least work for pay among the financially secure. But true work can permute itself into many forms. These include forms of play, artistic creation, and self-government that enable retired neighbors to "find another team, and rediscover the satisfaction that comes from working with a team, and doing your part as a part of the tribe."

More profoundly, reflects Frank, "We can see how people get sadder, more depressed, and isolated in retirement. We can learn from that how to move in another direction." This leads to new forms of community, he argues, with deep roots in American religious congregations, utopian communities, social movements, and liberal arts education. "Think Chautauqua, summer camps, and artist colonies," suggests this therapist. "Why not colonies for software engineers?" he asks, with a nod to nearby "campuses" where the best and brightest engineers at Google, Apple, and Intel eat, play, and work together around the clock. Beyond the technological and market-driven bounds of cyber-startups backed by venture capital, Frank sees a wider landscape that takes in many more Americans who "want to live more connected, happier lives as they get older. It's got to be practical, where people can experience doing and feeling different, or not much happens," he warns. "Just like depth psychotherapy, if you keep talking for a long time, most people will stop listening unless they can feel good things starting to happen."

At the same time, to achieve success, such experiments must spark the moral motives and draw on the everyday practices Americans have learned. "Not everyone wants to retire to work with kids or get into community service," allows Frank. "Some people want to keep working primarily with things or ideas, or work one-to-one in intense personal relationships, like most therapists do." Various forms of interpersonal relationship and organizational arrangement can embrace such differences, he proposes, while "enabling more people to do what they really want, to actualize unity. They want to become whole, not just fill in what's missing, or get more and get better."

Even highly educated and advantaged Americans can recognize entropy from their firsthand experience, Frank says, in working longer and harder to pay their mortgages, send their children to college, and balance their household budgets. That makes them even hungrier for "the tropism of a whole life, where every day you can live out your big picture of what it all means, and you can fill in that picture together with people around you. You can do it in a community that helps you figure out what to do with the big systems we are all just little cogs in." Virtually all Americans want to fall in love, or fall in love again with the one they love, adds this therapist with a smile. "We want to make the most of that idea, the love of your life is the special someone who wakes up the spark inside you that lights up the whole of life, and makes the world go 'round. If that *anima* is inside you, and all around you, too, then it's about more than romance, and there's more than one way to find it. There's more than one troubadour or teacher you can follow to awaken the spirit."

Resonating with communal, conciliar ideals of the congregation and the college as well as the summer camp and artist colony, this therapeutic sketch of alternative modes of retirement is emphatically moral. "It's a fact that people feel good when they do things that matter," Frank reports. "As a matter of fact, I have seen people become more direct, sensitive, loving, caring, and effective in the world, in their work and relationships, sometimes with the help of therapy. That's a real sign of what I mean by human integration," he judges, "and that's why I'm here."

This cardinal virtue and its related moral motives to remake retirement require no explicitly religious creeds or codes, argues this therapist, certainly none that turn on salvation in another world beyond this one. "Heaven, hell, and purgatory are all right here," he emphasizes. "It's all here. We don't have to wait until we die, physically, to get there. We do have to 'die,' psychologically, in order to let go of our delusions and difficulties, and allow the true self to come forth. 'Die before you die.' You can call that intimacy with God, and you can experience that in any moment," Frank concludes. "Especially when you don't think it's true, when you're feeling pain or difficulty or grinding wear and tear every day. You can give it to God, and see what happens."[31]

## WHAT'S NEXT?

In 1900 most American men worked from childhood to death, and they died on the job. Most women, too, worked in their households and family farms for as long as they lived. Only one in five elderly men was retired a century ago. By 1950 one in two were retired, then more than four in five by 2000.[32] Today only one in eight Americans over age

sixty-five continues to work full-time, and just one in twenty is still working at eighty, even though a third of baby boomers aged sixty-five to
sixty-nine are still on the job, and a sixth of those aged fifty to sixty-four
at work during the Great Recession said they expected never to stop
working.[33] In fact, we now retire at age sixty-two on average, and we
live to eighty or beyond.[34] Despite living longer, and longer in retirement, or indeed because of these changes, thinking about retirement
has come to touch more intimately than ever on questions of life's end
and how long we have to go, how healthy and able we will be to live out
retirement fully, without losing our joy of living or outliving our money.
How do ministers and pastors weigh these questions for themselves
and for those they guide and teach? How do the faithful feel and think
about what's next?

"I turned sixty-five a week ago, and I found myself thinking, *Holy
moly! When I was growing up everybody retired at sixty-five! Why
would they do that?"* wonders Fred Heiden, an energetic born-again
evangelical minister immersed in serving seniors in a large, thriving congregation in Silicon Valley.[35] "Whatever sixty-five feels like, I don't feel
like it. Then I looked in the mirror, and I thought, *How long do I have
left? Only fifteen years, maybe twenty? That's awful! Ridiculous! I'm
not going to be 80 in fifteen years!"* He shakes his head in denial, then
nods. "Oh, yes, I am." Working harder, longer, and more intensely than
he was doing in his forties, Fred wonders at how close to retirement he
is in age, and how far away from it he feels in practice. "Our kids are
grown, but my wife and I don't own a house here in Silicon Valley; and
we can't afford to buy one, so I'm not sure we can live here after I retire.
So do I think about retiring? No! I'll do another five years full-time at the
church and see, then maybe go part-time if they'll let me stay in the par-
sonage. Because, if I retired, then what? I don't play golf. That's boring.
I get energized by being with people." Empathic and responsive, Fred
finds spirited fulfillment in daily rounds of pastoral care, teaching Bible
classes, visiting the sick, leading funerals, and comforting mourners. He
worries about giving up all this. "Retirement should fill you with joy,

some sense of value that should continue. So sitting in a house by a lake is fine for a week or a month," he allows. "But after that, then what?"

Recalling an uncle who worked for decades in a steel mill, retired on a good union pension, and died soon after of a heart attack, Fred asks, "Is that how we want to live our lives? He hated going to work every day. He was forced to do it to support his family. He was all excited about retirement, but he was gone before it began. That's not how I want to live my life," Fred vows. Make sure you like what you're doing, when you go to work, he counsels members of his church. "If you don't like it, don't do it." God has nothing against wealth, he advises them, but God wants us to be fulfilled, to find joy and purpose in work and in life, because "we only get this life once. This life. I believe there's another one, but this one we only get one time, and this is the only one I know right now, so we better make sure we do the right thing."

Thinking of the funerals he leads several times a week, Fred testifies, "I absolutely know where I'm going after I die. I'm not afraid to die, not at all. I know I'm going to heaven. I don't know what it looks like. It doesn't matter to me. I just know I'm going to be with God, and I gotta believe that that's a good thing, so I absolutely believe it." He pauses, then adds, "But I'm not in a hurry to get there, because I got a lot of stuff I'd like to do yet." The reality of life everlasting takes in "the real spiritual hope we have in our Christian faith and the real feeling we have in actually living." Reason cannot pin down the whole of this reality and its revelation. "I think God has a great sense of humor," Fred laughs, by way of lifting up this mystery. "Some of those stories in the Bible, he had to be laughing when he wrote them, because they're just too funny. Like all those names in Samuel—fifteen verses—and nobody can pronounce them!"

The church has shirked its responsibility to help people prepare for death, and for retirement too, Fred reflects, not only because of our age-old fear of annihilation, but because people would rather not talk about the now familiar old-age story of drawn-out decline and departure. "It's inevitable, but it's still difficult," he says, particularly for him when families call on his beloved and reassuring presence to help them move their disabled, protesting parents out of their homes and into nursing-care facilities. "I'm there to comfort them, that God will be with them, and so will we"—he nods—"and sometimes the doctor is there, too, to give them something if they get too upset."

As we age, we can better recognize our partnership with God, affirms this born-again minister. "The older I get, the stronger I understand that partnership to be, so the less fear I have, the less worry I feel about the next step. Where are our plots? Do we have grave markers? Not yet," Fred answers. Spiritual preparation doesn't do away with the need to plan for what's next in this world, but it shifts its meaning. In response to his wife's suggesting that they relax and retire to a small town in the Sierras, where they can afford to buy a house at last, Fred asks, "So we're sitting there in the trees. For what? To drive to town or the nearest Indian casino to gamble? To watch reruns on satellite TV? What are we gonna do?" As a chaplain on call 24/7, including emergency calls from the local police and hospital to come at once from the family dinner table or a game with his grandchildren, Fred relishes a few days off, "especially Friday, when I don't need to think about tomorrow because Saturday's free, too." But he waves away the prospect of endless days of rest and entertainment, since they cannot take the place of days now filled with caring for souls. They cannot come close to the powerful feelings and rites of passage that mark the joys and sorrows of birth, marriage, sickness, and death. "It means the world to people for the pastor to be there when it counts, and it's the same for me," Fred testifies. "I don't want to give that up."

A mainline Protestant minister and biblical scholar in Atlanta, by contrast, underscores the power of sacred scripture to ring true to the depths of his own faithful experience of life's limits.[36] "My father died young, in his early fifties, and none of the men in my family lived past 70," Del Weaver recalls. Growing up in a rural world of hard physical labor, "I really wasn't around any retired people. Everyone I knew worked as hard as they could, as long as they could, because they had to."

Del retired early, because he could, after decades of disciplined saving and prudent investment. But he retired for deeper reasons, too, rooted in biblical convictions that "nothing is forever in the order of creation, within the limits of life," which underlie his sense of his own life's limits and stages. "You have to face the facts of getting older and losing a step, losing your full capacities. We wanted to retire in time to do the things we wanted to do, while we still could."

Waiting too long meant risking that "nothing would be left" of promises to travel the world, enjoy the great outdoors, explore the wilderness, and volunteer to preserve it. Do such concerns arise from a peculiarly modern kind of doubt or agnostic uncertainty about what the future holds? What of life everlasting? "Do you want the truth?" Del asks in turn. He answers:

> I'll tell you the truth. I have a thoroughly ancient Israelite understanding of that: This is it! Heaven? I would love to be surprised. I do not know, and I would not preach it from the pulpit on Sunday or at the funeral of a friend, because all this is part of folks' heart and soul. But the Old Testament doesn't really talk about the afterlife, two or three texts maybe, but they are late and problematic. Here you have a people who tried to live faithfully before their God and within their community, believing that this is all there is. Now that's a challenge,

Del acknowledges, "but since I've grown old enough to really think about these things, that's what I have believed."

A few years ago, when this scholar and his wife were cleaning out family files, she pulled out one she insisted on talking through in detail. "It was the file she wants to have handy if I die before she does. What to do at my funeral? Which texts, which hymns, who to call?" Del says softly, then raises his voice in reply. "Well, first, none of those resurrectional texts in the New Testament," he answers. "Two, Psalm 23, as long as you read it in the NRSV translation, which says not, 'I will live in the house of the LORD forever,' but 'I shall dwell in the house of the LORD my whole life long.' Yes, there is Romans 8. I *am* convinced that nothing can separate us from the love of God.[37] I honestly, deeply believe that. What that means after my body goes . . ." He lifts his palms and shrugs. "What I do know is that my body, and even my personality, is one little part of the cosmos, and there's more to it all than the cosmos."

What follows? Be true to God, and leave the afterlife to God, Del answers. Let near-death reports of the next world rest with half-remembered dreams. Instead, "Love mercy and do justice every day you can, and find a way to enjoy that day. Think of Ecclesiastes: 'It's all gone, we'll all die, and people will even forget all the great books we wrote,' which they will. So what is there left but to eat and drink and enjoy the wife of your youth?"[38] We live life in time. "We're all part of history, part of a people, a corporate reality, just like the Bible says. Yes, we're all individuals," Del laughs, "and I love my individuality and Americans cheering about 'I am who I am.' But it's not just me," he insists. "I am who I am because of all the people who shaped me—family, culture, shared understanding and shared genes—and that goes all the way back. So be a lover of life, not just a visitor. Try to make a difference, like Mary Oliver says in 'When Death Comes,' and it's our time to go through that door."[39]

This world and the next, this moment and life everlasting? A teacher in her sixties, raised Reform Jewish, married to an Episcopalian, and practicing Zen Buddhism in a small meditation group in Silicon Valley, weighs these questions of cosmic and acosmic truth, turning them back and forth, from eternity to here and now. "Look at burying the dead in the old Book of Common Prayer," Janet Silver invites.[40] "First, you see, 'I am the resurrection and the life, saith the Lord: he that believeth in me, though he were dead, yet shall he live.' Then you also see, 'We brought nothing into this world, and it is certain we can carry nothing out. The Lord gave, and the Lord hath taken away; blessed be the name of the Lord.' Amen, everything and nothing," Janet affirms. Christians recognizing that "in the midst of life we are in death," she suggests, is not so different from Buddhists seeing that "we are here, and we are not here; we don't have it just one way to hold on to." So when it comes to death and coming closer to it, she smiles. "Don't worry. Nothing happens."

But isn't that exactly what does worry us, the nothing that does happen and that we fear turning into? Or nothing that is not there and the nothing that is, when we imagine death turning out the lights and annihilating who we really are? In response, Janet recalls her Zen teacher visiting Yosemite Falls and wondering at how slowly the water seems to come down, with each drop going its own separate way before rejoining the river. "Before we were born, we had no feeling; we were one with the universe," her teacher observes in the light of "mind-only" Buddhism. "Whether it is separated into drops or not, water is water. Our life and death are the same thing. When we realize this fact we have no fear of death anymore, and we have no actual difficulty in our life."[41] If the water is glad to come back to the original river, what feeling will we have when we die? We will have perfect composure then, her teacher promises, but it may be too perfect for us now, attached as we are to our own individual feeling. If everything comes out of emptiness, one whole river or one whole mind, then life's true meaning and beauty flow from and into its oneness. Really? "It's easy to say, but not so easy to actually feel," Janet allows, "unless you can find a way to practice it with your whole body and mind."

A longtime Methodist pastor mulls such practical questions a few weeks after his retirement in Atlanta, and several years after the death of his wife and his own return bout with cancer.[42] "Every day is a gift. I appreciate that gift. Every day I have is grace. I try to live that theological truth," Jim Matthews says slowly. "There was a time, of course, when I thought I was immortal, just like my own kids," he confesses. "When I first got cancer twenty years ago and I was facing surgery, my little boy asked me, 'Daddy, are you gonna die?' I'm gonna die one day, I told him, but I'm not gonna die anytime soon. That brought my mortality home to me. Denial comes back in, thank God, and I'd probably be scared if I knew I was going to die tomorrow." He looks away, then back again. "But there is purpose and intention in creation. It inheres in who we are, from the moment of birth, and it runs all the way through. It doesn't start or stop with retirement. Today is the day to live it out. The only day."

In keeping with his faith, this Methodist minister stresses free will and willingness to commit our lives responsibly to fulfilling the purpose of creation. Jim resists countervailing accounts of determinism or fatalism, for example, when it comes to careers in corporate America or jurisdictional appointments of ministers to local churches in United Methodism. "I really struggle with the stories of people who retire all depressed or mad as hell that they didn't do something else or didn't make out better. Bitterness, remorse, and why not me?" If he ever felt that way, Jim told himself starting out, "I hope I have the courage to quit serving churches. I never have felt that way. I thank God for being able to connect with myself and what is going on, so that won't be me, and it hasn't been. Every place I went, I wanted to go. I stayed every place as long as I wanted to stay. I quit when I wanted to quit." And when he did, he recalls, "I was a little surprised and really gratified at that last Sunday, and the outpouring of love and nurture and support they gave me."

"I believe Jesus got up on Sunday morning, like Frederick Buechner says.[43] How he did that, I don't know," Jim reflects on the Resurrection. "That's a mystery. But I do believe that God overcame the power of death. Death is real. I'm not denying death, like a Greek holding out for the immortal soul like it's a Platonic form. I'm not there, even though I know that gets mixed in with faith for a lot of Christians," allows this pastor. "This life is all there is, but God has overcome what death can bring against us. So the future belongs to God, the immediate future and the ultimate future. What that looks like, the shape of it, I'm not so concerned about, like whether heaven has streets of gold to promise the poor."

On his deathbed, John Wesley supposedly said, "Best of all, God is with us," notes this life-long Methodist. "Not will be, but *is*. No matter what it feels like. Like I told my church when it was time to retire, thanking them for being who they are, 'You helped us believe when we couldn't. You said the words for us when we couldn't.' That's what the community does," Jim stresses. "It lives 'God is with us,' when you can't feel it yourself. It gets you through it together, when you can't do it on your own. Like I couldn't do it when my wife died." He breaks off, then ends, "I trust that the gospel story is the truth that sets us free. That's my story, and I'm sticking to it!"

Without denying the salvific promise of life everlasting and immortal souls going to heaven, an African-American pastor deeply committed to social justice and community service seeks first to bring the kingdom of God closer to the way we live here and now, in accord with the Lord's Prayer, "Thy kingdom come. Thy will be done on earth, as it is in heaven." Testifies Rev. Paul Richardson,[44] "The kingdom of God is what drives me. I don't see it, so I work for it." Instead of freedom from death, he stresses our freedom to live more fully. "You shall have life, and you shall have it more abundantly. That is what Jesus promises us. We don't have to lose our joy as we get older and closer to death. We can discover it."

"I don't like death," admits this activist Baptist minister, who leads the church Ella Mills attends. He grew up in a segregated Southern town where the Klan still marched by torchlight. "I lost my father when I was 12 and my mother when I was 16. I do funerals because I have to, not because I want to." At the same time, Pastor Paul holds, faith in a merciful God can free us at the limits of life from having to hold on to this world when the hour comes to leave it. So, for example, a church member now profoundly afflicted with Alzheimer's can truly pray, "Lord, take me. Take me home." Abundant life in the kingdom of God overcomes fear of death, vows this leader of a "servant church." It overcomes doubt or despair in the face of life's suffering and injustice. "How can I take part in bringing God's kingdom here into this life, as it is in heaven?" asks Pastor Paul. "That challenge moves me to think about retirement and plan for it," he replies, to help financially strapped members of his church to do likewise, and to urge other ministers to do so, too, especially those without personal savings or denominational pensions.

---

## Is retirement about freedom *from* work's discontent or freedom *to do* something different?

---

"I want my life to have meaning and value until I'm dead," Pastor Paul vows, "and so does everyone. A good work ethic goes beyond the day you retire. Whatever you give up when you retire, you want to replace it with something good, something that benefits others, not just yourself. Let that be what gets you up in the morning," he invites, "whether it's about taking care of children or other seniors, tutoring school dropouts, and learning how to help them." Is retirement more about *freedom from* work's discontents or about *freedom to* do something different? It's both, Pastor Paul replies, but it's more positive than negative. "Now you have more freedom to do the work you choose, select the work you want, dream about what you want to do and who you want to become. Listen to what God wants you to do!" he exclaims. "That can be all the more important for folks who have had less choice of a job because they have had to work further down on the economic ladders of this society in order to survive."[45]

In his congregation of more than a thousand members, mostly from working families, this black Baptist pastor can count fewer than ten "who have been able to retire without worrying that they have enough to see them through," he says, holding up the fingers of both hands and nodding toward their widespread losses in net worth over the last decade in particular.[46] "Most folks here cannot afford to retire, even if they have their house paid for. Those who can retire, they all depend on their Social Security check. That's the only check they get, just like 70 percent of all seniors in the African-American community. Medicare or Medicaid is the only way they can pay their doctor bills," he stresses. "So when politicians start talking about cutting Social Security, and taking away Medicare and Medicaid and Obamacare"—he raises his voice—"then we start getting concerned."[47]

That, too, is part of an ongoing struggle, from which the church and its members can never truly retire. "Don't let it get you down, but don't ever give it up," Pastor Paul urges. "Sing, pray, rest and rejoice in the Lord. And carry it on."

## Beginning to End

From midlife to old age, greater longevity has brought more years to most Americans. For some it has brought forth striking "encore" proposals about a new stage of life and a new world of work to create for the second half of life. It has led many Americans to imagine a big new step to take—liberating, exciting, and fulfilling—after retiring from full-time work, and long before entering into the "really old" age of declining health and capacity on the way to eventual invalidism and death. Almost no one wants to live forever, we can agree, yet we can expect that more than a few 99-year-olds want to live to 100. Who looks forward to "endless retirement, thirty years of R & R?" ask advocates of encore careers. Almost no one, we can agree, while we heed the faith of many Americans in a dynamic retirement shared with family and friends, stretching anytime from now into their eighties and beyond. That faith abides, even if many draw a curtain across what follows as decline and fall. They hope for a smooth, quick exit freed from drawn-out degeneration and disease, even if they do not pray for resurrection and the life to come in another world beyond this one.

We have heard stories of individual fragility and finitude entwined with mutual care and interdependence, begun by an upbeat chorus of voices celebrating youth regained in a timeless vacation paradise on earth, and followed by deeper doubts and reflections as well as denials of what will come later on. We have heard Americans vow that lifelong love is what they want most—love shared with a soul mate for life in a home of their own, with children settled securely nearby with kids of their own to hold in your arms and walk to the park.[48] True love endures, affirmed even as it is mourned by those who have lost a spouse or child; or questioned by those disappointed in romance or divorced in marriage, still seeking that special someone or serenity without them.

With these enduring goods and unfolding stories in mind, let us turn to the cultural sources of our visions and ideals of retirement in religious and civic traditions that begin in biblical Jerusalem and classical Athens. Let's see how they inspire modern market economies and nation-states in tandem with heartfelt romance and affectionate families over three centuries to make moral sense of retirement in the American grain.

CHAPTER

**3**

# WHERE RETIREMENT COMES FROM AND LEADS US

## BY THE WORD OF GOD, THE WILL OF THE PEOPLE, AND THE PURSUIT OF HAPPINESS

"What do you do?" How often have you asked that familiar question, and answered it? When and where does it usually come up? We can wonder, and recall a party or reception, a town meeting or vacation trip. Where does it become less likely, for example: deep in prayer or play, among the jobless poor or leisured rich? Why is the question of the work we do so important? It's hardly the whole story of who we are and whom we love. But it says a lot about what we know of life, where we stand in the social landscape, and how we got here, starting from the time and place of our birth, unfolding through our families and friends, charted by our schooling and careers. The importance of what we do at work, and how we feel and think about it—for example, as a job, career, calling, profession, or way of life—charges retirement with much of its meaning and drama. That drama takes in what we do at home and at play, in worship and in public. But it points up work in particular and counterpoints it, too, in shared melodies and morality tales of leisure, rest, prayer, and play.

Where do our dreams and visions of retirement come from? From our own firsthand experience and imagination, to be sure, but they trace a larger canvas and echo a longer story. Our visions and voices come through a cultural conversation we share, enacted in a moral drama we enter long after its opening, however we carry it on or change it by re-making our roles and rewriting our lines. In this cultural light let's look for retirement's sources and practical pathways to the present we inhabit, and the future we imagine, by turning toward traditions that go all the way back in the West to biblical Jerusalem and ancient Athens. Do these overarching images and underlying stories of life's unfolding and aim ring more or less true to our own experience and intuitions? Do their different angles of vision and narration—of God's will and human destiny, reason and passion, good and evil—shadow our understanding of retirement in shifting ways as well as shed bright light on it? Where do they lead us?

Where do we come from and go to? What are we here for? You need not be a Bible believer or a public-spirited citizen to ask these questions and wonder what we must do to be saved from sorrow if not sin. You need not read Deuteronomy or Plato to sense how the ways we live enact an ongoing conversation among moral traditions and express where we began, in the providence of our progress, the covenant of our constitution, and the sacred souls of our sovereign selves.

## EAST OF EDEN

The Bible has little to say about retirement as such, but everything to reveal about the world of work and rest, lit by prayer and service to God all the days of our lives, as we age over generations.[1] On the seventh day God rested from the work of creation, and the biblical story of Creation begins in the preternatural paradise of the garden of Eden, planted by providence with fruit hanging low for our first parents to pick at their pleasure. Created in God's image, humans are blessed by God and told, "Increase and multiply, and fill the earth, and subdue it" (Genesis 1:28 DRA) . . . "and have dominion . . . over every living thing that moves upon the earth" (Genesis 1:28 NRSV). There is plenty to do, but it's not all work and no play, prayer, or rest.

In the beginning God created the heavens and the earth. Let there be light, God said, and so separated the light from darkness, and work from rest. Let there be land, separating the seas; and on the second day the earth put forth vegetation at God's command, according to Genesis 1, with plants yielding seed and trees fruit, each according to its kind. Living creatures were likewise commanded to increase and multiply, before man was made and given dominion over them. In the distinct account of Genesis 2, God first created man, then planted the garden of Eden and made its every tree to grow, before putting the man in the garden to "till it and keep it," while commanding him to "freely eat of every tree of the garden," except the tree of knowledge of good and evil, with its fatal fruit. God created every beast of the field and bird of the air, then brought them to the man to name, that is, to order the world and make sense of it. Thus, God gave the man both headwork and handwork to do before the fall, making him an active co-creator of the garden with God, not simply a creature made in God's image or a consumer given the abundance of nature to live a life of leisure. Work is a duty that inheres in human life itself as a gift of God, formed from a union of earth and breath, made flesh and put in a place with work to do and moral decisions to make with freedom to choose and imperatives to heed. Gardening in Eden seems a task without toil, easily borne with no need to worry or retire, in a parklike paradise with the tree of eternal life set at its center (Genesis 2:4-20).[2]

Original sin yields paradise lost, along with divinely decreed pain in childbirth for women, spousal sexual desire, and social subordination of women to men. God then turns to Adam and curses the ground because of his sin: "In toil you shall eat of it all the days of your life. . . . By the sweat of your face you shall eat bread until you return to the ground, for out of it you were taken; you are dust, and to dust you shall return" (Genesis 3:16-19). Toil, trouble, and exile are all rolled into one dusty ball of human finitude and haunting awareness of mortality. Work is not essentially evil, but it becomes toil once sin breaks the originally blessed relationship between God and humans. Work becomes hard and uncertain on tilled ground no longer bound to yield grain but cursed to bring forth thorns and thistles. Then humans yearn for rest and release from toil, in this world or the next. God drives Adam out of the garden "to till the ground from which he was taken," and places cherubim and a flaming sword to bar Adam's way back to Eden, lest he ever reach the tree of eternal life, eat its fruit, and live forever like a god upon the earth (3:22-24).

East of Eden a division of labor arises between Cain and Abel, between the tiller of the land and the keeper of flocks. God favors Abel's offering over Cain's for unknown reasons that seem to stem from moral motives but nonetheless underscore the tensions between settled and seminomadic ways of life. Angry and jealous, Cain slays Abel, and God drives Cain off the land to wander on the earth. Six generations and a few verses later in Genesis (4:19-22), the sons of Lamech mark a further and fruitful division of labor among shepherds, musicians, and metalsmiths, with no contrast drawn between making music for a lifetime and sweating at a forge every day. But at the birth of his son Noah, Lamech prophesies, "Out of the ground that the LORD has cursed this one shall bring us relief from our work and from the toil of our hands" (5:29). Noah fulfills this prophecy after the flood as the first tiller of land in the new age, established by "the everlasting covenant between God and every living creature of all flesh that is on the earth," according to the priestly tradition (9:16). It bridges the times from the Creation to the flood without reference to the fall, but it rehearses the moral logic of human mortality and corruption (5:1-32). The Lord's spirit shall abide in humans only for a time, for they are flesh and but a breath away from death, and a human lifetime gradually descends in age from semidivine centuries to threescore and ten. (Cf. Genesis 5:4-32, Psalms 90:10.) Human corruption of the earth shall be punished by the flood. Then humankind shall be given a second chance and an everlasting covenant through Noah's righteousness and God's mercy, renewing the goodness of the earth corrupted by man's lawless deeds (Genesis 6:11-22).

The Hebrew Bible offers a view of work and rest set within the moral order of God's covenant and Law. In turn God establishes the Law within the biblical story that unfolds from Adam through Noah and Abraham to Moses, and centers on the crucial event of the Exodus. God rescues the people of Israel from slavery and delivers them from bondage in Egypt before the Mosaic covenant is given. They obey the Law in response to God's saving act. They obey out of love, trust, and gratitude, not from fear of fire and brimstone, prudent expectation of God's further favor, or a sense of duty bound by autonomous reason. In this redemptive light God ordains that humans work to earn their daily bread, and God commands that they rest from labor on the Sabbath. "Six days shalt thou labour, and do all thy work: but the seventh day *is* the sabbath of the Lord thy God: *in it* thou shalt not do any work" (Exodus 20:9-10 AKJV). The covenant embraces the whole of life to enable humans to become one and holy as God is one and holy. Work is set within the social order of the extended household as an institution that is at once political, economic, and domestic. A predominantly peasant society headed by a small political and priestly elite forms the hierarchy of an organic social body. Every person is a member with superordinate and subordinate social roles, moral duties, and practical virtues in corporate relationships that can shift as they age but never give way to the free and equal standing of modern individuals.[3]

> We must attain unity of the self in mind,
> heart, and appetite through singular
> attachment to God all our days.

At the same time, Israel is also the body of the people of God. All persons are members of one body, each created in the image of God. All Israel and each person are likewise commanded by God, as the King James Version makes clearest in English: "Hear, O Israel: The Lord our God *is* one Lord: and thou shalt love the Lord thy God with all thine heart, and with all thy soul, and with all thy might" (Deuteronomy

6:4-5). Relationship to one supreme God defines Israel as one people, and it defines each member of the people as an individual person in relation to "thy" God. Each person must attain unity of the self in mind, heart, and appetite through singular attachment to God all the days of his or her life. By being one, whole with and wholly with God, members of the covenant unify their own personality and the whole of the people of God.[4] Do we, too, still seek such unity? Or does the oneness we seek seem to flow more freely, unbound by God's will or God's people, and aimed at happiness not holiness?

From this covenantal life's work, no one can rest or retire. God commands Moses to teach every Israelite to do God's will in every concrete situation of daily life, "that you may fear the LORD your God, you and your son and your son's son, by keeping all his statutes and his commandments, which I command you, all the days of your life; and that your days may be prolonged" (Deuteronomy 6:2 RSV). Each person is to take to heart God's law and love, constantly contemplating, enacting, and teaching them through every act and hour of the day: "And these words which I command you this day shall be upon your heart; and you shall teach them diligently to your children, and shall talk of them when you sit in your house, and when you walk by the way, and when you lie down, and when you rise. And you shall bind them as a sign upon your hand, and they shall be as frontlets between your eyes. And you shall write them on the doorposts of your house and on your gates" (6:6-9 RSV).

God's laws are to come first and last to mind and to hand, ordering every human activity each day and every social relationship over a lifetime, inspiring each person not merely to follow the Law but to become the law in the whole of her or his life.

Israel must heed God's commandments and be careful to do them, "that it may go well with you, and that you may multiply greatly, as the LORD, the God of your fathers, has promised you, in a land flowing with milk and honey" (Deuteronomy 6:3 RSV). There God will give them "great and goodly cities, which you did not build, and houses full of all good things, which you did not fill, . . . and vineyards and olive trees, which you did not plant, and when you eat and are full, then take heed lest you forget the Lord, who brought you out of the land of Egypt, out of the house of bondage" (6:10-12 RSV). Echoing Eden's providential provision, neither human labor nor Canaanite nature gods will bring the blessings of fertility and prosperity in the promised land. Only Israel's God, the Lord of history, can bestow these blessings within the moral order and aim of the covenant that God's people must do their true work to fulfill every day of their lives. Thus Abraham, Sarah, and their children abide by a covenant with God, and sometimes break it, in ways that lead to God's blessing or punishment in terms of prosperity and peace, fruits of labor that increase and multiply like offspring over generations, or that come undone and come to ruin. Job rises from the ash heap of unjust loss as the terrible culmination of this covenant in the mystery of evil, redeemed by faith in God's love even if human reason cannot grasp God's will.

In the Gospels, Jesus Christ expresses the divine providence and power of this biblical tradition, epitomized in the prayer of petition he addresses to God as Our Father, to "Give us this day our daily bread" (Matthew 6:11). Thus the Gospels put work and wealth in their worldly place. Instead of saving for retirement or a rainy day, they urge us first and last to "lay up for yourselves treasures in heaven," for "where your treasure is, there will your heart be also" (6:19-21 AKJV). They ask us to consider the lilies of the field and the birds of the air, how they live and grow by the goodness of creation and the grace of God, without worry for the morrow. God knows humans need food, drink, and clothes. "But seek first his kingdom and his righteousness, and all these things shall be yours as well," Jesus teaches (6:28-33 RSV). Christians' chief work in the world is the work of God, to sow the Word and bring in the harvest of the kingdom of God (1 Corinthians 3:6-9; John 4:35-38).

More radical repudiation of the world comes to the fore in the apostolic era, as Christians' rising hopes for a new heaven and a new earth sharpen their indifference toward work in a world coming to an end. At the same time, Pauline visions of Christian life and community crystallize the "calling" of its members as a summoning by name or convoking an assembly, an assigning to a task or electing to an office. So they are called and chosen to join in a new community of the body of Christ, as an *ekklesia* of those called out and gathered in, given new work as apostles, prophets, evangelists, or teachers (Ephesians 4:11; 1 Corinthians 12:28). While waiting for the coming of the Lord, abide by your living, urged Paul, and continue to labor as before, for "If any will not work, neither let him eat" (2 Thessalonians 3:7-12 ASV). But let the godless run after worldly gain. Why? For the time is short, and the balance is clear. "For what shall it profit a man, if he shall gain the whole world, and lose his own soul?" (Mark 8:36 AKJV). God now calls Christians, whatever their worldly station, and assigns each to a new task in order to serve God and neighbor no less fully as slave or freeman, artisan or matron, Jewish or Gentile Christian. The Pauline metaphor of the cultic community as the body of Christ crucified and resurrected transforms ethics of the classical body politic from sustaining the lawful hierarchy of the Greek city or Roman empire to the ethics of mutual love and care among Christians as members one of another, equally embraced by the promise of being raised from the dead as imperishable "spiritual bodies," which God will provide (1 Corinthians 12:4-27; 13:1-13; 15:20-52).[5]

Constantine's favor shifted the construal of calling away from post-apostolic Christians as pilgrims in a pagan society seeking to withdraw from worldly work, toward those more willing to labor freely in this world for a time to build the church eternal. New monastic movements coupled withdrawal from worldly corruption with forms of communal asceticism that fixed hours of disciplined work, study, and rest within a daily round of prayer and worship to glorify God. Thus Augustine contrasts self-centered work and government in the earthbound city with cooperative social activity devoted to serving truth, justice, and peace as perfected in the City of God and embodied in this world by the church. "You have made us for yourself," Augustine prays to God at the outset of his *Confessions* (i. 1.1), "and our hearts are restless until they come to rest in you." The opposition of work and rest is resolved in "the peace of the Sabbath without end," which draws Stoic tranquillity and peace of mind in harmony with the lawful order of nature into worship and communion with God. For God will "then also rest in us, just as you are now at work in us; and your rest in us will then be as is now your work in us," since God is always at work and at rest, granting humans eternal rest and activity in heavenly chorus with the angels glorifying God.[6]

To keep holy the Sabbath as a day of rest means entering into the activity of the biblical God of creation, set in a time out of time ritually rooted in rhythmic patterns of work and rest that Genesis 2:1-3 reveals as woven into the fabric of all existence: "So God blessed the seventh day and hallowed it, because on it God rested from all his work which he had done in creation" (v.3 RSV). God's people remember the Sabbath to rejoice in the creation of the universe, recognize its wholeness, and emulate its Creator in dynamic rest, as Exodus 20:8-11 reminds us. They observe the Sabbath to recall their experience of enslavement and exile, and celebrate their deliverance, as Deuteronomy 5:12-15 reminds us. The Sabbath commemorates all creation and its goodness. It reenacts the redemption of God's people and re-creates their spirit by freeing them from enslavement to labor and material need. It renews the covenant between God and God's people, which forms and sustains their moral community, and it gives them a taste of a messianic time to come. As a day of active celebration and communion as well as prayer, "the Sabbath keeps Israel," no less than Israel keeps the Sabbath.[7]

Commanded by Mosaic law to keep holy the Sabbath and rest on the seventh day of Creation, early Christians rested and prayed on the seventh day of the week in the Greco-Roman world. But they also gathered on the first day of the week to break bread in eucharistic worship in remembrance of Christ at the Last Supper, to celebrate their deliverance from sin by the resurrection of Christ on Easter Sunday, and to reenact the birth of the church in the coming of the Holy Spirit to the apostles on Pentecost Sunday. For generations Christians continued Sabbath Eucharists to commemorate the creation, but by the fourth century they were observing only Sunday as their official day of rest and prayer. Metaphorical interpretations of the Sabbath by patristic writers uncoupled the covenantal constancy of its spirit from its literal observance on the seventh day, and applied it to the whole of Christian life through all time. In 321 CE Constantine decreed Sunday a day of rest in the cities of the Roman Empire, instead of another work day, and Roman civil law enabled the church to open its doors wider to Sunday worship and Christian rest without appeal to Mosaic law.[8]

Augustine further spiritualized the meaning of the Sabbath commandment to make the eschatological promise of sharing in God's eternal rest and activity, deepening ideals of Christian worship on Sunday as an offering of the church as the body of Christ. Its medieval practice spread in the sacrifice of the Roman Catholic Mass, which Luther protested as an offering from man to God instead of a gift from God to man. As a Thomistic expression of natural law binding all humans, however, the Decalogue's commandment to keep holy the Sabbath provided a point of departure for Protestant reformers to stress the need for all humans to observe the Sunday Sabbath as a day of holy rest and worship commanded of conscience bound by biblical duty. So decreed the Westminster Confession of Faith in 1646:

> As it is the law of nature, that, in general, a due proportion of time be set apart for the worship of God; so, in his Word, by a positive, moral, and perpetual commandment binding all men in all ages, he hath particularly appointed one day in seven, for a Sabbath, to be kept holy unto him: which, from the beginning of the world to the resurrection of Christ, was the last day of the week; and, from the resurrection of Christ, was changed into the first day of the week, which, in Scripture, is called the Lord's day, and is to be continued to the end of the world, as the Christian Sabbath.[9]

Do we keep holy the Sabbath? Can we sense its practical analogues in other religious traditions around the world, and heed their insights? Can we recognize the reality of ritual rivaling the world of daily labor and revealing the illusion of worldly desire? Like monks in the monastery or Protestant reformers in the world, can we embrace work itself as a meaningful and mindful calling, meditative and prayerful, flowing and full of grace?[10] Can we join in Augustine's prayer to put our restless hearts to rest in God's love, and give voice to God's glory forever? Or in retirement do we wish upon another star for happiness and sing another tune of love, march to a different drummer toward fulfillment, or dance in the moment to a melody all our own?

## THE GOOD CITY

By contrast to the body of Christ and the City of God, organic forms of the body politic in the classical *polis* lift up ideals of virtuous citizenship practiced for the good of the city as a whole, and they downplay the merit of individual work pursued for the welfare of any one person or household. Economic means serve civic ends. Lack of property and wealth stands in the way of civic virtue and participation in ancient Greek practice. So Hesiod and Phocylides made clear in the sixth century BCE by urging the needy man to seek first a livelihood, and then the excellence of a citizen secure and leisured enough to devote the time, energy, and learning to civic life that it demands.[11]

Given their civic virtue, bred by education and practical experience of the city's life over a lifetime, citizens grow more responsible as they age for the moral integrity and well-being of the polis as a whole, according to Plato's account in the *Laws* in the fourth century BCE (631e, 635a, 659d, 729c). Elders oversee the laws of the city in tune with the lawful harmony of the soul and the cosmos. They lead the city's schools and rites as "incantations of the soul," to inspire citizens to harmonize in the common good and detest the dissonance of injustice. Like good parents teaching their children by example, these servants of the law educate others and themselves less by the precepts they proclaim than by the way they live them out every day of their life in political community. Like courageous warriors, who risk death to defend the city against its enemies, just citizens who learn to rule and be ruled by coming to rule themselves, win the immortality of glory in the city's shared memory.[12]

In clans and households parents naturally claim to govern their children, Plato noted, as do the elderly to rule the younger, and the stronger to rule the weaker. Powerful warriors and kings were esteemed in Homeric Greece for leading the city in war and public life, and they were pitied if diminished by poverty and old age. By contrast, argued Plato, the most lawful and moral kind of rule calls for the prudent to lead the ignorant through "the natural rule exercised by the law over willing subjects, without violence" (690a–c).[13] The parent, elder, or ruler by birth, who imposes by force laws that "exist for the sake of some," becomes morally transformed into a servant of laws that exist for the sake of all (714e–717b). Through taking part in the educative common life of the polis, each person becomes transformed from a self-centered and conflicted partisan into the perfect citizen possessed of practical wisdom and justice, and possessed by these civic virtues:

> Let's consider each of us living beings to be a divine puppet, put together either for their play or some serious purpose—which, we don't know. What we do know is that these passions work within us like [iron] tendons or cords, drawing us and pulling against one another in opposite directions toward opposing deeds. . . . Each person should always follow one of the cords against the others; this cord is the golden and sacred pull of calculation [*logismos*]; and is called the common law of the city. . . . It is necessary always to assist this most noble pull of law because calculation, while noble, is gentle rather than violent, and its pull is in need of helpers . . .
>
> The core of education is a correct nurture, which draws the soul of the child at play toward an erotic attachment to what he must do when he becomes a man who is perfect as regards the virtue of his occupation [and the virtue] that makes one desire and love to become a perfect citizen who knows how to rule and be ruled with justice. . . . The knowledge of the nature and the habits of souls is of the greatest use for the art whose business it is to care for souls. That art is politics. (*Laws*, bk. 1, 643–45, 650)

In the good city Plato sets out in the *Laws*, public participation and the work of citizens subordinate the work of making money, and no one retires from good citizenship. Equally allocating land among citizens checks conflicts between more and less propertied classes. Excluding merchants and artisans from citizenship checks conflicts between landed and unlanded wealth. All property is both public and private, equally shared among familial households. They cannot divide by inheritance or sell their allotted lands, nor can they hold on to wealth of more than four times the amount the city guarantees them for farming their allotted land. So aging and illness bring no poverty to mutually responsible citizens within equally landed families (922b–925e). Checking poverty and wealth protects against civil conflict and faction. It enables the city to provide equality of opportunity as well as outcomes, while it encourages economic effort as well as civic virtue, rewarding both in due proportion by public office and honor (739c–745e).

Moral responsibilities and duties accompany the social roles of citizens through each stage of life. Young men must maintain the city's gymnasia and baths for themselves and their elders. Youths must court and marry in public to mate and bear healthy children. Women as well as men must take part in common meals and military training, while raising children at home. Afterwards, women, too, can enter public office, be called to military service in war, and lead larger lives in the public household (761c–d, 780a–785b). Instead of indulging their love of idle play, Plato calls on older citizens to study the sciences that are "noble, true, and beneficial to the city," such as philosophy and astronomy. These studies reveal the naturally lawful motion of the soul in synchrony with the motion of the stars, thereby anchoring the moral order of the city and checking blasphemy against the heavenly gods who oversee it (820c–824a, 964e–969d).

If active leisure is essential to the learning and work of citizens in Plato's account of the good city, in the *Politics* Aristotle followed Plato in commending the active life "both for cities and for individuals" (1325b14ff).[14] Virtuous civic participation is essential for the city's well-being, and human happiness inheres in activity in accord with moral excellence. Such a life of virtuous civic activity consists not merely of practices pursued for the strategic sake of the city's successful sur-vival but for the sake of its intrinsic good. Leisure is no less vital to the learning and life of contemplation that Aristotle sees enacting the high-est excellence of humans as rational animals in the *Nicomachean Ethics* (7.1177a–b), by contrast to our excellence as political animals and citizens in the *Politics*. Since intellect is "the best thing in us," our natural ruler and guide, its exercise in contemplating what is truly noble and divine is the best activity we can pursue. As the most continuously and purely pleasurable thing we can do, and the most self-sufficient, such contem-plation is the only human activity to be loved for its own sake, even if it tugs us away from civic involvement. So, argues Aristotle, "happiness is thought to depend on leisure; for we are busy that we may have leisure, and make war that we may live in peace." Military and political affairs aim at a happiness beyond their own nobility and greatness, let alone the mundane power and honor they win. For Plato life's ultimate end and good lies in the lawful harmony of the city itself, singing to itself in soulful harmony with the cosmos. For Aristotle the complete happiness of humans lies in the contemplative activity of intellect, which aims at no end beyond itself.[15]

In Stoic visions of divine providence and natural law that hark back to Plato as they come to inform Greco-Roman religion and early Chris-tianity, civic duties to honor the gods in a "state made up of gods and men" unite with the ultimate moral purpose of humans to grow in intel-ligence, goodness, and justice through authentic communion with the god whose being they share. Since spirit (*pneuma*) pervades and shapes all things as the vehicle of reason (*logos*) that governs and inheres in the cosmos, to act according to nature in Stoicism is implicitly to follow god. All the days of their lives, without ending or retiring, humans must praise God in every activity, public and private, as Epictetus urges in "On Providence":

> Why, if we had any sense, ought we be doing anything else, publicly and privately, than hymning and praising the Deity, and rehearsing His benefits. Ought we not, as we dig and plough

and eat, to sing the hymn of praise to god? "Great is God, that he hath furnished us these instruments wherewith we shall till the earth. Great is God that He hath given us hands, and power to swallow, and a belly, and power to grow unconsciously, and to breathe while asleep." This is what we ought to sing on every occasion, and above all to sing the greatest and divinest hymn, that God hath given us the faculty to comprehend these things and to follow the path of reason.

"What then?" Epictetus asks. He answers, "Why, what else can I, a lame old man, do but sing hymns to god?" So, he concludes by professing, promising, and summoning, "This is my task; I do it, and will not desert this post, so long as it may be given to me to fill it; I enjoin you to join me in the same song" (*Discourses*, 1.16.15–21).[16]

Does this natural song of praise and thanksgiving sound more inviting than Augustine's heavenly chorus? Do we, too, seek to twist the iron cords of appetite into accord with the golden thread of reason to serve the common good of the city? Can we trust in politics as the highest form of the art of caring for souls, or must we retire from conflicts of political interest and ideology in order to care for ourselves, if not to save our souls and love our neighbors?

## FROM SAVING WORK TO PLAYFUL PARADISE

From biblical Jerusalem and ancient Athens, traveling along Roman roads and medieval routes to the early-modern gates of the heavenly city of Enlightenment philosophers and the earthly paradise of Romantic poets, there emerges the quest we pursue in thinking about retirement today and weighing the life to come. The urban social order of the classical Greco-Roman world, with artisans and commercial traders added to peasants and ruling elites, gradually reshapes itself into the hierarchy of medieval Europe, headed by courts and monasteries and grounded in manorial agriculture.[17] Through late medieval towns and cities arise calls to heed the Bible alone to grasp the gospel truth of salvation and rightly guide the church, freeing the faithful to reimagine it less as a body politic headed by clergy and more as a body of worship made up of individual members and governed by the priesthood of all believers. Instead of exalting the "second baptism" of monastic vows of poverty, chastity, and obedience, this opens up Christians' calling to work, rest, and pray in the body of the church and the stations of society in wider ways that hark back to Paul in summoning each and every Christian by the word of God.

Martin Luther begins a revolution by carrying ideals of daily work as a divine calling out of the monastery, as Max Weber argued, and into the everyday life of the middle classes emerging in western Europe in the sixteenth century.[18] Work is prayer, and now everyone is to become a monk in the world, within a priesthood of all believers bound by conscience captive to the Word of God. The only way to live acceptably to God calls for no cloistered effort to escape the world or surpass its moral order of work and family life. It calls us to transform this life by laboring in our worldly calling to express our wholehearted love of God and neighbor. Everyday work and family life become a new kind of sacrament, an outward sign of an inward grace, consecrated and freed by faith alone from monastery walls and rites under clerical control. For Luther the concept of calling nonetheless remained traditional, insofar as God's will commands each person to stay in the feudal social station and economic occupation in which God's providence has placed him. Calvinism and the radical Reformation break this feudal mold, Weber argued, with a new kind of activism and asceticism that remake the world of work through methodically sustained and systematic efforts, inspired by the faith that God helps those who help themselves. By such work in the world, for the greater glory of God, we bring the kingdom of God closer to fulfillment on earth. We work to glorify God, not simply to make the world a better place or to enrich ourselves.

By proclaiming the workaday world as the theater of God's glory and the arena for fulfilling God's command, the Reformation inspires positive autonomous action in the world, taken through economic initiative and political self-government, rather than simply rejecting this world or enduring its autocracies for heaven's sake. Instead of cloistered rites and ascetic exercises on the monastic model, the service of God becomes a total demand in every walk of life. Salvation cannot be earned by deeds, acquired by law, or aided by indulgences. It can only be given freely by God as a gift of grace through faith alone in Jesus Christ as the Messiah. Stressing "faith" as a virtue of personhood in everyday practice, rather than particular acts as "works," makes it possible to accept the ambiguity of human ethical life in the world, and embrace the truth that salvation comes in spite of sin, not in its absolute absence. So we can accept a sinful world not simply as it is, but as an arena to work out God's will and human destiny through freely chosen yet conscientiously binding efforts of moral formation and social reform.[19]

Thus Max Weber compared the end of Dante's *Divine Comedy*, where the poet in Paradise stands speechless and still in timeless contemplation of the wondrous perfection of God's goodness, to the end of Milton's *Paradise Lost*.[20] It ends east of Eden, but now with a remarkable twist on the mortal toil and trouble of Genesis, and a Puritan's pointed dismissal of medieval visions of worldly work left behind in ascending to salvation on high. After their expulsion from Paradise, Adam and Eve look back at the gate barred by fiery arms. Then, wrote Milton:

> Some natural tears they dropped, but wiped them soon:
> The world was all before them, there to choose
> Their place of rest, and Providence their guide.

Indeed, the Archangel Michael has just advised Adam, "Only add / Deeds to thy knowledge answerable; add faith; / Add virtue, patience, temperance; add love; . . . / then will thou not be loth / To leave this Paradise, but shall possess / A Paradise within thee, happier far."[21] Paradise lies within each soul, a providential promise made to be kept by hard work and conscientious choice in one's own life, accepted as a lifelong task in this world that leads to salvation in the next.

Early Protestants and Puritans stress that one's work, station, and place as calling are something given, indeed imposed by the will of God.

This is a gift of God for Luther, but it may be a burden, too, a burden to be borne even if it weighs like a cross. A Christian does not select what he will do. He waits on what God commands of him, and then obeys. Calvin wrote that he accepted the calling to minister in Geneva against his own inclination, but according to God's will. He warns that "if a man lives by his own wits, without God's calling, he will wander and get lost all his life. Those who think they are very wise, and neither inquire of God nor receive his Spirit to govern their lives, are blind and grope in the dark. There is only one right way: to hold on single-mindedly to our divine calling and to have God always walking ahead of us."[22]

The godly are called to spiritual vocation by eternal election before the creation of the world. The ungodly follow their own disposition. Later Puritans defined callings in more diffuse if not more worldly terms, allowing that good works are "part of salvation" or even "contribute" to it, since they issue from the faith of the elect, but nonetheless they do not earn or merit salvation. Thus Cotton Mather declared that "much of our salvation consists in doing good works," for "good works are part of the great salvation which is purchased for you by Jesus Christ."[23]

By contrast to Calvinist callings given by God, a way of life that humans choose—*genus vitae* instead of *vocatio*—arises in the Stoic and humanist tradition, as it extends from Cicero through the Renaissance of Petrarch and Erasmus into the classical revival of eighteenth-century America exemplified by Thomas Jefferson.[24] Our work emerges from the selection and determination of the individual's way of life, a way of living and doing in human community. It depends on each person's innate aptitude and conscious selection. It is each person's work, not God's. Humanists followed a path pointed out by Epictetus's premise that everyone is born for something different, and his question, "How then shall we discover, each of us, what suits his character?" This question meant little to Luther and Calvin. But it crossed into Protestant thought in England in the sixteenth century, and it prompted notions of occupational aptitude, suitability, and choice vital to our own modern view of schooling and work based on talent, fitness, inclination and aspiration. Chapters on "the good choice of a calling" had grown familiar and conventional in English Protestant works on calling by the seventeenth century. They underlie modern aptitude and personality testing, beginning in the United States with the Army Alpha Test in World War I and the Stanford–Binet Intelligence Scale that spread into consolidating schools and expanding corporate businesses in the 1920s.[25]

The Protestant ethic of submission and obedience to God in a calling recombines with a classical humanist tradition stressing self-knowledge in the consciously specialized use of our natural abilities to frame modern visions of work as both a calling and a way of life. The worldly work of medieval Christians ascends from this world to the next in prayer and service to glorify God on monastic models that bridge the City of Man and the City of God. Puritans incorporate worldly work into a lifelong path of prayerful service to God as monks in the world of work and the family household. Retiring from this world of dutiful work to pray in the separate social sphere of the medieval monastery made no more sense to early modern Puritans than would our late modern retirement to relax and have fun in the world of leisure today, after we pursue demanding careers or endure grinding jobs that count neither as a calling given by God nor a way of life we were naturally born to love.

Puritans wanted to work in a calling given by God as a sign of faith in their predestined election, Max Weber judged, and care for the goods of this world rested on their saintly shoulders like a light cloak. "But fate decreed that the cloak should become an iron cage," he concluded, forcing us to labor within the immense machine of modern industrial capitalism to earn our daily bread and pay our monthly mortgage. Who among us still wears such a cloak or escapes such a cage? Who among us does not live in castles of romantic dreams as well? However fleeting or fulfilling, most of us seek shelter there, if only in fun-filled moments of middle-class leisure in the backyard or hours of play on the weekend, echoing youthful years of self-discovery for the privileged and orchestrating middle age in the counterpoint of bourgeois business with bohemian pleasure. So the rhythms of middle-class life couple the conscience of early-modern monks in the world with the Romantic quest of modern spirits to touch eternity in the moment, as we weigh the promise of retirement to free us to embrace the life to come, here and now.[26]

The long arc of middle-class life at work, rest, and play, by turns bohemian and bourgeois, unfolds across a changing Anglo-American social landscape. No rest is secure in the uncivil world of religious and political "war of all against all" that Hobbes describes in sixteenth-century England. Life is "nasty, brutish, and short," and humans are so vain that their solipsistic self-preservation demands mutual mistrust and wary vigilance until a sovereign state can impose peace by a forceful social contract, and a sovereign state church can defend it against conflicting construal of God's word and Nature's law. In the more sympathetic society Adam Smith set out around a free market and a fair administrative state in the eighteenth century, competitive risks demand stoic self-denial in the face of undeserved financial reverses, and compassion calls for aid to deserving others in need. The invisible hand of the market reaches from the sleeve of divine providence to guarantee progress overall. But it does not grant prosperity to all, Smith observed, in cities thriving with merchants and matrons but beset by beggars and ruled by princes. Market exchange divides good intentions from good outcomes, disintegrating moral deeds and virtues by unforeseen chance or fate. So good people can meet with misfortune in the marketplace, and evil can flourish at the expense of diligent workers who lose the fruits of their labor, including every prospect of retirement or rest in peace.[27]

Alongside the market's hard knocks and impersonal play of interests in the early modern city, there emerges a public sphere of citizens bearing rights and raising voices to enlighten self-interest and form moral opinion to guide republican self-government. There also emerges a private sphere of the bourgeois family and friendship, a softer circle of mutual care and kindness at odds with the competitive hardness of the public arena, yet offering a refuge from it and a rationale for it. "With what pleasure do we look upon a family, through the whole of which reign mutual love and esteem," asked Adam Smith, where the parents and children are companions for one another, without any other differences than what is made by respectful affection on the one side, and kind indulgence on the other; where freedom and fondness, mutual raillery and mutual kindness, show that no opposition of interest divides the brothers, nor any rivalship of favour sets the sisters at variance, and where every thing presents us with the idea of peace, cheerfulness, harmony, and contentment?

We prize the tenderness of this softer sphere, and we pity those punished for being too tender or trusting in public. We only regret, sighs Smith, that their softness is "unfit for the world, because the world is unworthy of it."[28]

Refuge from a commercial world unworthy of our deepest feelings and highest aims turns toward nature in Romantic terms that stress its resonance with our innermost instincts and its power to fulfill our true destiny. Thus Wordsworth's indictment of commerce and his vow to proclaim a higher faith in tune with nature's moods and the heart's true yearning:

> The world is too much with us; late and soon,
> Getting and spending, we lay waste our powers:
> Little we see in nature that is ours;
> We have given our hearts away, a sordid boon!
> The Sea that bares her bosom to the moon;
> The winds that will be howling at all hours,
> And are up-gathered now like sleeping flowers;
> For this, for everything, we are out of tune;
> It moves us not.—Great God! I'd rather be
> A Pagan suckled in a creed outworn;
> So might I, standing on this pleasant lea,
> Have glimpses that would make me less forlorn;
> Have sight of Proteus rising from the sea;
> Or hear old Triton blow his wreathed horn.[29]

Why shouldn't we have our own living poetry, philosophy, and religion of soulful experience to behold God and nature face-to-face, Emerson asks Americans accordingly, instead of looking backward to

111

entombed tradition? To find true solitude and oneness with nature, "a man needs to retire as much from his chamber as from society," Emerson proposes, and look at the stars to feel "the perpetual presence of the sublime." The soul seeks the beauty of nature, which satisfies this desire as "one expression for the Universe. God is the all-fair. Truth, and goodness, and beauty, are but different faces of the same All." Standing in the midst of such a sublime nature, Emerson testifies, we transcend ourselves: "I am nothing; I see all; the currents of the Universal Being circulate through me; I am part or particle of God."[30]

Not so fast, object latter-day saints and early-modern rationalists to Romantics urging us to become One with the All. We are sinners who must repent, for heaven's sake, they insist. We are thinkers who must work hard to know anything through the rigorous activity of discursive reason. Reason must examine, compare, distinguish, abstract, analyze, deduce, and demonstrate in order to gain knowledge, since no human knowledge comes through perceiving without conceiving. "Reason cannot intuit anything," declares Kant, "and the law is that reason acquires its possessions through work."[31] Thus Kant dismisses the pure "intellectual contemplation" of antiquity in scholastic usage, along with the enthusiasm of Romantics who have "only to attend to the oracle in one's breast and enjoy it, and so possess that wisdom whole and entire" that the "herculean labor" of true philosophy must work without rest or daydreaming to attain.[32]

Nevertheless, from Thoreau walking through the woods of Walden Pond in the "direction of his dreams," and Whitman taking to the open road to "loaf and invite my soul" at one with the universe, Americans in love with love have gone on to seek self-fulfillment in the arms of romantic relaxation, play, and ecstasy. Who among us wants to miss out on the fun, to lose out in love, or never to have loved at all? We dream under the stardust spell of movies that make the world go 'round, and we dance to melodies that haunt our reveries. We sing of feeling happy like a hot air balloon or a room without a roof, floating carefree in the air, with no reason to come down. Granted, the songs and movies that we know may just be passing fancies and in time may go, but for lovers who live on as companionate couples to share their golden years, it's very clear our love is here to stay, not for a year but ever and a day. Freed from bearing the bonds of faithful self-sacrifice or conscientious self-examination, we cannot rest until we rest in the embrace of the moment and the All, in the arms of our own true love, in touch with the infinity of feeling part of the whole.[33]

## AT HOME AND AWAY IN THE USA

Within warm circles of bourgeois families and friends, more indebted to Adam Smith than to Walt Whitman, modern ideals of rest and retirement take root as a reward for sustaining steady careers and staying on the job, no matter how hard or tedious, year after year. Yet rest and restlessness go hand and hand in the American grain, as Tocqueville observed in the 1830s. "An American will build a house in which to pass his old age and sell it before the roof is on," he marvels. If he has "a little spare leisure, his restless curiosity goes with him traveling up and down the vast territories of the United States." Why so? Compared to believers with their eyes fixed on heaven or gentry tied to the land in the Old World, Americans in pursuit of happiness set their hearts on the good things of this world. They are always in a hurry, Tocqueville thinks, for they have "only a limited time in which to find them, get them, and enjoy them." In this first new nation, "neither law nor custody holds anyone in one place, and that is a great further stimulus to this restlessness of temper. One will find people continually changing paths for fear of missing the shortest cut leading to happiness."[34]

Such restlessness stirs with a worldly faith of its own, instead of being driven by hardheaded doubt of the hereafter or poetic disdain for the marketplace. "Priests in the Middle Ages spoke of nothing but the other life; they hardly took any trouble to prove that a sincere Christian might be happy here below," Tocqueville explains. "But preachers in America are continually coming down to earth. Indeed they find it difficult to take their eyes off of it. The better to touch their hearers, they

113

are forever pointing out how religious beliefs favor freedom and public order, and it is often difficult to be sure when listening to them whether the main object of religion is to procure eternal felicity in the next world or prosperity in this."[35]

God helps them that help themselves, Ben Franklin preaches in "The Way to Wealth," and "there will be sleeping enough in the grave." Laziness rises so late and "travels so slowly, that poverty soon overtakes him," he warns, so "early to bed, and early to rise, makes a man healthy, wealthy, and wise." In the affairs of this world, trusting too much in others can be ruinous, and so "men are saved not by faith, but by the want of it; but a man's own care is profitable; for, saith Poor Dick, learning is to the studious, and riches to the careful, as well as power to the bold, and Heaven to the virtuous. And farther, if you would have a faithful servant, and one that you like, serve yourself." Faithfully serving yourself instead of falsely trusting in others paves the way to leisure through diligent labor, Franklin testifies, "since thou are not sure of a minute, throw not away an hour. Leisure is time for doing something useful; this leisure the diligent man will obtain, but the lazy man never."[36]

Restless and on the move in pursuit of happiness, or hard at work on the ground to build an enterprise and support a family at home, Americans inhabit a shifting social world that changes the ways their individuality takes shape in institutional practice. The concentric circles of colonial community in Puritan New England and the tiered "squirearchy" of Jefferson's Virginia open up into the parallel lanes of an entrepreneurial racecourse to track the greater movement and competition of spreading democracy, markets, and frontiers in the Jacksonian era. Gradually the grid of government grows to regulate economic enterprise, as it shifts from family farms and workshops into corporations in a national economy in the later nineteenth century.[37] Trust-busting Progressives check the sway of Gilded Age captains of industry, commanding a "governmentless government," while a growing middle class fills the age-graded ranks of a more standardized and carefully sequenced life course. It starts with child rearing in a home, apart from the office or factory, rises through legally required schooling outside the home, leads to a career organized into stages and steps in a corporate framework, then finishes in retirement expected if not mandated to follow at ages 62–70 or so.[38]

Building on the rules of free markets in labor, land, commodities, and capital, modern nation-states take the lead in setting rules to govern good parenting against neglect, and order compulsory elementary schooling and elective higher education to run worldwide on an age-graded system through a score of categories from kindergarten to postdoctorate. Standards for school curriculum and achievement for each age inform occupational credentialing in the world of work, evaluation on the job, and designation on the tax rolls that fund Social Security and Medicare accounts in the United States. Rules of occupational transition specify seniority, promotion, and career sequencing on the path to a formalized system of retirement, with its own rights and obligations set along a more or less mandatory timeline, for example, for continuing to pay Social Security taxes and beginning to draw Social Security benefits.

As nation-states expand in the eighteenth and nineteenth centuries, dimensions of selfhood once seen as sacred or natural forms of social membership—made in the image of God, given by nature's laws, embodied in religious-political communities interwoven with kinship in organic hierarchies and corporate metaphors of head, hands, and feet—emerge as dimensions of the individual life of each person seen as a citizen who is also a spouse, parent, child, student, worker, or retiree. Represented by government of, for, and by the people, society in turn is made up of individual citizens, rather than families, clans, villages, estates, classes, or castes. Each individual bears rights and responsibilities, with an inherently sacred standing and moral dignity, as the ultimate source and beneficiary of society. Society is constituted by a people for the sake of their mutual benefit as individuals, not only for their general welfare, justice, and progress in common. Since the turn of the twentieth century, nation-states have put this moral vision into social practice in expanding their institutions of socialization, education, occupational credentialing, career organization, and official retirement on a worldwide scale, however diverse the paths, anomalous the effects, or unfair the fates people actually experience in making their way through these institutions.[39]

Since the turn of the twenty-first century, however, more Americans have come to question the integrity of these institutions and their promise of a secure retirement, as their careers have grown choppier, their pensions spottier, and their savings scantier. Yet we still dream of retiring to enjoy our home sweet home and family, to answer the call of the open road to sunny shores and bright city lights, to plunge into arts and letters, to join more freely with friends in play and enjoy more fully the pleasure of their company. What's wrong with that? Nothing but the unfairness of breaking this promise and denying this freedom to everyone who deserves a chance to make their dreams come true. Why? Because they, too, have worked long and hard to earn the rewards of retirement, to realize their right to pursue happiness in this world, whatever their hopes for salvation in the next, and to secure the blessings of liberty to their posterity no less than ours.

## A New Deal for Workers in Retirement

Contested yet coherent ways of talking about what's right or wrong with retirement in America run back directly to the beginning of public deliberation over pensions and provision for old age in the New Deal. They run right up to the present in policy debates and political controversies over Social Security, Medicare, Medicaid, and Obamacare as well as kitchen-table talks over saving enough to retire, pay off debts, add insurance coverage, and care for aged in-laws.[40] "No greater tragedy exists in modern civilization than the aged, worn-out worker who after a life of ceaseless effort and useful productivity must look forward for his declining years to a poor-house," wrote then governor Franklin D. Roosevelt to the New York Legislature on February 28, 1929. "A modern social consciousness demands a more humane and efficient arrangement."[41] This conscientious demand to do our duty to help the needy and reward their hard work soon led to a portion of workers' wages being withheld to provide for their retirement. Defenders of the New Deal sometimes portrayed this arrangement as personal savings accounts safeguarded by government, while critics attacked it as taxes unfairly levied on earners and taxpayers' money unfairly doled out to dependents.

Consider, for example, the defense of public provision to help the needy by "protecting our most vulnerable," mounted in the image of FDR, as urged by Senator Bernie Sanders against budget-cutting Republicans in announcing his 2016 presidential campaign:

> At a time when millions of Americans are struggling to keep their heads above water economically, at a time when senior poverty is increasing, at a time when millions of kids are living in dire poverty, my Republican colleagues, as part of their recently-passed budget, are trying to make a terrible situation even worse. If you can believe it, the Republican budget throws 27 million Americans off health insurance, makes drastic cuts in Medicare, throws millions of low-income Americans, including pregnant women, off of nutrition programs, and makes it harder for working-class families to afford college or put their kids in the Head Start program. And then, to add insult to injury, they provide huge tax breaks for the very wealthiest families in this country while they raise taxes on working families. Well, let me tell my Republican colleagues that I respectfully disagree with their approach. Instead of cutting Social Security, we're going to expand Social Security benefits. Instead of cutting Head Start and child care, we are going to move to a universal pre-K system for all the children of this country.

Sanders concluded, "As Franklin Delano Roosevelt reminded us, a nation's greatness is judged not by what it provides to the most well-off, but how it treats the people most in need. And that is the kind of nation we must become."[42]

As President, FDR wove together moral languages of need and aid, earning and contribution, rights and responsibilities, duty and utility, too, to define Social Security and justify it. A century of startling industrial changes "has tended more and more to make life insecure," he noted on signing the original act in 1933. "Young people have come to wonder what would be their lot when they came to old age. The man with a job has wondered how long the job would last."[43] A year earlier he justified "the great task of furthering the security of the citizen and his family through social insurance," raised by "contribution rather than by an increase in general taxation," yet national in scope and leaving to the federal government "the responsibility of investing, maintaining and safeguarding the funds constituting the necessary insurance reserves."[44] Annuities built up by these contributions "in time will establish a self-supporting system for those now young and for future generations," FDR promised, with government directly providing pensions only for those too old to build up their own insurance, and encouraging "voluntary contributory annuities by which individual initiative can increase the annual amounts received in old age."[45] Within a few years, liberalizing old-age benefits paid early on in retirement, and beginning to pay them sooner, made for a pay-as-you-go system in practice. But the moral logic of individuals earning and saving continues to underlie debates over the system's enduring solvency in dialogue with questions over what it is that interdependent generations owe each other.

For example, in opposing cuts to Social Security proposed in the 2012 deficit-reduction package put forward by Alan Simpson and Erskine Bowles, Senator Sanders cited Simpson's "rude, inaccurate, and derogatory" characterization of Social Security as a "Ponzi scheme, not a retirement program," like "a milk cow with 310 million tits!"[46] The Simpson–Bowles plan would cut average annual benefits by $560 for a retiree at age seventy-five and by $1,000 at age eighty-five, Sanders pointed out, at a time when "two-thirds of senior citizens rely on Social Security for more than half of their income, and the average Social Security benefit today is about $1,200 a month," as health care and drug costs rise, making it "harder for today's average senior citizen to make ends meet." To this argument from need, Sanders added arguments based on workers' rights to receive benefits earned, not handouts given on the dole or claimed as entitlements. He attacked the unfairness of the Simpson–Bowles plan to "cause major economic pain to virtually every American, while lowering tax rates for millionaires, billionaires, and large corporations even more than President Bush."

By law Social Security is not part of the federal budget, Sanders noted, and it cannot add to the federal deficit. "This reflects Social Security's structure as an independent, self-financed insurance program, in which worker contributions, not general taxes, finance benefits," and benefits are paid only from its own revenues and trust fund, not by borrowing from general revenues.[47] "Even though Social Security operates in a fiscally responsible manner, some still advocate deep benefit cuts and seem convinced that Social Security hands out lavish welfare checks. But Social Security is not welfare," Sanders countered. "Seniors earned their benefits by working hard and paying into the program. Meanwhile, the average monthly Social Security benefit is only about $1,200, quite low by international standards." Principles of earning and contribution justify Social Security by the reciprocal rights of workers to receive the benefits they earn, and to earn the benefits they receive, along with their need for help to make ends meet. That help should be shared responsibly and fairly by privileged others to whom much has been given and too little asked in taxes in return.

FDR likewise justified New Deal reforms and reconstruction in light of "elementary principles of justice and fairness" consistent with individual liberties and freedoms as rights, and the responsibility of individuals to work hard to earn their own way. In late 1934 FDR asked not only, "Are you better off than you were last year?" as measured by less burdensome debts, more secure savings, better working conditions, and more firmly grounded "faith in your own future."[48] He also asked, "Have you as an individual paid too high a price for these gains" with the loss of individual liberty or constitutional "freedom of action or choice"? The public record of progress at a fair price, FDR argued, "is written in the experiences of your own personal lives." The most vociferous doubters he heard turn out to be the powerful few who sought special political and financial privileges for themselves, not the rights of all. FDR defended New Deal regulation of banking, the sale of "unsound mortgages," and "stock gambling" as efforts to clean up the evils of elites seeking to get rich quick by speculation. "The average person almost always loses. Only a very small minority of the people of this country believe in gambling as a substitute for the old philosophy of Benjamin Franklin that the way to wealth is through work."

In a 1938 radio address to the nation on the anniversary of the Social Security Act, Roosevelt sets out its moral and material accomplishments, including aid to 1.7 million "old folks [who] are spending their last years in surroundings they know and with people they love."[49] Through these accomplishments, he notes:

> Our government in fulfilling an obvious obligation to the citizens of the country has been doing so only because the citizens require action from their Representatives. If the people during these years had chosen a reactionary Administration or a "do nothing" Congress, Social Security would still be in the conversational stage—a beautiful dream which might come true in the dim distant future. But the underlying desire for personal and family security was nothing new. In the early days of colonization and through the long years following, the worker, the farmer, the merchant, the man of property, the preacher and the idealist came here to build, each for himself, a stronghold for the things he loved. The stronghold was his home; the things he loved and wished to protect were his family, his material and spiritual possessions. His security, then as now, was bound to that of his friends and neighbors.

Individual effort and earning go hand in hand with social interdependence and mutual aid. As the nation's industry and commerce have grown more complex, "the hazards of life have become more complex," Roosevelt reasons, and government rightly fulfills its obligation to respond to the needs of its citizens. In a more interdependent modern economy, each citizen "discovered that his individual strength and wits were no longer enough. This was true not only of the worker at shop bench or ledger; it was true also of the merchant or manufacturer who employed him. Where heretofore men had turned to neighbors for help and advice, they now turned to Government."

The first to turn to government and receive its protection, Roosevelt stresses, "were not the poor and lowly—those who had no resources other than their daily earnings—but the rich and the strong." Beginning in the nineteenth century, the United States passed "protective laws designed, in the main, to give security to property owners, to industrialists, to merchants and to bankers. True, the little man often profited by this type of legislation, but that was a by-product rather than a motive." The powerful had powerful voices, Roosevelt explains, loudly raised to protect their property, while workers only later organized for protective labor legislation, which "still gave no assurance of economic security. Strength or skill of arm or brain did not guarantee a man a job; it did not guarantee him a roof; it did not guarantee him the ability to provide for those dependent upon him or to take care of himself when he was too old to work." Here government does not stand apart from a free market that justifies unequal outcomes between rich and poor by their unequal efforts and merits. Instead government must respond justly to all its citizens, weak as well as powerful, to pass laws to make the economy fair for everyone and protect workers no less than property owners.

Long before the Great Depression, argues FDR, millions of Americans were living "in waste-lands of want and fear"—not a free-market state of nature—where their needs and rights combined to oblige government to respond by securing their capacity to contribute to the economy and find their place in society. "The millions of today want and have a right to the same security their forefathers sought—the assurance that with health and the willingness to work they will find a place for themselves in the social and economic system of the time." Government must help them lay the foundation to build their own security, just as it has done for business and industry. "We must face the fact that in this country we have a rich man's security and a poor man's security, and that the Government owes equal obligation to both. National security is not a half and half matter: it is all or none."

Justice requires security for all citizens for the good of the whole society. But it does not require government to offer anyone "an easy life" or "anything approaching abundance," FDR makes clear. Instead the Social Security Act "will furnish that minimum necessity to keep a foothold; and that is the kind of protection Americans want." Social Security provides the minimal protection that individual citizens need in order to work to earn their own way to sufficiency if not abundance. It fulfills their right to security, and it thereby enables them to exercise their right to earn a living. Equal justice under the law of the Social Security Act meant inclusion across the lines of rich and poor, first of all, then extending protection from mostly male members of the paid workforce to provide benefits to wives, widows, and orphans; and eventually to seasonal, temporary, and domestic workers, and finally to women and men of color.

Inclusion of all citizens, on the constitutional model of freedom of religion and speech as civil rights, figures in Roosevelt's formulation of an "Economic Bill of Rights" in his 1944 State of the Union address, and its rehearsal on the campaign trail.[50] Just as they have fought together in war, he reasons, so all Americans should return home to "a place where all persons, regardless of race, color, creed or place of birth, can live in peace, honor and human dignity—free to speak, and pray as they wish—free from want—and free from fear." So, he proposes, Congress should enact what the American people resolved, "a new basis of security and prosperity" established for all to realize their economic rights:

- The right of a useful and remunerative job in the industries or shops or farms or mines of the nation;

- The right to earn enough to provide adequate food and clothing and recreation;

- The right of every farmer to raise and sell his products at a return which will give him and his family a decent living;

- The right of every business man, large and small, to trade in an atmosphere of freedom from unfair competition and domination by monopolies at home or abroad;

- The right of every family to a decent home;

- The right to adequate medical care and the opportunity to achieve and enjoy good health;

- The right to adequate protection from the economic fears of old age, sickness, accident, and unemployment;

- The right to a good education.

"All of these rights spell security," Roosevelt sums up. "And after this war is won we must be prepared to move forward in the implementation of these rights, to new goals of human happiness and well-being."

Some people sneer at these ideals, Roosevelt acknowledges, as "the dreams of starry-eyed New Dealers." But the greater faith of the American people, he argues, stems from their recognition of the fact that the future of American workers lies in the well-being of private enterprise, no less than its future lies in their well-being, just as the "well-being of the Nation as a whole is synonymous with the well-being of each and every one of its citizens."

To assure the realization of these economic rights, therefore, Roosevelt promises adequate postwar programs to provide America with close to sixty million productive jobs. He proposes to help "private enterprise to finance expansion of our private industrial plant through normal investment channels" and increased tax depreciation rates to replace old equipment. This public help for private enterprise would create more jobs, increase business profits, cut consumer costs, and triple foreign trade. He pledges government to build new highways, and to help industry build new "homes with electricity and plumbing and air and sunlight," worthy of the millions of Americans who had never had them. FDR vowed to end postwar job discrimination on the wartime model of the Fair Employment Practice Committee. He promises that every "full-time job in America must provide enough for a decent living," since it is "only good common sense to see to it that the working man is paid enough" to buy the goods Americans produce "and keep our factories running." By this moral and institutional logic of argument, the economic rights of every American imply public provision, investment, and regulation to expand private-sector jobs, productivity, and profits for the common good. Every hardworking citizen deserves no less. Economic progress and social justice come together in prudent common sense.

## RETIREMENT FOR NOW: MORAL CHALLENGE AND AMBIGUITY

Much of this vision of great public works and fair public provision coupled with free enterprise and private profit to "give full employment to our people" came true over the generation to follow. The American middle class doubled in size and real household income from 1947 to 1973, as income grew more quickly at the bottom than at the top of society. Had this pace continued through the careers of baby boomers, median family income would have topped $124,000 by 2013 instead of stalling below half that amount. Since the 1970s, U.S. income has grown much more quickly at the top than at the bottom, and it has sagged in the middle. This has made our prosperity much less equally shared than it was a generation ago, even though per capita income grew by about two-thirds from 1973 to 2000 as the economy continued to expand, since most of the overall gain went to the wealthiest households. This has left our rates of poverty about the same and increased extreme poverty, with one in seven Americans still living below the poverty line, including one in five children, and two in five Black children.[51]

At the same time, public debate and personal quandaries over retirement have drawn old lines of moral argument about Americans' rights and responsibilities into this new landscape of widening economic hardship and inequality. One arena of this argument centers on questions of sharing fairly across generations, and what the old and young owe each other. Another surrounds questions of sharing fairly across economic divisions among rich and poor, struggling blue-collar workers, and a beleaguered middle class; between women and men; and among black, white, Hispanic, and Asian Americans. A third concerns questions of government's responsibility for public provision and spending, taxes and debt, in light of economic progress and social justice for all as democratic goods.

President Barack Obama framed these questions of public provision and sharing fairly the goods and costs of a secure retirement within a larger moral vision of American society indebted to FDR, indeed to Lincoln and Jefferson. To meet the urgent challenge of the Great Recession, Obama declared in his 2009 inaugural address that we must reaffirm our enduring spirit and carry forward our founding ideals: "the God-given promise that all are equal, all are free, and all deserve a chance to pursue their full measure of happiness."[52] By their labor our forebears have carried us up the long, rugged path towards prosperity and freedom. For us, they packed up their few worldly possessions and traveled across oceans in search of a new life. For us, they toiled in sweatshops and settled the West, endured the lash of the whip and plowed the hard earth.

Given the interdependence of our freedom with our forebears' struggle and sacrifice, we owe them in turn our shared commitment to "begin again the work of remaking America," and our shared recognition of this country as "bigger than the sum of our individual ambitions; greater than all the differences of birth or wealth or faction." Given the labor of many essential to our fate, not just the fortunes of a few, "The nation cannot prosper long when it favors only the prosperous." Our economic success depends not only on the growth of our GDP but on "the reach of our prosperity; on the ability to extend opportunity to every willing heart—not out of charity, but because it is the surest route to our common good." So, we should ask not "whether our government is too big or too small, but whether it works, whether it helps families find jobs at a decent wage, care they can afford, a retirement that is dignified."

Obama began his 2013 inaugural address by likewise invoking the self-evident truths of liberty and equality in the Declaration of Independence, then coupling Lincoln and FDR to urge Americans onward to "continue a never-ending journey to bridge the meaning of those words with the realities of our time."[53] Just as Americans learned by bloody lash and sword that no democracy can survive half-slave and half-free, so together, "we discovered that a free market only thrives when there are rules to ensure competition and fair play. Together, we resolved that a great nation must care for the vulnerable, and protect its people from life's worst hazards and misfortune." We celebrate initiative and enterprise, but we also "understand that our country cannot succeed when a shrinking few do very well and a growing many barely make it." America thrives when "every person can find independence and pride in their work; when the wages of honest labor liberate families from the brink of hardship." So "every citizen deserves a basic measure of security and dignity," without having to choose between "caring for the generation that built this country and investing in the generation that will build its future. For we remember the lessons of our past, when twilight years were spent in poverty and parents of a child with a disability had nowhere to turn."

Seen in this light, Obama argued, "The commitments we make to each other through Medicare and Medicaid and Social Security, these things do not sap our initiative; they strengthen us. They do not make us a nation of takers; they free us to take the risks that make this country great." Personal initiative and mutual responsibility go hand in hand with fairly regulated markets and public provision for the common good in this account on the model of FDR, by contrast to Mitt Romney's 2012 campaign depiction of 47 percent of voters dependent on government and convinced "they are entitled to health care, to food, to housing, to you-name-it" in exchange for their votes, without paying taxes or working hard to take personal responsibility for their lives.[54]

Mutual commitments and responsibility for our fellow citizens make America great, both political parties agree. But contrary to Democratic plans to strengthen public provision, the fact remains, insisted GOP fiscal conservatives such as the House Republican Study Committee (RSC), that government cannot afford to pay the rising costs of Social Security, Medicare, and Medicaid, let alone Obamacare. It cannot keep spending more without going deeper into debt for generations to come, or raising taxes unjustly on free enterprises that deserve to keep their profits in free markets. So do the business executives and investors who have earned the fruits of their labor and capital. Given free labor in free markets that naturally determine wages and wealth, moral questions of fairly distributing costs and benefits focus on public debt and spending across generations, not income earned across economic classes. "The mountains of federal debt being dumped on the backs of our children continue to grow and the window to rescue our economy is closing," warned the RSC in releasing its 2014 budget, "Back to Basics."[55] "We cannot let another year pass without taking the same commonsense steps toward a balanced budget that families have already taken with their budgets."

This means cutting federal spending to get "government out of the way so America's businesses can have the ability to grow and create jobs." It means cutting taxes on personal income, capital gains, corporate profits, and inherited wealth. The RSC vowed to balance the federal budget in four years by repealing "President Obama's job-killing healthcare law"; freezing federal funding for Medicaid and letting states control its benefits and eligibility; cutting Social Security benefits by tightening its cost-of-living adjustments; gradually raising eligibility to age seventy for Social Security and Medicare; and tightening work requirements for welfare programs.[56] The RSC budget is "just the opposite of what Barack Obama and the Party of Treason are proposing," judged the Tea Party Nation. "In short, this budget is a step toward sanity."[57]

On the contrary, argued progressives such as Bernie Sanders, fairer wages, taxes, regulation, and investment in public works programs that update the New Deal are needed to reverse the economic inequality and hardship that block economic growth and social justice alike in

America today. "Now is the time not for another Bill Clinton but for an FDR," Sanders recalled advising a newly elected Barack Obama. Instead of seeking to compromise with big business and finance to shrink big government, "FDR had the courage and the good political sense to understand that in the middle of terrible economic times the American people wanted to know what caused their suffering, who was the cause of it, and they wanted somebody to take these guys on, so he was very aggressive in his rhetoric in taking on the money interests," Sanders explained. "He said, 'Of course they're going to hate me, and I welcome their hatred. I'm with the working people of America. We're going to take on the money interests, and we are going create jobs through a variety of government programs. If you're prepared to deal with class issues, as Roosevelt did, if you're prepared to take on the big-money interests, you can rally the American people, and I think you can marginalize the Republicans," as extremists at odds with Lincoln and Eisenhower as well as FDR.[58]

Accordingly, in announcing his 2016 presidential campaign, Senator Sanders pledged to "begin a political revolution to transform our country economically, politically, socially and environmentally." Now is the time, he declared, "for millions of working families to come together, to revitalize American democracy, to end the collapse of the American middle class, to make certain that our children and grandchildren are able to enjoy a quality of life that brings them health, prosperity, security, and joy—and that once again makes the United States the leader in the world in the fight for economic and social justice, for environmental sanity and for a world of peace."[59] Instead of denying the American dream of progress and opportunity for all "by the grind of an economy that funnels all the wealth to the top," as millions of Americans work longer hours for lower wages and cannot feed their children, "we can put Americans back to work at decent paying jobs to rebuild our crumbling infrastructure." We can raise wages and taxes, and reform banking and campaign financing. We can provide health care, child care, and college for all in a country "where every senior can live in dignity and security, and not be forced to choose between their medicine or their food."[60]

As the 2016 Democratic nominee, Hillary Clinton likewise declared, "Social Security must continue to guarantee dignity in retirement for future generations."[61] There is no way to accomplish that goal, she argued, without "asking the highest-income Americans to pay more."[62] The 2016 Democratic Party Platform accordingly vowed to ask top earners to pay more on income over $250,000, and pledged to "fight every effort to cut, privatize, or weaken Social Security." By stark contrast, the Platform charged, Donald Trump "referred to Social Security as a 'Ponzi scheme,' and called for privatizing it as well as increasing the retirement age."[63]

"Does the name Ponzi all of a sudden come to mind?" asked Donald Trump as a presidential candidate in 2000 diagnosing Social Security, then prescribing the remedies of privatization and raising the retirement age to seventy. During the 2016 primary campaign, however, Trump broke with GOP fiscal orthodoxy to promise instead to "save Social Security and Medicare without cuts" and "leave Social Security the way it is. Not increase the age," as a matter of non-injury, benefits earned by contribution, and promise-keeping as well as political prudence. "We're not going to hurt the people who have been paying into Social Security their whole lives, and then all of a sudden they're supposed to get less," Trump argued during a Republican debate, as he vowed, "I'm the only one who is going to save Social Security, believe me." Against other GOP candidates proposing to raise the retirement age, Trump objected, "I think it's unfair that after all these years they want to cut you . . . It's not fair. You've been paying in for years." Even Tea Party members want to hold on to their entitlements, Trump noted, warning Republicans, "If you think you are going to change very substantially for the worse Medicare, Medicaid, and Social Security in any substantial way, and at the same time you think you are going to win elections, it just really is not going to happen."[64]

Donald Trump's "no cuts" stance on Social Security and Medicare won votes and deflected Democratic charges of threatening benefits.[65] The 2016 Republican Platform nonetheless reaffirmed House Speaker Paul Ryan's dire depiction of Social Security, since "everyone knows that its current course will lead to a financial and social disaster. Younger Americans have lost all faith in the program and expect little return for what they are paying into it." Republicans must therefore "modernize a system of retirement security forged in an old industrial era beyond the memory of most Americans" by assuring benefits to retired Americans and those near retirement, and then considering all options to reform it for the future. "As Republicans, we oppose tax increases and believe in the power of markets to create wealth and help secure the future of our Social Security system." If you rule out increasing revenue for Social Security by raising payroll tax rates or lifting the income cap for taxable earnings, then "securing" Social Security requires cutting benefits or privatizing accounts to fulfill faith in "the power of markets." Neither GOP budgets nor Speaker Ryan's "Better Way" policy blueprint spelled out these conclusions before the 2016 election. But soon afterward Republican congressional leaders proposed to slash benefits and cut taxes that high earners pay on benefits. Then President Trump and Speaker Ryan agreed to cut taxes by $3 trillion for wealthy households, leave Social Security and Medicare intact for today's seniors over the next decade, and turn Medicaid into limited "block grants" to the states, while Ryan continued plans to privatize Social Security and "voucherize" Medicare for tomorrow's seniors to help offset tax cuts financed by deficits.[66]

# FOR THE FUTURE: THE MANIFOLD GOOD OF RETIREMENT

Dreams and doubts drive the drama of retirement in the public square, and visions of a good life in a good society inspire its moods and motives, no less than good reasons justify its logic of moral argument in public debate. Social facts do not tell the whole story, but they frame it. Since most Americans are living longer, as a matter of fact, they will need more money and resources to sustain their lives in retirement, and pensions will play a greater role in both public and private life.

Nonetheless, as Americans live longer, they remain remarkable for judging that the elderly bear the greatest responsibility for their own economic well-being. One in two of us hold that view, compared to one in ten in most countries. Fewer than one in four of us point to the government as most responsible for the elderly, and only one in five of us point to their families.[67]

Yet most Americans today are deeply worried about retiring securely, in fact, and they want government to take action with employers to enable them to earn and save enough to retire.[68] Most think the existing retirement system is under so much stress that it needs immediate reform so workers, employers, and government can fairly share responsibility for retirement instead of shifting its risk to workers. Across political party lines—including two of three Republicans, three of four Independents, and seven of eight Democrats—Americans want Congress and the president to place higher priority on helping people retire securely. Most want to strengthen Social Security, not cut its benefits or raise its age threshold, and they support increasing payroll taxes to do so, including elimination of the taxable income cap for top earners. To supplement Social Security, Americans are open to a range of fixes to workplace pensions and retirement plans in tandem with private savings. But four in five favor requiring companies to provide a defined-benefit pension plan with guaranteed retirement income, set alongside an equivalent universal portable pension system and supplemented but not replaced by an automatic IRA. Few Americans understand the intricacies of the current retirement system or policy debates over its reform. But they want to strengthen its security for everyone who works hard for a living wage, pays their fair share of taxes, and saves enough for the life to come. That goal remains unreached. Whether citizens will mobilize and vote to attain it remains to be seen.

Deeper cultural convictions and moral insights run through imagining retirement and planning for it, even if we do not conceive it in terms of keeping holy the Sabbath or serving our country as unselfish citizens of a virtuous republic. Retirement beckons us with visions of the good life shared with family and friends in communities of care and love. It offers us a fresh chance to join with others to work for the good of the whole, to give something back, to make the world a better place with our own two hands. It invites us to reflect on what makes life worth living, not only what makes it fun. Moral ideals and norms run through chapters in the history of retirement, marked off by when, how, and why people *should* retire, and by the good or not-so-good social arrangements that help or hinder their retirement.

There is more than one way we think about the manifold goods of retirement, and about its difficulties, costs, and risks. What's fair, for example, when it comes to sharing them? It seems fair, at first glance, to think we should work hard and save enough of what we earn to support ourselves in retirement, and not take or beg what others have earned to do so. Consider Aesop's fable of the grasshopper and the ant, for example, or the Bible's commandment not to steal. Thou shalt not steal to pay for retirement or make it unaffordable for others, be it through unfair taxes, wages, or profits.

We also recognize that the needy who are aged and infirm should not go without food to eat, a roof over their heads, and some basic level of care for their health and well-being. For providing this aid to those in need, we are responsible, indeed duty bound as kith, kin, neighbors, or fellow citizens. That seems true, even if we disagree about precisely who is more or less responsible to help whom with what, how to do it, and how to pay for it. Shouldn't children take better care of the parents who raised them, after all, than of their neighbors or strangers? Or should quid pro quo norms of reciprocity give way to the Good Samaritan story? Then we should go and do likewise, taking to heart the "Do unto others" truth of the golden rule, and heeding the revelation that everyone is our neighbor, whom we should love beyond selfish measure.

Alongside the principles of earning and need, we can point to specific rights when it comes to retirement since the New Deal, and weigh our responsibilities to respect these rights. When it comes to Medicare and Medicaid, for example, we can argue over who is responsible or obliged to respect a "right to basic health care" or to bear the burden of providing for its fulfillment. Thus moral languages of goods, rights and responsibilities, liberties and duties, freedom and justice inform questions of policy and politics. What should be the role of government in providing for retirement? How should it balance spending and taxes in helping older and younger generations, in protecting those who have earned and saved as well as caring for the needy? These questions have grown sharper and come closer to us, as Americans' retirement savings, investments, and home equity sank in the Great Recession, and our government deepened its debt, just as the costs of caring for retiring baby boomers started to skyrocket. While jobs have since grown, markets bounced back, wages inched up unevenly, wealth gaps widened, and economic discontents boiled into political protest, the difficulty of reaching retirement continues to deepen for future generations. They ask what we must do to set things right, and we need to answer.[69]

> To fulfill our retirement dreams, we
> must share them with our neighbors
> and fellow citizens across lines of color,
> class, gender, and generation.

Thus the drama of retirement unfolds as heartfelt dream and moral demand, object of powerful personal commitment and contested public argument, defended as our just deserts and fair reward for a lifetime's labor, held dear and doubted as our God-given right to longer life, financial liberty, and the perpetual pursuit of happiness. To fulfill our dreams of retirement, we must share them with our neighbors and fellow citizens across the lines of color and class, gender and generation. Now the hour has come to wake up to deliberate and work together in light of our mutual debts and destiny, before our day is done.

Churches cannot solve the nation's problems of providing fairly for retirement by making laws or public policy. But at their best, as bodies of faith and bodies politic, they can live out good examples in practice of mutual care and shared responsibility across generations, economic divisions, and social differences between haves and have-nots, insiders and outsiders, our kind and others. In congregating across generations, as shown in the following two cases, local communities of worship can care for their own aging members, and enable them to nurture their offspring, reach out to help the needy, and welcome the stranger. As conscientious citizens no less than Good Samaritans, they can raise their voices in the public square to give good reasons for good laws, and vote the public interest over self-interest. They can join hands to teach by good example what it means to act justly and love mercy as members one of another, even as church and state remain separate institutions, each governed by its own members.

# CHAPTER 4

# Congregating Across Generations

## AGES AND STAGES TRANSFORMED

N early eighty million Americans born between 1946 and 1964 have begun to retire, at the rate of ten thousand every day.[1] As this tidal wave of retirement builds over the next twenty years, it will offer extraordinary opportunities and challenges to congregational communities to engage the aspirations of a legion of newly active volunteers and channel commitments of the faithful to serve the commonweal. It will open church doors wider to a generation of Americans remarkable for their selective, shifting participation in religious institutions, both in their organizational involvement and giving, no less than their spiritual enthusiasm.[2]

How can the flourishing life of congregations both ride and guide this rising wave of retirement among the largest, best educated, most active, and longest-lived generation of Americans yet, as it flows through the changing institutional channels of their work, rest, prayer, and play? Can it embrace the full range of their social difference and economic inequality? To find out, we need not compile a "how to" list of plug-in programs and activities for seniors to pursue in and out of the pews. Instead let's explore a "why so" landscape of best practices and callings true to bodies of worship and care that actually answers the hopes and fears of those at the threshold of retirement and beyond.[3] Many will be needy, since retirement has grown harder to reach and sustain securely. Many will be able to respond to their neighbors' needs, given their gifts, resources, and ideals, as they seek a fulfilling way of life in retirement. This takes in the hunger of those driven by demanding careers to find the time and space to connect and care for others across generations, buoyed by the flow of shared prayer, study, and play. It extends to tutoring and mentoring of many kinds, from unsettled students struggling to read or do math to jobless parents struggling to write a one-page résumé or get a ten-minute interview. It reaches out in missions to visit the sick, shelter the homeless, and feed the hungry. It reaches in to touch our own fears of dependency, debility, and isolation that lie beyond the vigor and freedom of active retirement, in the "really old" realm of longevity dimmed by chronic degenerative disease. "That's what I'm really afraid of, not death," aging retirees often confess.

## How can flourishing congregations ride and guide this rising wave of retirement?

We can ask leaders and members of exemplary congregations, and expert others, too, about what active retirees can do to keep good company with those slowing down or resting along the road ahead, not just delivering Meals on Wheels, but sitting by the bed and reading aloud or listening quietly, helping with home care or financial planning. We can look into the best practices of two exemplary congregations, one an evangelical church growing from Presbyterian roots in Silicon Valley and the other a vibrant United Methodist congregation in suburban Atlanta. Neither is typical in the remarkable extent of its social service, outreach, and witness. But both represent a range of such efforts, from food pantries to tutoring programs, evident in congregations of virtually every denomination and religious tradition in the United States.[4] Both feature outstanding missions of community service and social witness in step with pioneering initiatives to engage and care for seniors. Both pair up with particularly promising partners in such efforts as immigrant settlement programs backed by government, overseas mission trips with global NGOs, and food banks with corporate sponsors; teaching and mentoring programs with public schools and professional groups to match committed volunteers to needy students; and grief-counseling networks with trained caregivers to enable them to "just be there and listen, no matter what."

Across the church aisle or across town, around the block or around the world, we can weigh moral maxims that "charity begins at home" and Good Samaritan convictions that "everyone is our neighbor." We can recognize the shining examples of service and outreach set by congregations with relatively few material resources yet great generosity of spirit and love of neighbor in taking care of their own and their neighbors everywhere in need. These include the Black Baptist church in Atlanta noted in chapter 2 and the Hispanic Pentecostal congregation cited later in this chapter.[5] At the same time, much is expected of those to whom much is given, so we focus on two predominantly well-educated and well-off congregations to see what they are making of their blessings, how they are engaging their retired members in this mission, and why they are so inspired.

## TO SERVE IN THE SPIRIT: THE SOUL OF SILICON VALLEY

The evangelical vision of Alto Church in Silicon Valley is framed in biblical terms of the Great Commission to "go and make disciples of all nations" (Matthew 28:19-20 NIV), to proclaim "the good news of the kingdom" (Matthew 4:23), and to aspire to exemplary love of neighbor, for by this "everyone will know that you are my disciples, if you love one another" (John 13:35 NIV). At the same time, this vision of a church centered on Jesus with a life rooted in Scripture takes particular form in Silicon Valley today. "Everybody's welcome," it proclaims. "Nobody's perfect," it acknowledges. "Anything's possible," it promises. It opens its doors to everyone, and celebrates its diversity across the lines of generation as well as color, class, and denominational background. Given its locale and core composition of educated professionals, predominantly white with a growing Asian minority, the church is particularly noteworthy for embracing older and younger members in distinctive ways.

Age-graded day care and Sunday school classes from toddlers to teens, along with parenting and couples classes common to many mainline Protestant churches, are joined here by exceptionally large and lively worship services, "life groups," classes, and retreats for "18–35 singles." There are also "50+ singles" groups, "divorce and relationship recovery" groups, and dozens of groups based on age, neighborhood, and interests ranging from Bible study to bicycling, from "engaging extreme poverty" to playing tennis, and sharing high-tech work. "It has to be the biggest singles group ever in a church, or anywhere else," marvels a nonmember who works nearby. "You see them every day and night of the week, you walk by and hear the music. Everyone around here knows about it." Alto Church welcomes families with young children as "vital to the future of the church," notes a minister, "but we know more than half of all households in the Bay Area are single persons living alone, and we want to embrace them, too."

In the striking picture that Alto Church paints of congregating across generations, what often catches the eye and ear of outsiders, significantly enough, are all the single young adults, since they seem so conspicuously absent from many mainline churches.[6] Not only high school and college students attend the 18–35 singles services, because "that's where the heavenly girls are singing in the choir" of a high-energy rock band, says a young-adult minister with a smile. They keep coming, even if they don't meet the prince or princess of their romantic dreams, she adds, because "there's real connection and community here, where people really care about you for who you are, not for who you pretend to be on Facebook or Twitter. We know about looking great online and feeling bad about your life, feeling alone and feeling like nobody really knows you or likes you."[7] That's an everyday reality for many young adults, she points out, driven to achieve in highly competitive schooling and careers in Silicon Valley, studying and working on the side to pay inflated rents, meeting and dating in a fluid world of singles who can hook up and move on with no strings attached, but with wounds and wondering left behind to carry through years of iffy courtship.

"We're OK with mixed motives," adds another youth minister, "and we want to work with them. People go where people are. You come because someone you like invites you. You come back because there's a good crowd and a good vibe here. But you keep coming because there's something else, something you don't find in a club or a party: loving one another like Jesus loves us." Conversely, "Just because you love your parents and grandparents doesn't mean you want to go to church with them every Sunday, and then go to a bar to find someone to love," reasons a youth minister in his early thirties. "Birds of a feather flock together. I want to worship and hang out with other young professionals who are believers. We want a space of our own, with our own music and feeling to it. We want to be able to find our own way, to ask our own questions, and explore our own answers and doubts without threat. You can be biblical and Christian, without having to start with someone else telling you what you have to believe in order to belong."

Service projects and shared social activities also prove more accessible and engaging when they are generationally tuned. "School and careers here take almost all the time you have," notes an unmarried tax lawyer in his early thirties, "so I want to plug into something worthwhile with people I know and like from church. I can sign up to do something like helping serve dinner at a night shelter once a month, but not be tied down by it, because there are lots of other people involved in it. It's well organized, and it's scheduled online. Just go to the church website, and click." Social scale and resources also make a difference, allows this lawyer, "I've gone to smaller churches, and you can certainly find commitment and companionship there. But you can be known and connected in a church like this that's riding the wave, with lots of action you can choose to get in on."

139

An older minister explains why he pioneered the church's "contemporary worship" services, tuned to young singles in a separate "café" setting, stripped of "church trappings" and equipped with professionally designed theatrical lighting and staging, sound systems and projection screens:

> Personally, I love stained glass windows and choirs singing hymns. But the church itself felt stuffy and staid a dozen years ago, like the kind of place young people want to get away from, not come into. We wanted to flex that, and loosen it up into a "casual, coffee, kids, come-late" kind of experience. We wanted to open it up. Give it a big, wide front door, and create space inside where you can get involved and share with people your own age. You can listen to music you like, sing along, tell people your story and listen to theirs, without worrying about having to agree with some set of beliefs first, before you can belong. We consciously switch that around. We're not fundamentalist.
>
> It used to be "Believe first." Align your thinking with the way we think, do things our way. Then you belong. Now it's flipped on its head. Now it's like everyone can belong, and be known just as they are, *before* they choose to believe, and before they choose to conform. That's been a big switch, not just for churches, but for all sorts of community organizations. Some churches have been able to make that switch, and others haven't.

This recent shift in popular culture runs deeper in the American grain, this minister notes. It is rooted in revivalism's aim to awaken affections and save souls through personal experience of conversion in a Protestant priesthood of all believers that lifts up participatory practice as the first virtue of bodies politic, including the body of Christ.[8] It also springs from the gospel truth, this minister reasons:

> If God created every person and looks after them as his beloved children, then God pursues them, too. If Jesus died not to condemn the world but to save it, and the Holy Spirit acts in his people to be the people of God, the salt and light of the earth, then we shouldn't be afraid to welcome in everyone as they are. Just as Jesus did! Rich and poor, across all cultures, the obvious sinner

and the invisible sinner. Jesus flowed freely across all those lines. So we're being true to the gospel, even if it's a scary change for churches that used to have themselves all lined up with a more linear culture. This is more art form now. There is comfort, maybe even blessing in that more linear organization. But our culture won't accept that now.

Such construal of cultural change applies aptly to the counterpoint of educated middle-class work and play. It puts high-tech stress on problem-solving innovation and administrative efficiency bred by elite education and sustained effort at work in highly disciplined STEM fields, while relaxing its hold on personal life and leisure left free to flow along "art-form" currents of aesthetic appeal and individual taste bred by popular media and music.

Some critics see such cultural change enabling mushy, self-centered mystics to trump orthodox, self-controlled Puritans.[9] But this minister in the vanguard of "a new evangelical revolution" sees such cultural change not only favoring his own church's stance, but lifting up the unity of the true church across denominations:

> The body of Christ is becoming a truly small-c "catholic" church, free from harsh distinctions between denominations. Those walls are having to come down. Face it: that needed to happen. Many of us grew up in a world where everyone in our own church has the Bible all right and we're on the highway to heaven, while everyone in the church down the block has it dead wrong, and they're on the road to hell. That just cannot be true!

"It's sad." He frowns. "Why did we think they were our enemies? When there are so many real enemies out there" in a world torn by war, hunger, poverty, racial hatred, and ecological crisis, which the faithful need to face together.

This approach appeals to a generation educated to question and find their own way, notes a youth minister. They prize freedom of choice as well as conscience. They celebrate expressive feeling and emotional intimacy on the wide road to true friendship and communion instead of dogmatizing reason and revelation on the narrow path to orthodox faith. But this seeker-friendly approach can pose challenges of its own, allows an older minister, since it risks "the make-believe of discipleship without discipline, love freely given without obedience, and emotionally powerful worship experience without biblical authority."

Given these challenges, he vows, "We don't want to just spend more money to put on a better show with a bigger emotional bang for a bigger audience, and wind up with a depersonalized kind of Christianity lite. So we really call them to serve. Don't just sit there in the pew and watch the show. Stand up and pitch in. Become the hands and feet of Jesus! That's the 'why' of the body of Christ," he stresses, by contrast to the "how-to" of a high-performance megachurch built mainly to serve its own expansion.

At the same time, this "hybridized mainline, almost megachurch," as another minister put it, includes more traditional "hymn and choir" services of worship, favored by many middle-aged families as well as seniors. It features a range of Bible study classes that include seniors in groups that have grown together for decades, carrying their leather-bound copies of the King James Bible well worn by page-turning and dense with margin notes. It urges worshippers to join small "life groups" to deepen their faith, and enact it in service to others in the church and the community through dozens of projects that range from teaching Sunday school through helping the homeless to mission trips abroad.

Married couples in their sixties and seventies introduce spouses of several years or decades whom they have met and married in the church. Middle-aged divorcees and widowed or single-again seniors on their own have found new friends and companions, if not always new partners, in the church's large singles groups. They have found "a safe place to heal your heart" in "divorce and relationship recovery groups."[10] "Pain is the great leveler," sums up a minister responsible for leading these groups. "It makes people move and want to change, even if it takes a while. Here we're mostly midthirties and up," he explains. "When you're younger you know it's the other person's fault, not yours, and you're bound to walk around the corner and find some-one perfect the next time. Gradually you realize that it's you, too." He smiles slowly.

> You need to change, and you realize you can't just do it all by yourself. You need help, you need to do it with others, in the right kind of community where you can be accepted, and you can also be accountable. You can come here and not be judged. "Nobody's perfect." But you can become responsible, too, and if you keep coming, then you can come into relationship with Jesus in your life, and with other Christians who love one another.

"I've been coming to divorce recovery for a year, and nobody's pres-sured me to join the church," gratefully testifies a woman in her thirties. Such "healing groups" are open to those who are not church members, if they come in good faith and abide by rules of confidentiality and not dating other members. So are other church classes and life groups, as well as worship services. Indeed, the church lifts up such openness to outsiders in need as exemplary Christian charity and hospitality. It welcomes guests without obliging them to become formal church members, for all the personal encouragement and spiritual inspiration it devotes to embracing them in its community of worship, character, and contribution. "You can come to worship here for months or even years," notes a minister, "and you don't have to do the 'starting point' classes to move toward membership. You already belong, you're already part of us, and we already accept you and love you."

Wanting to change, to do better and become better in life, marks one starting point of initiation for this evangelical church with a rel-atively educated and psychologically fluent population. "Did you ever want to do something different, and you just jumped in and tried, and you couldn't do it?" asks one minister in a starting-point class for new-comers. "I thought I wanted to run a marathon," he says by way of example. "I went out to run for the first time since high school PE, and I got a hundred yards before I had to stop and rest, because I was out of breath and exhausted. So you have to train. You have to practice. The best way to do that is with other people, including people who know how to do it, who can show you how by example."

So the church holds up "spiritual practices," and offers itself as a community of traditional Christian practices, including prayer, Scripture reading, confession, and worship. But it also invites newcomers to try out "unplugging, solitude, silence; taking nature walks, taking the slow lane, taking a day of rest; caring for a friend, and serving the poor." Weekly starting-point classes invite newcomers to try out spiritual practices such as introducing themselves sincerely to say what they most hope for at the first class, or recalling who was the most loving and accepting person in their childhood. What were their key experiences of faith and community, of spiritual gifts and callings? Only after a month of such classes does a low-key altar call "invite people to come up for prayer, come over to join a life group, and take the next step to join the church," explains a minister. "But we don't press them. We don't need them to become members. In fact, we tell them, if you decide to become a member, this is a place where members serve, not where they get served first. Guests get the front seat. Members take the backseat."

For guests on the way to becoming church members, while planning or entering retirement, it is friendship that usually comes first and leads them forward. It is bred in life-group networks devoted to common interests and activities, as informal as sharing a weekly walk in a local park or a bike ride in the nearby hills. They need commit themselves to nothing more than a regular round of golf, indistinguishable in practice from any other except perhaps for a shared prayer and the absence of expletives, off-color jokes, and stiff drinks in the clubhouse.

Good friends and good causes often go hand in hand. The African-American director of a large food bank just a few miles and a world away from the church looks out her window at a half dozen retired electrical engineers smoothly swinging hammers and guiding Skilsaws to build a new food-storage annex for the project. "They've known each other for years," she reflects. "Some came from the church; then they brought others over from Habitat for Humanity. They don't hang out much with everyone else; they don't wear their hearts on their sleeves. But they like each other. They're good workers; they know what they're doing. They're worth their weight in gold, and we love them."

Does anything distinguish members of the church from other volunteers? "More of them actually show up than some of the others, even other church folks," replies the food-bank director. "Not because they're better people or more Christian," she adds, "but because they get more hands-on encouragement, especially from a few longtime volunteers who come over a lot and bring them along. They don't just send a check, like some other churches, although we are grateful for that too," she smiles, "and we couldn't get along without it." Recalls one leading veteran volunteer, "I just happened to come the first time, because they asked at church for someone who could do electrical repairs. I did it. I saw they were meeting a real need for food and clothing, and they didn't turn anybody away. I met some of the people there. They were honest and organized. I liked them, so I kept coming back. I talked about it at singles meetings and Bible classes, and I brought other people back with me. Mostly word of mouth, even though after a while we put it up on the online bulletin board for service projects."

The food bank relies on donations from local grocery stores, corporations, and chambers of commerce, along with civic and religious groups, to feed and clothe needy members of a majority-minority community pinched by low wages, high jobless rates, and skyrocketing housing prices in Silicon Valley. So food-bank leaders appreciate volunteers committed to their cause without seeking to politicize it. "Our community needs political activists and organizers, but that's not our role here," says one. "We have to make that clear to some more 'progressive' church folks who want us to get into it, but not to these folks. They are mostly white and educated, but they're pretty diverse politically, and they know how to get along. They accept that, and they want to do good without making it left-wing or right-wing good."

Church members in or near retirement have also become immersed in a weekly teaching and mentoring program to share "fundamental financial paradigms, life and job skills" with a thousand "under-resourced" high school students at risk of being caught in generational cycles of poverty in Silicon Valley's poorest neighborhoods. The program's focus on "how money works" ties together education and earning with practical insight for students in high schools where most fail to graduate, start college, or enter the skilled workforce. It aims to teach by example as well as information, and it hunts for exemplary volunteers.

"We partner with high school principals and teachers in their own classrooms during regular school hours," explains Dick Rice, the program's director. "So we need retirees, professionals, and executives who can free their time to take part. We go out to local churches, civic groups, corporate groups. We talk to them about what we can do person-to-person to break the chain of poverty and financial illiteracy by enabling teenagers to learn about budgeting, credit, loans, interest, and foreclosure. Not just how to balance your checkbook and avoid predatory lenders," Dick makes clear, "but how to balance your life and negotiate the American financial system. So these kids can start making good decisions about school and work, find a mentor, get on a career path, and self-determine."

Where does this "FutureProfits" program start with volunteers? "With a brainwave and a heartbeat," laughs Dick, a veteran community organizer with local roots and a seminary degree. "Actually, we're looking for people with a good heart, and a certain level of sophistication in how they see race and economics. Poor people don't just need to try harder," he stresses. "You need to get that to get into this. But you don't need to be liberal or conservative politically. We welcome capitalists!" he exclaims. "We want them to help these kids learn how to become good capitalists themselves in terms of being smart and responsible about money." Volunteers need a certain amount of skill to handle the material, and "the confidence to stand up in front of a bunch of terrifying high school kids," notes Dick with a smile. The program appeals to Rotarians as well as Unitarians, he adds, while pointing out:

Church people are some of our best volunteers, because they also bring a feeling for justice and empowerment as caring for all God's children, and answering God's call to be responsible for creation and work for the beloved community. That's how I approach it, coming from Dr. King and Bonhoeffer, and not just with liberal churches. Most of the evangelical churches we work with recognize that now in their own way. They're not just about saving souls, and letting the body of the world go its own way. Some church volunteers come to us after they've done things like short-term mission trips to Mexico or Central America, and they've become frustrated by drive-by do-gooding. We're practical, and we stick with it for a whole school year. That's an hour in class every week plus prep, and ten hours of training up front. That's a pretty deep commitment. It engages you, if you're ready for it. If you're ready for a relationship with kids who don't really know any people like you. People who wear khakis and button-down shirts to work in an office or lab, who have advanced degrees and good jobs and investments. That relationship can make a difference in how these kids see the world and their chances in it going forward, even if you don't wind up mentoring them to get into Stanford or get a job with Google by the end of the year.

What can churches do better or do differently in serving the community and the world? "Most churches put their own members first," answers Dick. "They come to us in order to serve their members by serving the community. We do this, first of all, to serve kids in need and their community," he counters. "Then, second, to give volunteers good experiences." These two aims don't always line up, he notes, and community programs that depend on volunteers who are also donors feel the tug toward putting them first. Church leaders know this feeling firsthand, and they can draw on it to help keep these priorities straight, and keep these partnerships focused on serving the needy instead of the wealthy.

Churches can also help community projects hedge against the temptation, typical among high-tech firms and civic groups led by elite problem solvers in Silicon Valley, to "look for the quick fix and the big tech breakthrough to solve community problems from above instead of working away on the ground," observes Dick. "Yes, we need systemic solutions to come through legislation and investment, but you don't fix four hundred years of African-American slavery and exclusion with a great app!" Churches, too, can find themselves forgoing the long view of history and the long, hard work needed to remake the future, Dick warns, in favor of the "short-term mission flavor of the month," when they should instead sustain their commitments to social witness and service.

Churches centered on educated professionals also face the challenge bred by their own success, notes this community activist, of valuing their own experience and opinions above those of the community they seek to help. "People who live on this side of the freeway are smart and hardworking, too," Dick declares. "They have to be in order to survive. Wealthy folks who haven't carried the burdens of the poor need to recognize that if they really want to help them." Mutual recognition and learning inhere in biblical ideals of justice and love by this account, and churches need to put them into programmatic practice.

For example, recounts Dick, a good-sized and well-funded congregation in the heart of Silicon Valley came to him with an offer to send its junior pastors to train leaders of a local Hispanic Pentecostal church to help it become more effectively organized. "More effective how?" asked Dick in reply, since the local church in question numbered a thousand members, and counted four of five adults in small groups and as many children in Sunday school. It organized scores of volunteers to feed four hundred hungry people every week, shelter the homeless, and welcome new immigrants. "What do you have to give them?" queried Dick before suggesting an exchange program in which leaders of both congregations would participate in mutual learning and planning. "There's a lot to learn on both sides," he notes, "including the explosion of Pentecostal Christianity in the Global South that most mainline church folks know almost nothing about."

Underlying the practical challenges of tutoring and mentoring needy high school students, and related programs sponsored by Dick's community organization, runs the riptide of larger social changes against efforts to enable the least of these to enter the middle-class mainstream of American society. "We're working to enable poor people and immigrants to rise up and contribute and thrive," he attests, "when middle-class opportunities and security are shrinking for everyone. So how do we preach redemption and liberation to the captives, when fewer and fewer folks are free?" Dick pauses, then adds, "The churches in America need to ask that question, and press forward with that conversation. Sometimes I wonder if they're ready to do that."

Why not start on the ground in key congregations in Silicon Valley, Dick asks, particularly where some church members are worth $100 million and others lack $100 in net worth. Commit to no hunger in the church, first of all, to food and clothing for all. Then work for jobs, housing, and schooling for everyone in the pews. "God made enough for the whole of creation," he affirms, "so let's live that way in community, with peer accountability and responsibility in discipleship. No freeloading. You couldn't keep people out of the churches then, instead of straining to get them in!" We have to dig deeper to live out the unity of our faith in a more deeply divided society, Dick stresses. "That's why we want to get well-off, well-educated faithful people into the schools with kids in need. Because after a while it's not 'those brown kids.' It's these kids I've come to know and care about—Jamal, Luis, Eduardo. That's a start on building relationships across cultures and classes that depend on love instead of power." Dick lifts up his hands. "It's a step to bring the kingdom closer, to follow Jesus washing the feet of the disciples."

Just such a heartfelt spirit of service motivates one longstanding volunteer in this tutoring and mentoring program. So testifies a high-tech executive led to take part by his experience of the church and its born-again pastor, "He made Jesus real for me. So I wanted to follow him and do something for the least of these, not just sit on a church board or committee." At the same time, he can draw on his professional experience of mentoring junior executives following in his corporate footsteps. "That's a Christian calling too," he reflects, "to enrich the lives of the people we work with, not just materially but spiritually. I actually want to walk alongside people and share what's on their hearts, and do that at work, not only at church or at home."

Tutoring provides "really practical skills that can help these kids change their lives by earning and saving money," affirms this executive. "But it also opens up person-to-person relationships and feedback, where they can go beyond feeling powerless and helpless, and broaden their view of what their lives can be. Even if they don't go on to college, they can find a way to learn how to make a decent living." At the same time, he adds, "doing this has taken me out of my own comfort zone as a rich white guy, and reminded me of how other people live by actually entering into their lives." It has "deepened my understanding of poverty," he reflects, "but it has also freed me from my big ideas of what to do about it," which cannot replace the personal attention and engagement of a Good Samaritan needed to love your neighbor.

The hands-on example of church volunteers at a local VA hospital likewise inspired a visitor there to come to church. "Who are these people? I wondered," he recalls over the course of several months spent visiting an old Navy friend undergoing inpatient cancer treatment at the hospital. "They were always there, they were really dedicated and kind, and they weren't preachy. They helped out. They read and talked with patients who were in bad shape. They put on a party with local artists who did portraits and sketches of patients with their loved ones and families. That's what I saw first, and that's what drew me to the church." He attended worship, then gravitated to helping ministries that included many of the hospital volunteers. He enrolled in twenty weekly classes of training in the church's Stephen Ministry to give "Christ-centered emotional and spiritual care to others" through one-on-one peer counseling.[11] "I came to the church through the volunteering and service, not to the volunteering through the church," he sums up. "And that is what's kept me here, even though now I'm branching out a little. I'm in a group for older singles, and maybe I'll join a Bible class. I'm trying to find a new balance here."

Local service projects and short-term mission trips abroad can spark larger commitments to helping others that shape plans for retirement. "I went to Africa for ten days last year with a group from the church," recalls an IT specialist in composing corporate budget reports in Silicon Valley. "It opened my eyes to a whole new world. I felt the huge gap between really making a difference there, and dropping in someplace for a week or two, building a school room or painting a church, taking a picture of it with everybody out front, then taking off." A few years from retirement, in his midsixties, with a solid pension to match his wife's, he is planning to go back for a year and see where it leads. "I can teach people there how to put together a spreadsheet and do word processing—use Excel and MS Word—and get plugged in so they can get a good job working for a company, a nonprofit, or a government. Say I teach just three people, Christians in their twenties or thirties who are motivated and educated enough to learn, and I ask them to pass it along, once they get a steady job, and teach three more people for free. That can make a real difference!"

Another church member in her fifties, Laura Ponti, has already made such an "encore career" move after twenty years near the top of a thriving high-tech corporation. "I had a good run, and the company was very good to me," she recalls. "But I was ready to do something different." Her father's death and the breakup of a long romantic relationship came together to bring her to a crossroads that led to Alto Church and to a new kind of calling. After taking time off to help her widowed mother, then rest and travel on her own, she realized, "I actually love business, and I'm good at it, so why not find a pro bono business to get involved in?" She began volunteering in a community program to help single mothers find jobs, affordable housing, and day care. She started fund-raising for it, then joined its board of directors, and eventually became its chief executive. "I took it step-by-step," she explains, "and I decided this is something I really care about. I love children, but I put my career first. Now here I am, with no kids but enough money and freedom to do something to help mothers with kids, but no husbands and no money."

Working for a fraction of what she earned before, Laura reflects, is "a choice I was free to make, since I wanted to give something back, and not just give money. Lots of nonprofits need the kind of skill set I have, and I'd rather be helping to do this instead of making more money for people who already have plenty." In fact, leading a non-profit organization with an annual budget of several million dollars has proven more complicated than managing units of a billion-dollar corporation. "Before, all I had to do was keep things organized and make my numbers," she observes. "Here I have to inspire people to take part and contribute, since we're mostly volunteers and donated money. It's not just teamwork and the bottom line. It's really about who we are as a community."

Joining Alto Church also centered on community for this executive. "I always believed in God, but I stopped going to church years ago," Laura recounts. "Then I look up and, abruptly, I'm single again. I'm seeing a therapist, but I hit bottom, and I don't know how to get out of it. I'm really struggling with the breakup, and I want to go someplace where I'm not the only one. I start looking around online and asking friends, and I find out about the relationship-recovery groups here." An exploratory first visit turned into a homecoming. "I was blown away," she recalls. "I knew I wanted a community connection, and I wanted God in on it, but I didn't know how to put the pieces together. So, I go to the group on Monday night, and it was like twenty years of seeking all came together in the unity of spirituality, psychology, and Christianity. When it comes to boundaries and how people grow, being loving doesn't mean being a pushover."

Put off by traditional Christian language of sin and repentance, heaven and hell, Laura realized she "had been throwing out the baby with the bathwater."

> Words like *sin* and *kingdom* and *righteousness*—when you take them at face value in today's world, they're incredibly off-putting. But that's not really what they mean. You have to translate them into something much more practical, and you have to have

a community to do that in. That's where the big "Aha!" was for me. Being "saved" doesn't mean you're damned if you don't, or Christians are better than everyone else. It means that we're all walking around with pain in our heart, and that pain needs to be healed. It needs to be healed by a love that's greater than any one human being. Knowing that love, and trying to show up every day as the best person I was made to be, that's what it means to be saved. Being a "sinner" doesn't mean you're evil if you go and rob a bank. It's not good and bad like black and white. To sin means to miss the mark. If I'm in a bad mood and I snap at someone instead of really listening to them, I miss the mark, because I was taking out my frustration on someone else who didn't deserve it. We're all sinners because we're all human. "Nobody's perfect." We have good days and bad days. But God loves us, and we can do better.

Belonging before believing, given God's love exemplified by Alto Church members for seekers in need of a caring community of character, "made all the difference in the world," testifies Laura. So did capable church leaders "willing to show their vulnerability and model that for the people around them. Wow! That really moved me. Practice what you preach So I said, 'This is where I want to be.'"

Will this executive ever retire from her new nonprofit role? "I'll stay involved and find ways to help out as long as I can," Laura replies. "This kind of operating role takes a lot of energy, so I can foresee the time when I'm ready not to be in charge, and not be responsible for everything, for all the people and all the money." Helping out, by contrast, turns on "letting others come into your heart, letting yourself feel their need and their goodness, so it's not just give-and-take. You give each person you love a piece of your heart. But it's not just one size. Your heart grows larger."

Synergy and shared moral transformation among members in a body of common prayer, practice, and play also figure in discussions at Alto Church on the limits of generational groups and activities, and how to span them. A clinical psychologist who belongs to the church and admires the ingenuity of its age-specific activities for enabling distinct generations to congregate with their peers, and worship with the familiar feeling of traditional hymns or the surging heartbeat of Christian rock, nonetheless underscores the good of activities that bring young and old together. "Put a nursery in a nursing home, or a Christian preschool in a church hall," she urges, "and something wonderful can happen. People can reach across generations to care for each other, teach each other, and play with each other."

Service projects, day care, shared study, and social concerns can shape community across age cohorts, this psychologist affirms, "But people should have a good time together in church, and not just do good. It's important to play together, celebrate and enjoy one another, and have a good time in good company." This church does a much better job of play than most, she allows. It can do better still, she is convinced. So she is eager to help in ways that span the arts, healing, listening one-on-one, and conversing in small groups within the chorus of common prayer and worship.

Thus, for example, many older members of the church center their week around an early Sunday service, featuring organ and choir music instead of Christian rock. Some younger families join them there, says one mother, "for hymns we love and want our kids to know too." This service leads into a two-hour Bible study class, led by the seniors' pastor, Fred Heiden. It begins and ends in coffee and conversation among several hundred seniors. Birthday greetings and friendly banter at the outset segue into personally detailed requests for prayer. These elicit and update news of illness and recovery, medical diagnosis and treatment, changing states of mind and emotion as well as physical health, deaths in the family, along with children wed and grandchildren newly born.

In response to a wife's report to this seniors' Bible class that her husband nearing eighty has just been diagnosed with a brain tumor, forcing them to cancel a long-planned anniversary vacation to await a prognosis, Fred Heiden asks, "Yes, and how is *he* feeling through all of this?" Disappointed and worried, she answers, and Fred reflects, "This is when family really kicks in. We really need each other, and we need Jesus in the middle of us, just like he promises, just like he really *is* here in our midst, even when we think he's not."

Doubt and despair can be voiced in sharing such news and prayers. "Cancer, what's that about?" Fred asks in the case of a woman faithfully undergoing round after painful round of chemotherapy. "Why does God permit pain and let the world go on this way instead of fixing it?" God's in charge, the pastor affirms, and God will heal us, even when we cannot see how or why. "God disciplines us from love, and God heals us from love, even when we don't get it. We don't get it! We don't follow God's will—just like my forty-year-old children still won't do what I say!" protests Fred in not-so-mock exasperation to shared laughter. Then he turns serious, "So God comes down himself! He knows we don't get it. He knows we need him."

Week by week in the seniors' Bible class, Fred Heiden tells the story of a longtime church member in her eighties, lingering at death's door, until at last she can no longer talk or eat. "Why is God waiting around when she is ready to go?" We can ask that question, he acknowledges, but do we know the whole of it, he wonders. On a visit to the family the day before, Fred finds the dying woman's "granddaughter holding her hand, stroking her hand and talking to her, quietly and lovingly," as the woman smiles in peace. "So God is doing something wondrous in this family, for this family, here and now," the pastor reflects.

> And God is giving us the wonder of faith that we are really going to be with him. It's not just lights out, or going to some ER waiting room. It's the promise Jesus makes in John 14:3: "And if I go and prepare a place for you, I will come back and take you to be with me that you also may be where I am." [NIV]
>
> God has already done it! So once we accept Christ, we are saved! We can stop whining and worrying. We don't need to add anything on. We can stop right here, and thank God.

"Let us pray," Fred Heiden concludes, with a prayer of thanksgiving that rehearses the lines of the hymn opening the class, "It is well with my soul, whatever worldly trials and sorrows surround me, since Jesus has shed His own blood for my soul."

Instead of dismissing death or hiding it behind the curtain that separates actively pursuing "young again" retirement from "getting really old," the church can instead open eyes and hearts in a community of mutual care and recognition of persons as they age, decline, fall ill, and die. It can give them a sense of shared continuity, too, with one another across the years and generations, with hope for their children and their children's children in this world as well as the next. "Though outwardly we are wasting away, yet inwardly we are being renewed day by day," Fred quotes Paul (2 Corinthians 4:16 NIV) on God's constant renewal of the spirit that enables us to live our lives in community day by day. In the face of death we can feel fear and doubt and anger, he allows. But we can trust that God will abide with us, he affirms, that "Jesus will put his arm around us and take us home." No one gets over death, but we get through it together in the communion of the church as family and body. "We take nothing with us when we go. What do we leave behind? What lives on? How we love God and each other."[12]

## AGES AND STAGES TRANSFORMED IN ATLANTA

Pine Glen Methodist Church in suburban Atlanta likewise lifts up mutual care and recognition within "life changing communities," attentive to differences across generations that it seeks to honor and span. The church welcomes all of God's children to "experience acceptance, affirmation, opportunity, and life transformation" through "ministries to all ages and stages," including adults and children, senior adults and youth. Yet generational changes have shifted these stages in practice. "Twenty years ago, the seniors knew exactly who they were, and we knew exactly what to do with them," recalls a minister responsible for adults over fifty. "Get them all together in a bus to go to the art museum downtown or take them to a retreat center on the coast for a few days. Let the ladies bake cookies and run the altar society, and let the businessmen lead the pastor-parish relations committee," she laughs. "But it's not that way anymore." Why not? She replies:

> Now we have seniors in their eighties and nineties, and we have baby boomers turning seventy, in their sixties and fifties, who don't think they're "seniors" at all, or even older adults. They don't feel "old," and they don't feel like they belong with people who do. They go to museums and concerts on their own, thank you. They drive their own cars to the beach, and they're not so big on church retreats. They want to explore new things, and get involved more actively out in the community, beyond the church. They want to do things, not just sit and watch.

In response to these generational changes, and the greater longevity that enables distinct cultural cohorts to form among its older members, the church has opened up its programs and partnerships with community centers, schools, and social agencies across metro Atlanta and beyond. It has plunged into helping resettle refugees in a small town nearby that has mushroomed into a remarkably diverse and crowded gateway city for first-generation immigrants. They come from the Horn of Africa, the Middle East, and Southeast Asia. They speak more than thirty languages. There you can stop behind a school bus, notes a church volunteer, "And you'll see twenty children get off the bus, every color of the rainbow, and not one white face. It's a different world, just fifteen minutes from the front door of this church, and it's our world. We can't be scared of it, even if some of us still are."

Besides providing volunteers and funds to these new partners, the church has gathered more actively around core volunteer groups of "younger retirees" to start and sustain key ministries. "We pack two hundred meals and snacks into snack packs every Thursday evening for needy students to take home from school every Friday to help their families make it through the weekend," points out the seniors' minister by way of example. "A dozen or so volunteers can get that done in an hour," she explains, "but only because of a committed core of five or six we count on to organize the packing, and do all the ordering and purchasing. They pick up everything beforehand from the food banks and markets, and they get it all out to the schools afterwards." The church's mobile soup kitchen likewise relies on a large rotation of volunteers to serve the hungry and homeless in one of the city's neediest neighborhoods, but a core group of volunteers reliably provides the expert food purchasing and preparation essential to the program. "We partner with a church downtown to serve hundreds of meals every week on a just-in-time schedule" notes a minister. "Believe me, none of us on staff could make that happen by ourselves."

Such concentric circles of church volunteers in tandem with local, metro, and regional partners mark other programs that Pine Glen sponsors. Its longtime support for a nearby Methodist Children's Home has multiplied into metro-wide partnerships with children's social-service agencies, refugee groups, and "Angel Tree" networks to provide Christmas gifts to needy children. "We're concentrating on new shoes for children this year," notes a volunteer with a clipboard standing by a mountain of bright shoe boxes in the church hall, as she checks donations against a long list of needed shoe sizes and styles sent earlier from the agencies and assigned to church members to go out and do the purchasing.

"Every winter good-hearted people used to bring in their old summer sandals," notes the clothing director of a local refugee resettlement agency. "Now we can actually match the shoes to what our families need in cold, rainy weather, because the church makes the extra effort to coordinate with us and buy winter shoes that fit our kids." Because "head volunteers" from Pine Glen, especially retirees, come so reliably and learn roles played by support staff of the refugee agency, adds its director, "We can count on them to lead others, and show up every week for months," to sustain the agency's work, by contrast to local college students who sign up for course credits, drift away at semester's end, and take hours of valuable training time with them.

Pine Glen Methodist does not boast the extraordinary scale and resources of Alto Church in Silicon Valley. But its three thousand members, many of them well-educated, well-connected professionals and managers, make it one of Atlanta's largest and most resourceful mainline congregations. It lacks the high-profile "18–35 singles ministry" of Alto Church. But it draws three hundred members and visitors every Sunday to a "contemporary worship" service that sets Methodist liturgy to the beat of Christian rock music played by a band of church members led by professional musicians. The crowd swaying to the music here includes more married young adults with school-age children and teens in tow, and fewer singles than Alto Church, especially of college age and beyond. "We're more about young families here," reflects a youth minister, "not because we don't want singles in their twenties and thirties, but because of the neighborhood."

Pine Glen is a suburban enclave of single-family ranch homes built in the 1950s and '60s, many still occupied by their original owners with their children and grandchildren living nearby. Predominantly white by race and college-educated by class, it draws young families to its outstanding public schools, safe streets, and convenient commutes. Adjoining university neighborhoods offer apartments and congregations that attract more single young adults, including Methodist campus ministries, youth fellowships, and social groups. "Three-generation families anchor this church," notes a longtime member. "That may seem like a throwback, and I don't know how long it can continue, with more of the kids going away to work instead of coming back after college. But it gives us tremendous strength, if you can get everyone to agree on something."

When the church first faced the choice to sponsor refugee families more than a decade ago, "not everyone jumped on board," recalls the persuasive retiree with overseas business experience who led the initiative to partner with local agencies to rent and furnish housing for refugees, fill their cupboards, find them jobs, and tutor them in English. "Should we really be doing this, we wondered, and doing it for folks who were not going to join the church, or even become Christians?" he shakes his head. "I went around to every agency. Then we met and talked it over in church, again and again for months, until we finally agreed to try it with just one family." That family turned out to be Muslims from Jordan. A month after they arrived and got settled, the family of five came to church with a translator, and "the mother got up and she spoke from the bottom of her heart," reports this leading layman, with a smile. "It brought tears to your eyes. By the time she got through, there wasn't a dry eye in the house, and there wasn't any more worrying about whether we were doing the right thing or not. We voted unanimously to go ahead and take families of any color or creed."

Reflecting on this critical moment as a moral turnabout, Greg Williams, another lay leader of the church's refugee program affirms, "Put a human face on suffering, and we respond. It's not a million people at the border or a thousand who want to come over the state line and take our jobs and handouts." He frowns. "People here want to help others in need, person-to-person, just like they help each other. They don't want to 'change society,' or get into politics. They want to make the world a better place, one soul at a time." He pauses, then adds, "We have a big, active scout troop here, and a lot of us really are Boy Scouts, you know. We want to do our duty and help others, and we want them to do everything they can to help themselves. That's what the refugee families do, and that's why we've been able to double down and keep upping our support for them, without strings." He explains:

> Nine out of ten of these families are pretty much self-supporting after six months. We help them find jobs, and they keep them. They get to work on time, and they get home safe every night. They're paying their own rent. The kids are in school and learning English, playing soccer. The parents are studying for their citizenship exams, memorizing the questions and answers. We have sponsored families from Jordan, Turkey, Somalia, Ethiopia, Kenya, Nepal, Thailand, Malaysia, and Myanmar. All over, and that's just a start. Some of them get off the plane with no baggage, just what they're carrying in their arms. You see that, and you wish everyone else who needs help could get it and make the most of it like this. It makes you feel you're doing something

good that will last, that will give people a new life for themselves and a future for their children.

Securing that future and building its long-term support in the church remain concerns for the founding organizers of the refugee program. "We want to hand it on to the next generation," vows Greg.

> Not just the volunteers and donors it takes to do the job, but the lasting commitments and networking we need to do our part in a complicated setup that runs from the State Department down through national church groups to the local refugee agencies we work with here. When we started, we were the main event in the church. Now we've got competition from other big projects, and we want to make sure there's enough support to go around.

Lay leaders of other outreach projects in the church share such concerns, including the professional women who have led in raising substantial funds to build a school in a rural area of West Africa long beset by civil war, poverty, and scant public services, then devastated by the Ebola virus. "We've raised the money to build the school, and we're working to endow it," explains a lawyer involved in the church's fund-raising efforts and short-term mission trips to the school and a nearby Methodist congregation. "We've set up a foundation to do that and provide scholarships. You can donate to it, and you can sponsor a student for a year for $150." These efforts build on generations of Methodist women active in missions, she notes, but they mark a generational change as well. "We can still bake cookies, but we can do a lot more and a lot better. We have a higher calling that connects us to the world *and* the church."

These continuing commitments in turn lead members of the church to weigh its own trajectory across generations. "The older generation here is joined at the hip," observes Greg Williams, now in his seventies. "We've known each other for years, our kids have gone to school and scouts together, married each other. It's almost like a small town in the middle of the city." Can that last? "I hope and pray it does," Greg answers. "But it has to change, too, and sometimes I worry that things are loosening up, you know, when I see the kids just sitting there listening to the rock band on Sunday morning, then heading out the door. Seven minutes, seven words, seven chords—and a dozen exits."

A youth pastor speaks to such concerns with reassurance, "Loosening up maybe, but not falling apart," she observes. "The Boy Scouts help move furniture upstairs into the apartments for refugees. We do a lot with the kids in classes and activities grouped by age. We're really intentional about keeping them engaged through junior high and high school, giving them room of their own, giving them new places and people to connect with. Like the mentors they can choose in confirmation class, someone older they can share things with, like piano or painting, horses or computers. It's almost like having an extra grandmother you get to choose."

"Time will tell," Greg allows, with appreciation for such intergenerational efforts. "You have to give credit to the church for trying, and to all the mothers doing their all to keep their families on track." In the present he is focused on shaping his own active retirement in light of his parents' telling example:

> When my father hit sixty-five and retired from county government with a good pension, they moved to a retirement community in Florida, because they wanted to relax and enjoy life together. They went from a place where they knew everybody to a place where they didn't know anybody. It was actually like being deported! Eventually they put down some roots there, but Dad got bored with sitting around after six months, and began working part-time, right up to when he started to slow down and didn't know what day it was. He died at eighty-two. "The reason I came here is gone," my mother says, and she's still going strong at ninety-three. So I figure I have ten to twenty years left, and our kids live a few miles away. I want to stay where I am, and do all I can to make a difference right here. The people you know are more important than the weather.

Greg's successful career raising funds for nonprofit private hospitals with strong philanthropic support in the region enabled him to move smoothly into volunteering to raise funds for other good causes when he retired. "It's honorable work," he reflects. "It teaches you that most people want to do good and be remembered for something besides making money. You get older and you want to do something else." That moral insight combines with his practical experience of how crucial it is for nonprofit groups to overcome the risks of iffy donations and budget projections to assure their future. Greg continues:

> Our local partners in caring for refugees rely a lot on grants from the federal government, funneled through national church groups. But those grants depend on the State Department deciding how many refugees to let in and where to send them, and they go through middle steps that take time. So we really need to grow our own donor base. That's what I'm working on, and I'm willing to give it the five or six years it will probably take to get done, not just in the church, but with one hundred families across this city who make this one of their top philanthropic priorities.

Why take on such a demanding task in retirement, even as an "encore career" in line with one's earlier experience and expertise? "Because these people with nothing are giving everything they've got to make a new life here. This organization is helping them," Greg answers directly. "That makes me want to give them my skills and experience, my aggravating persistence, so they don't have to worry about where their next meal is coming from. They deserve it."

What do older members of Pine Glen deserve and need in turn from the church? "Participation, responsibility, and attentive care," readily answers Mary Davis, a minister to seniors, "along with inspiring love." Mary pauses for emphasis before continuing.

"We need to help them wake up to everything we can do together to change the world, and to what we can't do," she reflects. "You can't separate the meaning of life from the meaning of death. It has meaning, too, and we can face it, by living our life every day as if it counts. It does," she affirms, then elaborates:

Retirement is a big step. You sign papers. You move your stuff out of the office one day. But it's a process. You can overload with things to do and get tired, even if it's "leisure." You can underload and get bored. You can volunteer all over the place, and get frustrated.

You have a dream beforehand, like getting a boat and sailing it on the lake or the Inland Waterway, like a long vacation. But retirement is a way of life, where you have to find a balance and rhythm. That may take some experimenting, not just sailing away from it all.

Does that hold for congregational life as well? "Yes," replies Mary. "We have a handful of retired people, a small bunch, who help out all the time. They're an example for everyone of what it means to be in mission." Some tutor African refugees after school four days a week, for example, and others take the lead in buying school supplies for needy students in a nearby rental corridor crowded with Hispanic and South Asian immigrants. They take the initiative to invite older adults from the neighborhood and nearby retirement homes to join schoolchildren, their parents, and hundreds of other volunteers at a yearly church "super-event" to assemble more than fifty thousand packaged meals for Africa in three shifts over one weekend. It was a privilege to take part, wrote one grateful visitor afterwards. "We felt engaged, useful, and happy. Something we seniors don't always feel."

Others in retirement are not so tireless or encompassing in the reach of their commitments. But they are nonetheless longstanding in their loyalty to Bible classes that have flourished for decades as "churches within the church" of the congregation at large. "Those classes are huge, and they're tight, because people fellowship together there. They interact," reports another minister to seniors. "Not so much for the younger ones, and we wonder why." It may stem from more dual-earner families with less free time among middle-aged adults, he suspects, and it may involve the alternative appeal of "contemporary worship" to younger parents and their teen-aged children. "It's popular, and we're committed to it, but it can seem more like a rock concert with an audience. It's dark in there, it's loud, and people don't really talk to each other."

Greater longevity and better health to enjoy it have opened up churches to more adults living longer in retirement, reflects Mary Davis. "Once we had five members over 90. Now we have more than sixty, including two over a hundred. Some of them are still driving themselves to church every Sunday. One just shot her first hole-in-one playing golf at age ninety-two!" Longer life opens up new opportunities and ministries for the church, she affirms, but it poses new problems, too, in a shifting social landscape. She explains: "We have many more 'elderly,' eighty and over. We have more in the middle, sixty-five to late seventies, mostly but not all retired. We have those in their 50s and 60s, mostly still working, but some retired. So more different things are going on, and we're doing some things better than others."

> We're taking more care of the elderly, with more lay visitation teams going to see shut-ins every week. Seeing about health care and home care for those who need it. Making sure people have their wills and directives done. We're working with people on their life stories, doing albums and letters to their grandchildren. You can pick out your favorite poem, or write one of your own, and share it in the senior newsletter we do. You can get a DNA test and use it for a family genealogy. We're helping people plan ahead with peace of mind but also to look ahead with hope. Sometimes even when their own grown children are saying, "Let's not be negative. Let's not think about death."
>
> In the middle group it varies more by what they choose to do, whether they're still working, how much time they have free. We have some great servant leaders and full-time volunteers, and some who come once a month to pack lunches, or just to eat lunch and visit. That's it, and that's fine too. We probably have the most to do to catch up with the 50-and-up group. They're still working and really busy, trying to get their kids through college, and take care of their parents, trying to save money. They're really busy. But they're also in denial if they think they're not aging. We can do more to help them with their planning, their health, *and* their faith.

"We're trying to figure out how to work around that denial to do this," explains Mary, "without calling it seniors' ministry." Intergenerational care plays a key part in this effort, including a network of in-home care providers for the elderly and services to enable "aging in place." So do larger metro and statewide networks for senior housing, health care, and counseling. "You have to do your homework to find out who's who," notes Mary, "and who you can count on to come through. We have a contract with a really good pastoral care and counseling center, so we can send our folks there and ask them to come here, too, for talks and training. We've brought people in from the metropolitan commission on aging to talk about Alzheimer's, behavioral medicine, and focusing your mind through exercise."

"Start in early on caregiving and planning for the future," urges Mary. Occasional "lunch bunch" events to discuss such matters have led to an ongoing class, with guests who range from theologians and grief counselors to remodeling contractors who specialize in ramps and bathroom bars to ease mobility for the elderly in their own homes. A counselor began the first class by asking if every husband and wife were planning to die the same night, startling more than a few couples and setting off a discussion of living alone or in new kinds of community. A contractor began the next session by advising, "First move the microwave down to the tabletop, so you don't burn yourself," to approving nods, Mary recalls, "and I knew we were headed in the right direction. The third week we talked about retired husbands and wives getting in each other's way around the house." She smiles. "About wives cooking for retired husbands and wondering if *they* were ever going to get to retire, too. Go out to dinner more often. Get more help in the kitchen. Now's the time to think about this, in your fifties and sixties, before it's on top of you."

The congregation's coherence comes to the fore among its older members in response to eventual decline and diminishing capacity. "We watch each other. A lot of people have been here for a long, long time," comments Mary. "They know each other, the older set. They notice when someone seems a little weaker or confused. They talk about it quietly. They get worried. Then they call somebody on the staff, and we worry together. We can talk to their distant family, if no one is close by. We get them involved, so we can start walking through this together, and make sure you stay safe, you're not alone, as you slow down."

For example, in the case of a former choir member in his eighties with Alzheimer's for more than a decade, now widowed and living in a nursing home, weekly church visitors brought a "fidget quilt" they made of differently textured and patterned pieces of textile. "I wasn't sure he would like it," recalls one visitor. "But he loves it. It's always in his hands. One time he dropped it, and I picked it up and put it back in his lap, and he said, 'I can do this!' A sentence! A sentence! It was the first time I've heard him say anything in two or three years. Then he looked up at his walker, with his name written on it, and he said, 'Albert James!' He read his name! This was a wonderful day in our life with Albert, I thought, because he is still in there!"

Mutual recognition and care can be sustained, even as we decline, reflects another minister to seniors, and even under the stress of separation. "Sometimes children come from out of town and whisk their parents away, and never tell the church," regrets this minister. "That's a shame. We miss them, and we try to stay in touch with them." The church seeks to recognize and respond to related changes in age-specific groups and classes with their own rhythms and rites of passage. "We try to merge Bible classes and activity groups when the older folks can't come anymore, or their kids move them away, or they die. We're good at mergers. But still there's grieving to go through, when you're down to just a few people in that big room that used to be full." He pauses, then adds, "Institutions need to grieve too. Not just say we're fine, or we're madder than hell, but we're not grieving. No, we miss you when you can't come anymore, when you're not here anymore. The church goes on, but we have to re-create ourselves for it to be a living body."

Personal and professional concerns overlap in congregations, observes Mary Davis as a middle-aged minister at Pine Glen, when she thinks of seniors at the church and her own aging parents nearby. "My father retired at seventy from personnel work at a big company, because it was mandatory," she says. "He didn't want to. He loved working with people, and he kind of lost his identity when he left. He stayed home for a year, doing yard work. Then he started doing temp jobs, just to be out doing something instead of feeling useless and depressed." What larger lessons has she learned from her father's example? "Don't wait too long to retire, but don't go too soon either," she answers. "Don't just put your life up on the shelf in the den with your retirement plaque from Georgia-Pacific or AT&T, and start following your wife around. Yes, we want to see you at church all the time, but we want you to find your own way here!"

These are "traditional problems" of the privileged among an older generation of executive and professional breadwinners, acknowledges Mary, with homemaker wives actively engaged in serving the church and community as well their families. "That's not all bad, when it comes to doing for others. But it's even less typical today. So we need to ask ourselves, what can congregations do now to model a good life in retirement?" Try to enable people to learn from each other by example in church, she urges, not so much in "retirement classes," but in conversations and activities shared by those already actively retired and others still working "with no idea of how to retire or what to do next. Except maybe give up and start grieving for what you've lost, or start running after all the excitement and fun you can find." Mary grimaces. "Boy, is that scary!"

Conversely, the congregation itself needs younger members to step up and into the volunteer roles vital to the church's common life, from the choir and vestry to Sunday school and refugee programs, and to remake these roles too. "For years a volunteer in the church office ordered and purchased all our office supplies, until he finally got too old to do it," recalls the church's office manager. "Someone else came in, and the bills went up. We checked back through the accounts and found out our old friend had been paying for all the paper himself, and not turning in the receipts. He made up the paper ministry! Now we have to redo it."

The congregation devotes thought and energy to forming its children and holding on to them, particularly in their teens, as well as drawing in young families with children. It engages older members in all these efforts, for example, in low-key outreach to neighbors to share in concerts, barbecues, and local service projects. Retirees take the lead in day care and preschool programs. They connect with youngsters in confirmation classes by mutual choice and congenial interests. "More and more now we don't live near our parents. We're both working, and we can't send the kids over to grandma's house after school," notes a youth minister. "So it can be a godsend to find folks in church who love children and become like family to you."

Older members of the congregation no longer take for granted continued churchgoing by children of their own and others in the pews. Their willingness to step up in response encourages ministers at Pine Glen. "It's a wake up call," says Mary Davis. "They get that we all need to be involved to raise up and train these children, so that they'll be here when they're our age. They'll become who God wants them to be, because we've kept them here." She emphasizes:

> Older adults in the church feel an urgency today, more than ten years ago, to hold on to the children, teenagers and young adults, and keep them close. They're gonna fly away if we don't really put our arms around them. That feeling in the older community of wanting to reach out to the kids, and plant roots in them, helps us reach across the age groups in the church.
>
> For parents that starts at home. My seven-year-old said to me the other day, "When I grow up, I'm not gonna go to church on Sunday." Why not? I asked. "Because I can't think of anybody else in my class that goes to church on Sunday. I think I'm the only one." She said that, in the first grade! She just dropped it like a lead balloon right there at the dinner table, and my husband and I didn't know what to do. We sat there for a second in silence.
>
> **Q:** Then what did you say?

"Yes, you will. That's what our family does. Because it's important to us. Because it *is* important." That's what my parents would have said to me, I realized. I saw the words coming straight out of my mother's mouth and into mine, coming right through me to my daughter.

This scene in an intergenerational drama brings to mind her own college years, Mary recalls, as she headed off to help with university worship every week. "I can still remember getting up early every Sunday and being the only person awake on my dark dorm hallway. 'Every week, really?' my roommates would wonder. They couldn't believe that I would do this!" Echoing in her daughter's declaration, such wonderment underscores her own sense of what is at stake for churches today. Look at intown suburban neighborhoods built a century ago in Atlanta, she notes, "and you see a church on every corner, because that's what everyone did. Now we all struggle to get people to care enough to come for one hour, or maybe two. Now, when you can drive! You don't even need to walk like they did then."

In response to such social change and spiritual inertia, Mary reflects, churches can and should attend to the goods inherent in congregating. "People do want to be known. In bigger churches it's even more important to pay attention to this and help people get to know each other, because I can't know everyone." Look at service projects, she suggests, especially one-off projects, like the church's annual Habitat for Humanity "build" or a weekend "super event" like the one that draws hundreds of people to Pine Glen to pack thousands of meals for Africa. "Do something together as a team, like picking up or delivering food, and you bring people together. It's not just men driving trucks." Mary smiles. "They look forward to doing something else together the next time. Maybe they start their own Bible study class on Saturday morning or Sunday after service. One group like that meets Saturday mornings at 7 a.m. at Herb's house, men in their forties to seventies. He's retired, and they'll talk about work and retirement, he says, along with everything else."

Where does the church fall short when it comes to inspiring and caring for its members in retirement or nearing it? "Parents in their forties and fifties are on our rolls, but we don't know a lot of them, because they're not around," replies an associate minister responsible for programs across age-groups at Pine Glen. "Sure, they should be looking ahead to retirement, and doing more good in the world. But they're incredibly busy at work, and taking care of their kids, driving them everywhere in junior high, trying to keep track of them in high school. They want the church to help with their kids and fit into their schedules, but not make demands on them," he reflects after fielding protests from a mother over required confirmation classes crowding her daughter's sports schedule. "I couldn't believe it," he marvels. "Church is just another extracurricular activity!" Age-specific selective participation also shows up, he finds, in cases where "the little children bring young parents back to the fold" of day care, preschool, and Sunday school classes. Then parents of older children sometimes tune out and drift away. "Especially for midweek events you see that gap between parents with young children and retirees. The ones in the middle are not there. That's a challenge for us," he recognizes. "We're working on it. But so far we haven't seen a flock of fifty-year-olds fly back for dinner and fellowship on Wednesday nights."

Pine Glen cares for its older members and mourns their passing as it nurtures their successors. "We know we can't just do it the same way all over again," allows Mary Davis. "These are people who have been sitting together every Sunday at worship and Bible class, some of them, for forty or fifty years. When funerals come, they all come together and fill up the first five rows." What does the future hold? "It's in the hands of God, but we're trying to do our part," she vows, "even if we can't figure out how we got from there to here. Yes, there are people on the rolls we never see except for an hour every now and then. But we want to face the future together."

One good sign for the future is a Sunday Bible class of some twenty-five couples in their early thirties with young children. "They're really tight," notes Mary. "Every weekend they're over here with the kids together in the playground behind the church. They do birthday parties together, and retreats. They all come when we baptize their children." Their church life overlaps with their social life, she observes, even though most of the women work outside the home, and "we don't see so much of them during the week. Sometimes they skip worship, but they all come to Sunday Bible class. They volunteer, they contribute financially. So we're trying to rethink and respond to them while we stay the course," with an eye to better appreciating age-specific groups and activities even when they seem to tug against common worship that aims to embrace and ground the church as a whole.

Pine Glen has dramatically extended its outreach and service beyond its local community to missions that welcome refugees, feed the hungry across Atlanta, and support a school in Africa. At the same time, it wrestles with how to bring the wider world into the church. "That's a challenge for us," acknowledges a youth minister. "Can we learn about other religions? Can we learn from them, and partner with them? Can we face problems of social change and sexual identity, for example, in the debate over marriage equality? That's hard for us," he admits. Theological and moral, such disagreements in the church can cut across generations and denominations. "Some parents of teens really don't want us to talk about controversial stuff, even though it's all around the kids, and it's in the churches too."

While United Methodist pastors elsewhere struggle over performing same-sex marriages, and delegates to denominational conferences argue over its prohibition in the "Social Principles" of the United Methodist *Book of Discipline*, some parents at Pine Glen are all the more determined to protect their children by agreeing, "We should love the sinner, but don't be one of them," notes this youth minister, "and leave it at that." "That's hard to accept," he confesses. "When the beauty of the church comes from our freedom of conscience to wonder and learn what God wants for us, and what God's love means for us."

What then? "Protect your children, and trust your pastors, too," urges this minister. "We can trust one another, and take care of one an-other. We can live with differences. Most older members of the church feel that way," he observes gratefully. "They are peacemakers. 'Come on,' they say. 'We love our grandchildren, straight or gay, and we love our church.'"

Thus questions of how congregations can better enable and inspire those entering retirement, and why they should do so, become matters of intergenerational relationship, dialogue, and participation in practice. Distinctions between "the church and the world," even in the most traditional or sect-like congregations, prove paradoxical. The larger so-ciety's difficulties and divisions enter into the church through its own members' socially-situated intuitions, interests, and experience over generations, even as their common convictions, worship, and ideals of what makes life worth living go out with them to inspire their work in the world and inflect their way of life, if not to transform society.[13] "De-part and Serve," urges a sign posted at the exit of the main parking lot at Pine Glen Methodist. "It may seem sappy or preachy at first," allows Greg Williams. "But it's actually a prayer that gets to you after a while, about what we can do and who we can be, by the grace of God."

## BODIES OF WORSHIP, COMMUNITIES OF CARE

The ideal of the congregation as a body of worship that lives out its prayers in a community of care inspires these two exemplary cases in terms that reach from the church as the Pauline body of Christ to the Judaic people of God, and beyond to the Islamic *umma* and the Buddhist *sangha*. Americans are indeed great joiners, and both churches open their arms wide in welcome, including the "more art form" model at Alto Church of coming to belong before choosing to believe or conform. Crit-ics of this user-friendly approach of seeker churches as "Christianity lite" can doubt its champions in the vanguard of an evangelical revolution to usher in a new unity among born-again, Spirit-filled Christians beyond denominations. But they can both agree on the need for the faithful to stand up and pitch in to serve others as "the hands and feet of Jesus."

Everyone wants to be seen and known, to belong to each other and to God, to find "a safe place to heal your heart" and an unselfish love to move you to be the best person you were made to be. Everyone is our neighbor, both congregations affirm, to love and care for on the model of the Good Samaritan, even when—especially when—they do not look or sound like us. In calling the people of God to become the salt and light of the earth, both churches embrace love and justice as practical personal virtues bred by communities of character that share their exercise in regularly recurring activities and teach them by example, face-to-face and side by side. Right and wrong acts cannot be abstracted from relationships rooted in rites of common worship and practices of mutual care. Nor can they be contained within the church alone as a world set against or above and beyond the larger society.

Let the light of our love shine in the world, leaders of both these resourceful churches urge, in the face of its neediness and unfairness, its indifference and evil, if everyone is to know the faithful as children of God, not merely pious and privileged Americans of a particular color, creed, class, and generation sheltered in affluent suburban enclaves. Both churches seek to reach out beyond these boundaries to help the needy in neighborhoods nearby as well as in distant lands. In these efforts they draw on the talents, skills, and experience of their members to do good, and feel good about doing it, in ways we have heard praised by rich and poor, counselors and pastors alike as essential to life before and after retirement. In particular they draw on the activist drive and organizing ability of younger retirees in core volunteer groups to sustain key ministries with apt community partners.

At the same time, these churches care for their own members across generations, for example, in aiding seniors in decline and protecting teens at risk. They struggle with the brittle certainties and persistent anxieties tied to their ethical rigor and social advantage. They seek to shelter their children from moral controversy and confusion. They meet temptation to uplift the poor by high-tech problem solving and upbeat cheering to try harder. In studying Scripture, caring for souls, and sharing in fellowship, both churches enable their aging members to plan for the future and to face it—to express and heed hard truths of human frailty and finitude, to answer the call to respond to suffering and sickness, to mourn together those they love and lose.[14]

As treasure in earthen vessels and a living body of faith, every congregation interacts with society as a whole. Its communion is shaped by the ages and stages of its members' lives, unfolding in social space and historical time. In turn it shapes their individual dreams and shared stories across generations in common prayer and practice, Sunday by Sunday and day by day, in light of the life to come.

By way of conclusion, taking congregational community as a touchstone, let's go back to the beginning of our inquiry into the emerging ethos of retirement, with a feel for its saving promise of self-renewal and fulfillment in this world, however shining or unsure salvation seems in the next. "What must we do to be saved?" we can ask. We can answer by examining the ways we actually live, here and now, to make moral sense of retirement more clearly, to remake its promise more truly, and keep it more fully.

# CONCLUSION

What does it mean to live a good life? What does it feel like? Can we tell for ourselves, even if we can't say for everyone? Even if we can't make sense of it all, surely we can judge some of how life has gone for us up to now. We can tell the difference between a happy family and a troubled marriage, finding love at first sight or winding up unlucky in love. We can distinguish a true calling from a golden career or a grinding job. So we can think and dream about what's next, as we age, even if we wonder whether our retirement plans will pan out and our dreams will come true.

Can we complete life or redeem it, in this lifetime or in this world? The good life has no shape, some say, or at least no one shape or size that fits all. But we can know what's good when we see it, we may answer, and recognize happiness when we feel it. Must we really wait to judge a person's life until he dies, his children are grown, and his legacy is known? Must we wait until the trumpet sounds, and our fate finally comes from the hand of God, the law of nature, or the arc of history?[1] Not if we believe in latter-day dreams of retirement, and accept their promise of a slice of paradise on earth.

There is more than one way to plan and dream about retirement in light of how we think about love and work, and how we imagine life

177

and death. What if we imagine life amounting to pleasure and pain, giving and getting, costs and benefits that each one of us can add up side by side in debit or credit columns and calculate along a bottom line? Then we can certainly conceive of retirement as "time for myself," to be spent as freely as I please and as fully as I can afford. After all, I have earned it by years on the job. It's a reward for work done and wages saved, debts paid and investments made. I may enjoy the good things of life in retirement with others, to be sure, but I choose them as fulfilling for myself, like desirable items entered and crossed off on a shopping list or "bucket list" of places to go, things to do, and peak experiences to pursue. If you can dream it, you can do it, and credit it to your account. By such accounting, can we ever get enough? Not as long as we keep living and desiring what comes next. Whether given by God or nature, our rights to life, liberty, and the pursuit of happiness begin with freedom from the constraints of workaday life that retirement promises to lift from our shoulders and minds. Retirement invites us into a bright-lit future, curtained off from the dim limits and decline of old age. Instead it frees us to get back in shape and go back to feeling young again, to plunge into play and fall in love again.[2]

## Retirement is an opportunity to shape your legacy for family, friends, and the world.

If instead we imagine each one of us living here and now, feeling in tune with the romantic moment instead of shopping around in the retail marketplace, then we can aim to experience the present as fully and deeply as possible, as vividly and vitally as we can. Adding up pleasures or possessions is not the point of freedom from constraint, or freedom to do what we want and have fun. We should do what will make us feel happy, not only more satisfied but really fulfilled, joyful, serene, at one with ourselves and others in the moment. Instead of worrying about the future or regretting the past, we should enter into the present moment and make the moment last—whether in the swing of a sweet melody or a sharp cross-court volley, cradled in the arms of the deep or the love of your life, out on the town or at home around the dinner table with family and friends—just as familiar images of retirement urge us to enjoy the bright dawn breaking over the first day of the rest of your life, or savor the golden sunset ablaze in the evening sky.[3]

Is there anything wrong with this picture of retirement, or anything missing from it? Is there something more than this story of individuals, freed from Faustian paradox as well as religious roots and civic bonds, and now seeking all they can get from life, or all they can experience in each moment? You can never get enough of what you don't really want, warn financial advisors of clients with "disordered desires." Amen, agree critics of individualism overgrown along the utilitarian bottom line of the bourgeois market or the romantic self-expression of the bohemian moment. We can weigh such warnings and wonder what we *really* want, be it lifelong love or peace of mind here and now. Is it true enlightenment in the moment, as Janet Silver suggests, or life everlasting in heaven, as Fred Heiden proclaims? If we can know what makes life worth living and embrace it in practice as a good way of life, as therapist Frank Costa seeks to do with his patients or Pastor Paul Richardson with his congregants, then there may be enough for us to share without always wanting more. There may be enough for us to get what we need and accept our own limits without outdoing others to get it, or feeling cheated and denied our due if we fail to get more and more, or even if we succeed.[4] We can dwell in the house of the Lord all our days, however finite their number, as Del Weaver affirms the promise of Psalm 23. We can accept every day as a gift of grace, as Jim Matthews testifies to the gospel truth that sets the faithful free.

## You cannot lead a good life without a good society.

Instead of seeing others mainly as means to our own ends of doing and feeling better as individuals, such critics say, we can recognize ourselves as members of larger bodies, not only voluntary associations we choose to join or leave, but social bodies we are born into and live through, from formative family and faith to country and civilization. Retirement, then, can give us a fresh chance to open up to the mutuality of all social life, and embrace the common goods we share. We can take part in social networks not just to give back because we have gotten something in a quid pro quo market exchange between self-interested individuals, but for goodness' sake, to "give back to the community" we come from and inhabit as inherently social selves bred and bound by membership, suspended in webs of relationship and significance we ourselves have spun together.[5]

As activists, therapists, and pastors urge, retirement can help us join hands more fully in efforts to "make the world a better place with your own two hands," whether it is the world of a neighborhood school or park, a local church or food bank. Each of us is inextricably social, even when—especially when—we are expressing our own unique selves to one another through words and gestures we share in everyday rites of interaction, from shaking hands to saying good-byes, and in lifelong rites of passage from baptisms to funerals. For it is the hands of others that lift us from the womb and lower us to the grave, that give us aid in our labor, joy in our affection, and consolation in our sorrow.[6] Turned toward this touch and seen in this light, retirement can open our arms and hearts, in and out of church pews and community projects. It can widen our way across common ground in seeking to realize common goods diverse enough to share, that is, moral and social goods diverse enough to pray for and pursue, to debate and experience together in practice, for example, clean water and air, safe streets, good schools, and decent jobs at living wages.[7]

Retirement gives us more time and space to take part with others in public practices that make us members one of another in bodies politic—not only churches, temples, and synagogues, but clubs, teams, community groups, town councils, and political parties. Through such practices of membership in communities of character, we can find our place in social bodies that are at once bounded and interconnected, possessing and possessed by institutional virtues of trustworthiness, prudence, and wisdom, for example, not only faith, hope, and charity. At once personal and institutional, these are virtues that we can practice together without breaking the rules and contracts that bind us. These are virtues we can teach by example and learn together without ignoring the passions and interests that drive us, or overlooking their vicious power to corrupt persons and institutions alike in need of transformation.[8] Thus Bill Hanson condemns short-sighted corporate leaders in defense of prudence and integrity exercised by principled managers in free markets, for example, and Noah Morris denounces structural conflicts of interest built into employer-based 401(k) plans in the name of economic rationality taught in Econ 101.

Through such practices of membership, we can come to experience the manifold ways we belong to one another as social selves in relationship and participation within social bodies we inhabit and traverse over the whole course of our lives. We can come to see who we are as a whole, each of us and all of us, as Ella Mills testifies in the light of God's Word and Frank Costa spells out in terms of developmental psychology. This sense of integrity carries with it intuitions and convictions of what is *enough*—enough stuff, space, and time—within a moral community that moves and holds us all, mortal and immortal, in the rhythm of generations, until it is time to go.[9]

Such sense of a beginning and ending to each lifetime within the whole of a social fabric unfolding in history across generations arises in Western traditions embodied in the biblical synagogue and church, alongside the ancient *polis* and classical republic. In fact, we cannot grasp the modern common sense we take for granted of equally informed and self-interested buyers and sellers transacting honestly in a free market, and equally endowed citizens bearing universal rights in a free country, without sensing their religious and civic roots. They

181

spring from the covenantal communal fellowship and unforced public dialogue that give rise to the Protestant priesthood of all believers and the democratic self-government of all citizens, who are created equal in the sacred souls of their sovereign selves.[10]

> The good of each person is inseparable
> from the good of the community they
> make up as its self-governing citizens.

Given these roots, the question of whether you can lead a good life without a good society becomes problematic if not incoherent. For the good of each person is inseparable from the good of the political community they make up as its self-governing citizens. The good of each member of the people of God is inseparable from the good of all God's people, one with God in lawful covenant and so all united as a people and each unified as a personality. Dissenting believers may join and leave myriad denominations in America today. But no practicing believer can love God without loving everyone as their neighbor, or belonging to the whole of the body of Christ or the Judaic people of God, the Islamic *umma* or the Buddhist *sangha*.[11]

As a member of God's people, no one can retire from the lifelong calling of Deuteronomy to be one with God, and wholly with God, by heeding the covenant and following its every law every day in order to become the Law over a lifetime and teach it by shared example over generations. As a citizen of a true republic, seen as a living body of self-governing members, no one can retire from the lifelong calling Plato posits to learn to serve the good, to make good laws through shared deliberation and discipline, and come to rule oneself in order to rule and be ruled justly.[12]

If retirement offers no release from such a calling, then it's not so easy to retire as it sounds in terms of an endless vacation that frees us from work to get away from it all to relax and have fun in the sun. Certainly not, every moral tradition agrees, each in its own way. Desires are end-less and often at odds with one another in any one individual, classical economists point out, while individuals driven by desire often struggle over scarce goods. So we need to discipline ourselves conscientiously in order to earn and save steadily, and invest wisely, as Ben Franklin and latter-day financial advisors agree. We need to analyze the costs and benefits of what we desire in order to balance our priorities prudently. We need to coordinate our interests, and check prices set by supply and demand in a free market we order by fair contracts and equal rights.[13]

However endless and at odds, desires can also prove elusive and obscure, psychologists and poets add, or obsessive and compulsive. We cannot always know what we want from moment to moment, and we cannot always get what we want from day to day or year to year over the course of our lives. Neither can we expect to shape a coherent way of life simply through seeking one peak experience after another, therapists caution, and living from leap to leap in their pursuit. So we should sublimate libidinal desires, therapeutic thinking reveals, or get in touch with what we really want in order to feel good. Instead of seek-ing pleasure as a sensation, pursuing happiness as a passive feeling, or calculating costs and benefits to serve self-interest, we should strive for satisfaction through novel experiences inherent in the process of achiev-ing creative and compelling aims.[14]

Realizing forms of excellence inherent in practical activities—rang-ing from the practice of carpentry or medicine, through playing base-ball or chess, to making music or laws—leads back from modern moral psychology toward classical ethics of practical virtue. As exemplified by Kelsey Tyler in a town hall meeting or Bill Hanson in collegial conference no less than Pastor Paul in the pulpit and Ella Mills in the pew, these are virtues of justice, wisdom, prudence, and courage bred by practicing re-current activities within exemplary forms of social relationship in bodies politic and professional, educational and productive, as well as virtues of faith, hope, and charity bred by prayer in bodies of worship and by parental care in families.

As in learning to pray, preach, or play ball, we take up or improvise new practices, or we are inducted into them, and so we share experiences to which new visions of a good person and a good way of life ring true. Such visions in turn make sense of these practices, and inspire us to pursue them more clearly—for example, to practice our art, sport, meditation, or studies more steadily and seriously. So we realize imaginary visions by enacting them. We particularize theoretical ideals by embodying them. We revise moral traditions by making them our own in specific spheres of common practice that can regenerate implicit understandings and reshape overarching ideals in turn.[15] So Del Weaver, Janet Silver, and Bill Hanson rework the antinomy of orthodox faith and skeptical reason into distinctive moral stances to affirm the meaning and goodness of life in their everyday action.

Actual social practices and relationships are framed in classical republican perspective by the institutional ordering of households, schools, legislatures, courts, and temples seen as an integral moral ecology arranged to nurture virtues in practice, by contrast to modern instrumental models of institutions seen as sets of coordinating social mechanisms designed to serve the interests of individuals and protect their rights. So instead of seeking simply to advance our own interests and assert our own rights in the pursuit of happiness, we are bound to struggle together in practice against the power of our own passions to shape the steel cords of appetite in accord with the golden thread of lawful reason. In democratic deliberation through informed and reasoned argument, lit by Enlightenment ideals of conscientious truth-telling and mutual sympathy, we are bound to struggle, too, against the powers of political partisanship and oligarchy. Only by such effort can we shape institutions in accord with the practical wisdom and justice of a republic that enables everyone to contribute fully to its well-being and share fully in its liberty and prosperity. To be true to these principles in practice, we must provide and pay for the social conditions that enable citizens to work, earn, and save enough to retire securely.[16]

America seen as a shining city upon a hill, blessed by liberty, harks back to temples in both Athens and Jerusalem. Pride goeth before the biblical fall from preternatural leisure and creative cultivation in the garden of Eden, which consigns us to toil in the dust. But the fall also stems from the peculiarly human capacity for rational discernment and deliberative choice to tell the difference between what is good and bad, fruitful or futile. As cultural animals, left unfinished by instinct, humans develop the capacity for thoughtful symbolic representation and language to communicate and cooperate. When they eat of the forbidden fruit of the tree of knowledge, their eyes are opened to reflective self-consciousness, and they see that they are naked. Exercising this complex cognitive capacity in original sin exiles Adam and Eve from the garden of Eden, but it enables humans to flourish almost everywhere else. They fan out from Africa, and thread the eye of the evolutionary needle by adapting to all sorts of environments so cleverly that they outhunt every other species and out-farm the earth itself, until at last they outpace the adaptive capacity of the planet's ecosphere in the millisecond blink of barely three centuries.[17]

Made in the mysterious image and likeness of the God of Zion, humans prove as clever as the far-seeing gods of Olympus, yet fatefully unable to foresee the ultimate outcome of their decisive action. So we have come to "subdue the earth" and exercise dominion over its creatures, as a matter of sheer fact overwhelming an arguable biblical premise. Now we must face the consequences of our presence on this planet and the real possibility of eco-catastrophe. Like Noah's offspring after the flood, we must turn from doing as we will toward the lawful order of a covenant with the whole of creation and the human species, transcending the wealth of nations and limited-liability corporations, if we are to be "a blessing and not a curse upon the earth."[18]

As the fallout of our carbon-fueled choices begins to be visited upon our children for generations to come, we must awaken to the crisis of climate change with an unselfish courage and wisdom we have yet to summon. We can no longer dream that a technological fix will give birth to a new heaven and a new earth. But we can hope and pray that the biblical mystery of "what was, and is, and is to be" in deep time will enable to us act responsibly in our time, by the grace of God, to heal this world of wonders, not as pristine wilderness or paradise regained but as a city redeemed, shining and singing to itself in harmony with all creation.[19]

From this work and this world we cannot retire. Let us join in, move heaven and earth, and tread lightly.

# NOTES

## PREFACE

1. Social Security Administration, "The Future of Social Security," SSA #05-10055, 2008; and Social Security Administration, "Annual Performance Plan for FY 2012," page 36: "Nearly 80 million baby boomers will file for retirement benefits over the next 20 years—an average of 10,000 per day," excluding decedents and recognizing that some will retire before or after turning age sixty-five. From 1946 to 1964 some 72.5 million persons were born in the United States, increasing via immigration to a cohort of 78.8 million by 1999 and numbering just under 77 million when the oldest baby boomers began turning sixty-five in 2011, with 60 million projected by 2030, when all baby boomers will be sixty-six to eighty-four years old and almost one in five U.S. residents will be aged sixty-five or over, compared to one in eight in 2010 and one in ten in 1970, according to Sandra L. Colby and Jennifer M. Ortman, "The Baby Boom Cohort in the United States: 2012 to 2060," U.S. Census Bureau Current Population Reports, May 2014, https://www.census.gov/prod /2014pubs/p25-1141.pdf. The population sixty-five and older will increase 34 percent in 2017–2027, while the working age population increases 2 percent, with Social Security and Medicare accounting for 63 percent of the increase in all federal noninterest spending, to hike the deficit from 2.9 percent to 5 percent of GDP, projects the Congressional Budget Office (CBO), *The Budget and Economic Outlook: 2017 to 2027*, January 2017.

2. See Richard Madsen, "The Archipelago of Faith," *American Journal of Sociology* 114, no. 5 (2009): 1263–1301; Steven M. Tipton, *Getting Saved from the Sixties: Moral Meaning in Conversion and Cultural Change* (Berkeley and Los Angeles: University of California Press, 1982); Mark O. Wilhelm, Patrick M. Rooney, and Eugene R. Tempel, "Changes in Religious Giving Reflect Changes in Involvement: Age and Cohort Effects in Religious Giving, Secular Giving, and Attendance," *Journal for the Scientific Study of Religion* 46, no. 2 (2007): 217–32.

3. Cf. Max Weber, "Science as a Vocation," and "The Social Psychology of the World Religions," in *From Max Weber: Essays in Sociology*, ed. Hans Gerth and C. Wright Mills

(Oxford: Oxford University Press, 1946), 129–56, 267–301; and Robert N. Bellah, "Religious Evolution," *American Sociological Review* 29, no. 3 (1964): 358–74.

4. Charles Taylor, *Sources of the Self: The Making of the Modern Identity* (Cambridge, MA: Harvard University Press, 1998) and *A Secular Age* (Cambridge, MA: Harvard University Press, 2007); Michael Walzer, *Thick and Thin: Moral Argument at Home and Abroad* (Notre Dame, IN: University of Notre Dame Press, 1994), 85–104.

5. Steven M. Tipton, "Social Differentiation and Moral Pluralism," in *Meaning and Modernity: Religion, Polity, and Self*, ed. Richard Madsen et al. (Berkeley and Los Angeles: University of California Press, 2002), 15–40; Tipton, *Getting Saved from the Sixties*; Robert N. Bellah et al., *Habits of the Heart* (Berkeley and Los Angeles: University of California Press, 1985, 1996, 2008) and *The Good Society* (New York: Knopf, 1991).

6. Matthew 20:1-16; Isaiah 65:21-22.

7. Bellah, "Religious Evolution"; Tipton, *Getting Saved from the Sixties*; Madsen, "The Archipelago of Faith."

8. Richard Douglas, "Talent and Vocation in Humanist and Protestant Thought," in *Action and Conviction in Early Modern Europe: Essays in Honor of E. H. Harbison*, ed. Theodore K. Rabb and Jerrold Seigel (Princeton, NJ: Princeton University Press, 1969), 261–98; Taylor, *Sources of the Self*, parts 4–5.

9. Weber, "The Social Psychology of the World Religions," 280–92; Charles Taylor, *Modern Social Imaginaries* (Durham and London: Duke University Press, 2004), 23–30.

# CHAPTER 1

1. Social Security Administration, "The Future of Social Security." See Raj Chetty et al., "The Fading American Dream: Trends in Absolute Income Mobility Since 1940," Stanford University, December 2016, on the percentage of children outearning their parents falling from 90 percent for children born in 1940 to 50 percent for children born in 1980, and boomers falling from 85 percent in 1946 to 60 percent in 1964, with the largest declines concentrated in the industrial Midwest states and in cities with higher levels of residential segregation, poorer public schools, a smaller middle class, weaker families, and less social capital. The aggregate value of pension plan assets of the S&P 500 companies fell to $1.82 trillion USD, some 24 percent and $568 billion short of aggregate liabilities of $2.32 trillion, estimated Mercer Investment Consulting on July 6, 2016. U.S. public employee pension systems for all fifty states and Washington, DC, totaled $5.599 trillion in pension debt ($49,388 per household in the United States) for 2015 as calculated on a market basis, and $1.306 trillion total ($11,055 per household) as calculated on an actuarial basis, estimated U.S. Pension Tracker, Stanford Institute for Economic Policy Research, February 2017, at http://us.pensiontracker.org, with California ranked second, at $92,748 market pension debt per household, and Georgia thirty-third at $33,590.

2. Employment Benefit Research Institute (EBRI), "The 2016 Retirement Confidence Survey," March 2016, esp. 1–6, 13–18, 27–30; National Institute on Retirement, "Retirement Security 2017," February 2017; and Pew Research Center, "Most Middle-Aged Adults Are Rethinking Retirement Plans," May 28, 2009, http://www.pewsocialtrends

.org/2009/05/28/most-middle-aged-adults-are-rethinking-retirement-plans/. By 2017 three in four workers reported worrying about reaching retirement securely and planning to work longer and spend less to do so. By 2016 one in five American workers felt very confident they would have enough money to meet their basic living expenses in retirement, up from only one in eight in 2009, but still below one in four in 2002. Cf. D'Vera Cohn and Paul Taylor, "Baby Boomers Approach Age 65—Glumly," Pew Research Center, December 20, 2010, http://www.pewsocialtrends.org/2010/12/20/baby-boomers -approach-65-glumly/; and Rich Morin and Richard Fry, "More Americans Worry about Financing Retirement: Adults in Their Late 30s Most Concerned," Pew Research Center, October 22, 2012, http://www.pewsocialtrends.org/2012/10/22/more-americans-worry -about-financing-retirement/, reporting retirement worries more concentrated among middle-aged adults (53 percent, up from 18 percent in 2009) than among boomers aged 60 to 64 (34 percent), given their greater percentage losses in home equity and net worth since 2001. Half of millennials and Gen Xers fear they will receive little or no Social Security benefits, compared to 28 percent of boomers under sixty-five, reports Pew Research Center, "Millennials in Adulthood," March 7, 2014, http://www.pewsocialtrends .org/2014/03/07/millennials-in-adulthood/.

3. Employment Benefit Research Institute, "The 2016 Retirement Confidence Survey." Labor force participation rates of those aged sixty-five to sixty-nine rose from 18.4 percent in 1985 and 21.8 percent in 1990 to 31.6 percent in 2014 and 32.1 percent in 2015, with men rising from 26.8 percent to 36.1 percent in 1994–2014 and women rising from 17.9 percent to 27.5 percent, reports the Bureau of Labor Statistics (hereinafter BLS), "Labor Force Participation and Work Status of People 65 Years and Older," January 2013; and BLS, "Table 3.3. Civilian Labor Force Participation," *Monthly Labor Review*, December 2015 and December 2016.

4. Gordon B. T. Merwin, Richard W. Johnson, and Dan Murphy, "Why Do Boomers Plan to Work So Long?" (Working Paper #2006–19, Center for Retirement Research at Boston College, November 2006), http://crr.bc.edu/wp-content/uploads/2006/11/wp_2006-191 .pdf; Employee Benefit Research Institute, "The 2009 Retirement Confidence Survey." Claudia Goldin and Lawrence Katz, "Women Working Longer: Facts and Some Explanations," National Bureau of Economic Research (NBER), November 2016, finds that women who enjoyed their jobs earlier in life were employed longer, independent of their education or earnings, although women often choose to work longer after deciding to pursue higher education and build a career. Cf. Annamaria Lusardi and Olivia Mitchell, "Older Women's Labor Market Attachment, Retirement Planning, and Household Debt," NBER, November 2016, finding older women work longer remedially due to higher debt than prior cohorts, financial fragility, and low financial literacy; late divorce, more dependent children, adverse Social Security changes; and loss of pension, job, pay, or home equity.

5. Erik H. Erikson, "Life Cycle," *International Encyclopedia of the Social Sciences*, ed. David L. Sills (New York: Macmillan/Free Press, 1968), 286–92; John W. Meyer, "Self and Life Course: Institutionalization and Its Effects," 242–60 in George M. Thomas et al., eds., *Institutional Structure* (Newbury Park, CA: SAGE Publications, 1987).

6. Marc Freedman, *Encore: Finding Work that Matters in the Second Half of Life* (New York: PublicAffairs, 2008); Sarah Kershaw, "Ready for Life's Encore Performances," *New*

*York Times*, March 21, 2010; Council of Economic Advisers, "Work-Life Balance and the Economics of Workplace Flexibility," Executive Office of the President, March 2010.

7. See Teresa Ghilarducci, "Guaranteed Retirement Accounts" (EPI Briefing Paper #204, Economic Policy Institute, November 20, 2007), http://www.gpn.org/bp204.html; and Jennifer Erin Brown et al., "Shortchanged in Retirement," National Institute on Retirement Security, March 2016, showing women 80 percent likelier than men to be impoverished at age 65 or older and three times likelier at age 75–79, given median wages at 80 percent of men's, and income 25 percent lower at 65 and above and 44 percent lower by age 80, with pensions and 401(k) account assets one-third lower than men's, linked to higher costs for women of family caregiving, divorce, and health care paid out of pocket over a longer average life span of 81.2 versus 76.4 years. Women with higher education, earnings, and savings have been one-fifth likelier than others to delay retirement beyond age 65 by choice, find Goldin and Katz, "Women Working Longer" (NBER Working Paper 22607, Sep. 2016), but later employment is now rising among the less educated at roughly the same pace, while women not working are likelier to have poor health and little savings, and to rely on Social Security benefits and sometimes SSI disability benefits. By contrast to earlier cohorts and their higher rates of employment in middle age, African-American women aged 50–72 in recent cohorts are less likely to be working longer than their white counterparts, due to worse employment outcomes, fewer resources, worse health, more physically demanding jobs, and improved disability programs, according to Joanna N. Lahey, "Understanding Why Black Women Are Not Working Longer" (NBER Working Paper 22680, Sep. 2016).

8. See note 3 above; and BLS, "Labor Force Projections," December 2015, showing that workers over sixty-five composed one-tenth of the labor force in 1985 and reached one-sixth by 2010, with 7.2 million working late by 2012, twice as many as in 1997. Courtney C. Coil and Phillip B. Levine, "Reconsidering Retirement: How Losses and Layoffs Affect Older Workers," NBER, September 2010, report that retirement rates began falling in the mid-1990s in response to restrictive changes in pensions and Social Security, then flattened out after 2006, suggesting that job loss and long-term unemployment in the Great Recession pressed the jobless aged 62–69 to retire early at the cost of lower life-long Social Security benefits, while employed workers delayed retirement to increase Social Security payments and rebuild savings and investment portfolios. More educated and affluent workers thereby respond most directly to falling stock markets and the threat of lower investment income in retirement. Likelier to be jobless, less educated and less affluent workers respond most directly to slackening labor markets and rising long-term joblessness by retiring early. Those working past sixty-five since 2007 reached record generational highs, while overall labor force participation rates through 2016 remained below 60 percent, under peaks of 63 percent in 2008 and 66 percent a decade earlier, due to millions more dropping out of the labor force as well as baby boomers reaching retirement age, according to BLS, "The Employment Situation—October 2016," November 4, 2016.

9. Society of Actuaries, *Working in Retirement*, July 2012, p. 8, found 55 percent of older Americans working late in 2011 in order to stay active and involved, they said, and 51 percent in order to earn additional income, reported by Steven Greenhouse, "Working Late, by Choice or Not," *New York Times*, May 10, 2012, F1.

10. Sun Life Financial U.S. Unretirement Index 2011, pp. 16–18. Cf. Tavia Grant, "Freedom 68: Canadians Feel Retirement Dreams Fading," *Toronto Globe and Mail*, March 8, 2011.

11. Cohn and Taylor, "Baby Boomers Approach Age 65"; financial planner interview, San Francisco, June 2011.

12. I am indebted to Ann Swidler for clarifying this point and related dilemmas of retirement.

13. Dana Dratch, "7 Things to Know about the 'New Retirement,'" *Bankrate*, http://www .bankrate.com/finance/retirement/new-retirement-1.aspx, accessed August 7, 2017.

14. Cf. Jacob Hacker, *The Great Risk Shift: The New Economic Insecurity and the Decline of the American Dream* (Oxford: Oxford University Press, 2006); and the promise of President George W. Bush's 2005 inaugural address to build an ownership society: "We will widen the ownership of homes and businesses, retirement savings and health insurance—preparing our people for the challenges of life in a free society. By making every citizen an agent of his or her own destiny, we will give our fellow Americans greater freedom from want and fear, and make our society more prosperous and just and equal." msnbc.com, "George W. Bush 2nd Inaugural Address," NBCNews.com, updated January 20, 2005, http:// www.nbcnews.com/id/6848112/ns/politics-george_w_bush_the_second_inaugural /t/george-w-bush-nd-inaugural-address/#.WYhn7lGGOUk.

15. Prudential Insurance Company of America, "Retirement Needs a New Plan," *New York Times*, October 17, 2012, F10.

16. Dratch, "7 Things," 1; and Walter Upgrave, "Convincing Someone to Save for Retirement," *Money* magazine, July 10, 2012.

17. Dratch, "7 Things," 1; Center for Economic and Policy Research (CEPR), "2000–2010 Was a Lost Economic Decade," *Data Bytes*, September 13, 2011. Average health care costs are expected to rise by 6 percent annually for the foreseeable future, well above the rate of Social Security COLAs, Medicare, and employer health plans, report HealthView Services, "The High Cost of Living Longer," 2016, pp. 4, 7–8, http://www.hvsfinancial .com/wp-content/uploads/2016/12/Women_Retirement_Health_Care.pdf.

18. See, for example, Paul Pettillo, "Now What Retirement?" August 24, 2011, at target2025.com; and Harry Phibbs, "Retirement Is a Mirage," *Daily Mail*, October 6, 2009. Net productivity rose 73.4 percent in 1973–2015, and average hourly pay rose 11.1 percent, compared to 96.7 percent productivity growth and 91.3 percent pay growth in 1948–1973, reports the Economic Policy Institute, "The Productivity-Pay Gap," August 2016. In 1947–1973 U.S. income grew 31 percent more slowly in the top quintile than in the bottom quintile, while in 1973–2000 income grew 55 percent more quickly in the top quintile than in the bottom, report Lawrence Mishel, Jared Bernstein, and Sylvia Allegretto, *The State of Working America* (Ithaca, NY: Cornell University Press, 2005). The middle-class share of U.S. aggregate gross household income before taxes fell from 62 percent in 1970 to 43 percent in 2014, as middle-income Americans fell from 61 percent to less than 50 percent of the adult population; and the middle-class share of aggregate disposable household income after taxes and transfers fell from 62 to 56 percent from 1991 to 2010, calculates Rakesh Kochtar et al., "Middle Class Fortunes in Western Europe," Pew Research Center, April 2017, 4, 29–30, available at http://www.pewglobal .org/2017/04/24/middle-class-fortunes-in-western-europe/; and Kochtar, "The American

Middle Class Is Losing Ground," Pew Research Center, December 2015, available at http://www.pewsocialtrends.org/2015/12/09/the-american-middle-class-is-losing-ground/.

19. CEPR, "2000–2010 Was a Lost Economic Decade"; Edward N. Wolff, "The Asset Price Meltdown and the Wealth of the Middle Class" (NBER Working Paper 18559, November 2012). Declines from 2007 to 2010 in median net worth to $77,000 per household on average and $179,000 for households aged fifty-five to sixty-four are based on Federal Reserve data, with losses in home equity, foreclosures, and underwater loans based on data from Moody Analytics and the AARP, reported in "The Road to Retirement," *New York Times* editorial, September 15, 2012.

20. See Emmanuel Saez, "Striking It Richer: The Evolution of Top Incomes in the United States," University of California, Berkeley, updated June 2016 from *Pathways* magazine, Winter 2008, 1–10, showing bottom 99 percent incomes up by 7.6 percent from 2009 to 2015, while top 1 percent incomes rose by 37.4 percent, capturing 52 percent of all 2009–2015 income gains. Median household income increased by 5.2 percent between 2014 and 2015 to $56,516, still 1.6 percent lower than in 2007 and 2.4 percent lower than in 1999. With 3 million added jobs and unemployment declining to 5 percent by 2016, job growth rather than wage growth cut poverty rates most sharply for African-American and Hispanic households, nearly half of those below the poverty line, but 2015 gains by lower-income households did not improve overall measures of income inequality or alter the economy's long-term trajectory of slow growth, reports the U.S. Census Bureau, *Income and Poverty in the United States: 2015*, September 2016. Income polarization and declining middle-class incomes curbed consumer spending by 3.5 percent in 1998–2013, about $400 billion annually, and retarded economic growth, estimates Ali Alichi, Kory Kantenga, and Juan Sole, "Income Polarization in the United States" (IMF Working Paper WP16/121, June 2016), https://www.imf.org/external/pubs/ft/wp/2016/wp16121.pdf. Board of Governors of the Federal Reserve System, "Report on the Economic Well-Being of U.S. Households in 2015," May 2016, 1–3, reported 46 percent of 5,600 respondents could not cover $400 in emergency expenses, 31 percent were either "struggling to get by" or "just getting by," and 31 percent of workers lacked retirement savings, including 27 percent of non-retired respondents age sixty or older. Tony James and Teresa Ghilarducci, *Rescuing Retirement: A Plan to Guarantee Retirement Security For All Americans* (Austin and New York: Disruption Books, 2016), report 68 percent of all working-age Americans lack employer-sponsored retirement plans, and 25 million will face poverty in retirement by 2050, given retirement savings averaging $14,500 for those aged forty to fifty-five.

21. Henry Siu and Nir Jaimovich, "Jobless Recoveries," Third Way NEXT Initiative, April 8, 2015, http://www.thirdway.org/report/jobless-recoveries; Michael J. Hicks and Srikant Devaraj, "The Myth and Reality of Manufacturing in America," Ball State University, June 2015, 5–6, http://conexus.cberdata.org/files/MfgReality.pdf. See David Autor, "The Polarization of Job Opportunities in the U.S. Labor Market," Center for American Progress and the Brookings Institution, April 2010, at https://www.brookings.edu/research/the-polarization-of-job-opportunities-in-the-u-s-labor-market-implications-for-employment-and-earnings/; Pew Research Center, "The State of American Jobs," October 6, 2016, http://www.pewsocialtrends.org/2016/10/06/the-state-of-american-jobs/; Anton Cheremukhin, "Middle-Skill Jobs Lost in U.S. Market Polarization," *DallasFed* 9, no. 5 (May

2014): 1–4; Daron Acemoglu and Pascual Restrepo, "Robots and Jobs: Evidence from US Labor Markets" (NBER Working Paper 23285, March 2017), http://www.nber.org/papers/w23285; David Autor et al., "Concentrating on the Fall of the Labor Share" (NBER Working Paper 23108, January 2017), at http://www.nber.org/papers/w23108; and Jae Song et al., "Firming Up Inequality" (NBER Working Paper 21199, May 2015), at http://www.nber.org/papers/w21199.

22. Robert Reich, "Speech: The Revolt of the Anxious Class," Democratic Leadership Council, November 22, 1994, https://www.dol.gov/dol/aboutdol/history/reich/speeches/sp94 1122.htm ; Frank Levy, *The New Dollars and Dreams* (New York: Russell Sage Foundation, 1998), 3–4; Jason Furman et al., "Artificial Intelligence, Automation, and the Economy," Executive Office of the President, December 2016, 13–14, https://obamawhitehouse .archives.gov/sites/whitehouse.gov/files/documents/Artificial-Intelligence-Auto mation-Economy.PDF. On STEMpathy jobs and industrial jobs lost to microchips instead of Mexicans, see Thomas Friedman, "Trump Voters, Just Hear Me Out," *New York Times*, November 2, 2016, A23; and David J. Deming, "The Growing Importance of Social Skills in the Labor Market" (NBER Working Paper 21473, August 2015), at http://www.nber .org/papers/w21473. On the rise of the on-demand economy, see Lawrence F. Katz and Alan B. Krueger, "The Rise and Nature of Alternative Work Arrangements in the United States, 1995–2015," March 29, 2016, http://scholar.harvard.edu/files/lkatz/files /katz_krueger_cws_v3.pdf.

23. Thomas Piketty, Emmanuel Saez, and Gabriel Zucman, "Distributional National Accounts: Methods and Estimates for the United States" (NBER Working Paper 22945, December 2016), at http://www.nber.org/papers/w22945. Cf. Saez, "Striking It Richer," 2016, https://eml.berkeley.edu/~saez/saez-UStopincomes-2015.pdf; Emmanuel Saez and Gabriel Zucman, "Wealth Inequality in the United States since 1913" (NBER Working Paper 20625, October 2014), https://gabriel-zucman.eu/files/SaezZucman2014.pdf; and Jesse Bricker et al., "Measuring Income and Wealth at the Top Using Administrative and Survey Data," Brookings, Spring 2016, at https://www.brookings.edu/bpea-articles /measuring-income-and-wealth-at-the-top-using-administrative-and-survey-data/.

24. Piketty, Saez, and Zucman, "Distributional National Accounts," 16–22, 25–32.

25. Bureau of Economic Analysis, U.S. Department of Commerce, reported in Floyd Norris, "For Business, Golden Days; for Workers, the Dross," *New York Times,* November 26, 2011, B3; William Lazonick, "Profits without Prosperity," *Harvard Business Review* 92, no. 9 (September 2014): 46–55.

26. See U.S. Census Bureau, "The Research Supplemental Poverty Measure: 2010," November 2011, https://www.census.gov/prod/2011pubs/p60-241.pdf; U.S. Census Bureau, "The Research Supplemental Poverty Measure: 2011," November 2012, https://www.census .gov/prod/2012pubs/p60-244.pdf; and U.S. Census Bureau, "The Supplemental Poverty Measure: 2015," September 2016, "Table 3. Percentage of People by Ratio of Income /Resources to Poverty Threshold," at https://www.census.gov/library/publications/2016 /demo/p60-258.html, showing 22.6 percent of Americans under 150 percent of the poverty line in 2015 by the official measure and 30.6 percent by the more comprehensive supplemental poverty measure.

27. World Economic Forum, *The Inclusive Growth and Development Report 2017*, January 2017, fig. 6, 16, at https://www.weforum.org/reports/the-inclusive-growth-and-develop ment-report-2017; and Saez, "Striking It Richer," 5.

28. Morin and Fry, "More Americans Worry about Financing Retirement," shows different levels of household income and education defining the largest gaps in Americans' confidence over retirement, along with age differences coinciding with percentage losses in median wealth since the Great Recession.

29. Sean F. Reardon and Kendra Bischoff, "The Continuing Increase in Income Segregation, 2007–2012," Stanford Center for Education Policy Analysis, 2016, at https://cepa .stanford.edu/content/continuing-increase-income-segregation-2007-2012; "Residential Segregation by Income, 1970–2009," in J. Logan, ed., *Diversity and Disparities* (New York: Sage Foundation, 2014); and "Income Inequality and Income Segregation," *American Journal of Sociology* 116, no. 4 (2011): 1092–1153.

30. Raj Chetty et al., "Where Is the Land of Opportunity? The Geography of Intergenerational Mobility in the U.S.," NBER Working Paper 19843, January 2014, http://www .rajchetty.com/chettyfiles/mobility_geo.pdf; and Chetty et al., "Is the United States Still a Land of Opportunity? Recent Trends in Intergenerational Mobility" (NBER Working Paper 19844, January 2014), at http://www.nber.org/papers/w19844. On a "30 million–word gap" between three-year old children from low-income and high-income families, linked to the "achievement gap" in elementary education via differential language acquisition in early childhood, see Betty Hart and Todd Risley, *Meaningful Differences in the Everyday Experience of Young American Children* (Baltimore: Paul H. Brookes, 1995).

31. Alan Berube, "Where the College Graduates Are: Degree Attainment in Metropolitan Areas," Brookings Institution, May 31, 2012, https://www.brookings.edu/blog /the-avenue/2012/05/31/where-the-grads-are-degree-attainment-in-metro-areas/; and Jeremy Greenwood et al., "Marry Your Like: Assortative Mating and Income Inequality" (NBER Working Paper 19829, January 2014), at http://www.nber.org /papers/w19829. See Shannon M. Monnat, "Deaths of Despair and Support for Trump in the 2016 Presidential Election," Penn State University Research Brief, December 4, 2016, http://aese.psu.edu/directory/smm67/Election16.pdf; Ann Case and Sir Angus Deaton, "Rising Morbidity and Mortality in Midlife among White Non-Hispanic Americans in the 21st Century," *Proceedings of the National Academy of the Sciences of the United States of America* 112, 49 (November 2015): 15078–83; and color-coded data on life expectancy, joblessness, and wages in Department of Health and Human Services, *National Vital Statistics Reports* 64, no. 11 (September 2015), fig. 1, 5; Valerie Wilson and William M. Rodgers III, "Black-White Wage Gaps Expand with Rising Wage Inequality," Economic Policy Institute, September 20, 2016, 4, table 1, http://www.epi.org/publication/black-white-wage-gaps-expand-with-rising-wage -inequality/; BLS, U.S. Department of Labor, "The Employment Situation—October 2016," USDL-16-2095, https://www.bls.gov/news.release/archives/empsit_11042016 .pdf, Summary Table A and Table A-10. In 2016 Clinton won 489 of the wealthiest, most populous U.S. counties, encompassing 64 percent of America's economic activity; Trump won the remaining 2,623, and turnout fell below 55 percent of all voting-age adults, reports Louis Jacobson, "Mike Pence Says Trump Won Most Counties by a Republican since Ronald Reagan," PolitiFact, December 4, 2016, from

data compiled by David Leip, "Atlas of U.S. Presidential Elections," November 2016, http://www.politifact.com/truth-o-meter/statements/2016/dec/04/mike-pence/mike-pence-says-donald-trump-won-most-counties-rep/.

32. Barack Obama, "Remarks by the President on Economic Mobility," December 4, 2013, https://obamawhitehouse.archives.gov/the-press-office/2013/12/04/remarks-president-economic-mobility. Cf. Club for Growth, "Our Philosophy: Prosperity and Opportunity through Economic Freedom," 2012, at www.clubforgrowth.org/philosophy.

33. Pew Research Center, "Most See Inequality Growing, but Partisans Differ over Solutions," January 23, 2014, http://www.people-press.org/2014/01/23/most-see-inequality-growing-but-partisans-differ-over-solutions/; Chris Kahn, "U.S. Voters Want Leader to End Advantage of Rich and Powerful," Reuters/Ipsos Poll, November 8, 2016, http://www.reuters.com/article/us-usa-election-poll-mood-idUSKBN1332NC, reporting agreement with these two statements by 72 and 75 percent respectively of 10,604 voters with ballots already cast.

34. Americans save at an estimated median rate of 1 percent of their annual income in the bottom quintile of the income distribution, 11 percent in the middle quintile, and 24 percent in the top quintile, with the top 5 percent saving 37 percent and the top 1 percent saving 51 percent of their income, estimate Karen E. Dynan, Jonathan Skinner, and Stephen Zeldes, "Do the Rich Save More?" *Journal of Political Economy* 112, no. 2 (2004): 397–444. The Congressional Budget Office, "The Budget and Economic Outlook: 2017 to 2027," January 2017, projects that mandatory Social Security and Medicare spending will jump from a third of all federal spending in 2017 to 42 percent by 2027, leading a rise from 37 to 45 percent in all federal spending on older adults (including federal retirees and veterans and the elderly on Medicaid) at current benefit levels and tax rates, thereby squeezing discretionary spending from 6.3 percent of GDP to 5.3 percent in 2027, the lowest level since 1962, including spending on children already reduced from 20 percent of the federal domestic budget in 1960 to 15 percent in 2011, reports Yamiche Alcindor, "Contradictions as President Prepares a Budget," *New York Times*, February 24, 2017, A1, 14. Rising pension costs and debts at the state level will also transfer wealth from young to old by crowding out spending on schools and child welfare to cover unfunded pension liabilities, ranging from $92,748 per household in California (second to Alaska at $110,538) to $33,590 in Georgia (thirty-third, with Tennessee fiftieth at $19,586) in 2015, estimates the Stanford Institute for Economic Policy Research, at http://us.pensiontracker.org. See note 1 above.

35. Here and below see Thomas B. Edsall, "How the Other Fifth Lives," *New York Times*, April 27, 2016; Reardon and Bischoff, "The Continuing Increase"; Timothy Smeeding, "Gates, Gaps, and Intergenerational Mobility: The Importance of an Even Start," in Irwin Kirsch and Henry Braun, eds., *The Dynamics of Opportunity in America: Evidence and Perspectives* (New York: Springer, 2016), 255–95; Richard Reeves, "The Dangerous Separation of the American Upper Middle Class," Brookings, September 3, 2015, https://www.brookings.edu/research/the-dangerous-separation-of-the-american-upper-middle-class/; Federal Reserve System, "Report on the Economic Well-Being of U.S. Households in 2015," May 2016, 1–3; and Diane Whitmore et al., "Money Lightens the Load," Brookings, December 12, 2016, at https://www.brookings.edu/research/money-lightens-the-load/.

36. Jon Huang et al., "Election 2016: Exit Polls," *New York Times*, November 8, 2016, https://www.nytimes.com/interactive/2016/11/08/us/politics/election-exit-polls.html. Voters earning $100,000 or more split their votes for president in 2016, as in 2008 and 2012, instead of favoring Republican candidates by two to one as they did in the 1980s. Donald Trump won white voters without a college degree and earning less than $30,000 by a margin of 62 to 30 percent in 2016, compared to Mitt Romney's narrow win by 52 to 45 percent in 2012, as almost one in four of Obama's white, working-class supporters in 2012 defected in 2016, according to the Cooperative Congressional Election Study, reported Nate Cohn, "Turnout Was Not Driver of Clinton's Defeat," *New York Times*, March 28, 2017, A17. Emily Elkins, *The Five Types of Trump Voters*, Democracy Fund Voter Study Group, June 2017, identifies less educated, lower-earning "American Preservationists" and "Anti-Elites" less loyal to the GOP as Trump's strongest primary voters and 39 percent of his general-election vote, based on their support for entitlements and jobs in response to their personal economic distress, by contrast to more educated, higher-earning "Staunch Conservatives" and "Free Marketeers" more loyal to the GOP and other primary candidates, who made up 55 percent of Trump's general election vote, with another 6 percent coming from "the Disengaged."

37. Pew Research Center, "The Public's Policy Priorities for 2016," January 21, 2016, http://www.people-press.org/2016/01/22/budget-deficit-slips-as-public-priority/1-21 -2016_06/; Joan C. Williams, "What So Many People Don't Get about the U.S. Working Class," *Harvard Business Review*, November 10, 2016; and Eduardo Porter, "A Budget Reflecting Resentments," *New York Times*, March 8, 2017, B1, 6. Cf. Senator Bernie Sanders, "Bernie's Announcement," Bernie.com, May 26, 2015, http://www.berniesanders .com/bernies-announcement; and Donald Trump, "Donald Trump's Presidential Announcement Speech," *Time*, http://www.time.com/3923128/donald-trump-announce ment-speech/. A Washington Post–ABC News poll released April 23, 2017, at www .washingtonpost.com, reported 67 percent of Americans think "the Democratic Party is out of touch with most people," and 62 percent think likewise of the Republican Party. "President Trump is Least Popular President at 100-Day Mark," https://www.washing tonpost.com/page/2010-2019/WashingtonPost/2017/04/23/National-Politics/Polling /release_466.xml?tid=a_inl.

38. Michael J. Sandel, *What Money Can't Buy: The Moral Limits of Markets* (New York: Farrar, Straus and Giroux, 2012), 203; Andrew Del Banco, *The Real American Dream: A Meditation on Hope* (Cambridge, MA: Harvard University Press, 1999), 67.

39. Estimates of the rising ratio of CEO compensation, with the value of share options realized, at America's 350 biggest companies to the pay of an average worker in the U.S. private sector rise from 20:1 in 1965 to 383:1 in 2000, 185:1 in 2009 and 231:1 in 2011, according to the Economic Policy Institute, "The State of Working America," 2011, at http://www.stateofworkingamerica.org/charts. Median household income in Silicon Valley's most expensive residential communities exceeded $200,000 in 2009, and the median home price exceeded $2.4 million according to MLS data.

40. Lee Rainwater, *What Money Buys: Inequality and the Social Meanings of Income* (New York: Basic Books, 1974).

41. See Aristotle, *Nicomachean Ethics*, books 1–2, on the practical nature of virtue bred by habit, and books 8–9 on the social relations and civic good of friendship. *The Complete*

*Works of Aristotle*, ed. Jonathan Barnes, vol. 2 (Princeton, NJ: Princeton University Press, 1984).

42. See Robert E. Lane, *Political Ideology: Why the American Common Man Believes What He Does* (New York: Free Press, 1962), chap. 4, "The Fear of Equality," 57–81; Joan Huber, *Income and Ideology: An Analysis of the American Political Formula* (New York: Free Press, 1973), esp. chap. 6, "Why Are the Rich, Rich and the Poor, Poor?" 100–116, showing more or less emphasis, varying along class and race lines, placed on individual agency and desert to rationalize unequal economic and social status; and Alberto Alesina and Edward L. Glaeser, *Fighting Poverty in the US and Europe* (Oxford: Oxford University Press, 2004), showing Americans more likely to credit wealth to the "pluck" of individual effort and merit by 70 percent to 30 percent, and Europeans more likely to credit it to the "luck or stuck" effects of social position by a similar 70 to 30 margin.

43. Richard Ravitch and Paul Volcker et al., "A Statement from the Task Force Co-Chairs," in *Report of the State Budget Crisis Task Force*, July 2012, at http://www.statebudgetcrisis. org, concludes, "Pension funds for state and local government workers are underfunded by approximately a trillion dollars according to their actuaries and by as much as $3 trillion or more if more conservative investment assumptions are used. . . . Unfunded liabilities for health care benefits for state and local government retirees amount to more than $1 trillion," pp. 1–2. Howard Silverblatt et al., "S & P 500 2011: Pensions and Other Post-Employment Benefits (OPEB)," July 2012, http://www.spindices.com/documents /research/sp-500 2011-pensions-and-opeb-201207.pdf, shows record underfunding of pensions of major U.S. companies, with only 10 of 338 defined-benefit pension plans fully funded, and shortfalls of $10 billion or more posted by General Electric, Exxon Mobil, AT&T, Boeing, Ford, IBM, and Lockheed Martin. "For baby boomers, few options remain for securing a comfortable retirement. There are too few years left for boomers to significantly add income to their retirement resources, outside of staying in the workforce," judges Silverblatt, 1.

44. Jason DeParle, "Two Classes, Divided by 'I Do,'" *New York Times*, July 15, 1, 18.

45. See, for example, Silicon Valley Community Foundation, "2012: The City of San Jose's Budget Crisis," April 2012, https://www.siliconvalleycf.org/sites/default/files/SanJose Budget%20FactSheet%20FINAL.pdf; and California Tax Reform Association, "High-Tech, Low Tax," March 2012, http://arev.assembly.ca.gov/sites/arev.assembly.ca.gov/files/hear ings/Goldberg_Testimony_3-12-12.pdf.

46. Transition United States, "Transition 101," http://transitionus.org/transition-101; and Rob Hopkins, *The Transition Handbook: From Oil Dependency to Local Resilience* (White River Junction, VT: Chelsea Green, 2008).

47. Cf. Jeffrey Stout, *Blessed Are the Organized* (Princeton, NJ: Princeton University Press, 2010); and Robert Coles, "Social Struggle and Weariness," *Psychiatry* 27 (November 1964): 305–15.

48. Transition Towns, "In Transition 1.0," 2009, at https://vimeo.com/8029815, and Laura Whitehead, "In Transition 2.0," March 19, 2012, https://transitionnetwork.org/news-and -blog/in-transition-2-0/.

49. Ernst Callenbach, *Ecotopia* (New York: Bantam, 1990).

50. Alexis de Tocqueville, *Democracy in America*, ed. J. P. Mayer (Garden City, N.Y.: Double-day Anchor, 1969), vol. 2, pt. 2, chap. 5, "On the Use Which the Americans Make of Associations in Civil Life," 517.

51. See Chetty et al., "The Fading American Dream," on downward trends in absolute income mobility for cohorts born since 1940. On the uneven impact by age cohorts of losses in net worth see R. Morin and R. Fry, "More Americans Worry about Financing Retirement," showing adults aged thirty-five to forty-four losing 55 percent of their net worth between 2007 and 2010, those forty-five to fifty-four losing 40 percent, those fifty-five to sixty-four losing 33 percent, and those sixty-five and older losing 9 percent.

52. Congressional Budget Office, "The Budget and Economic Outlook: 2017 to 2027," January 2017, https://www.cbo.gov/publication/52370. In fiscal year 2015 24 percent of the federal budget paid for Social Security, 16 percent for Medicare, and 8 percent for federal retirees and veterans, excluding the elderly on Medicaid, calculates the Center on Budget and Policy Priorities, "Policy Basics: Where Do Our Federal Tax Dollars Go?" March 2016, from Office of Management and Budget data. See note 34 above on rising mandatory federal spending on older adults squeezing out discretionary spending on poor children and their families.

53. See Teresa Kroeger, Tanyell Cooke, and Elise Gould, "The Class of 2016," Economic Policy Institute, April 21, 2016, http://www.epi.org/publication/class-of-2016/; Patricia Cohen, "Young, Without Degree or Prospects," *New York Times*, May 12, 2016, B1, B8; and Nelson Schwartz, "Salary Gap Widens as Top Workers in Specialized Fields Reap Rewards," *New York Times*, July 24, 2015, on top-tier bright-collar pay pulling away from pay near the bottom in fields such as health care over the past decade; and pay for graduates in science, technology, engineering, and math likewise pulling away from liberal arts graduates, as engineers from the class of 2014 started at $65,000 a year, compared to $42,000 for the liberal arts. See note 31 above on life expectancy, jobless rates, and wage gaps diverging by race and ethnicity.

54. Sabrina Tavernise, "Whites Account for under Half of Births in U.S.," *New York Times*, May 17, 2012, http://www.nytimes.com/2012/05/17/us/whites-account-for-under-half -of-births-in-us.html, as non-Hispanic whites, given a median age of 42, accounted for only 49.6 percent of births, while racial and ethnic minorities and mixed-race births rose to 50.4 percent of all births from July 1, 2011, to June 30, 2012, and made up 92 percent of all U.S. population growth from 2000 to 2010. Hawaii, California, New Mexico, and Texas now count as majority-minority states; and nonwhites count for a majority in 348 of the 3,000 or so counties in the nation, a share that doubles when it comes to the population of toddlers.

55. See Sean F. Reardon, Demetra Kalogrides, and Kenneth Shores, "The Demography of Racial/Ethnic Test Score Gaps" (Working Paper No. 16-10, Stanford Center for Education Policy Analysis [CEPA], 2016) at https://cepa.stanford.edu/content/geography-racialethnic -test-score-gaps; Sean F. Reardon and Ximena A. Portilla, "Recent Trends in Income, Racial, and Ethnic School Readiness Gaps at Kindergarten Entry" (CEPA Working Paper No. 15-02, June 2016, https://cepa.stanford.edu/content/recent-trends-socioeconomic-and -racial-school-readiness-gaps-kindergarten-entry); Martha J. Bailey and Susan Dynarski,

"Gains and Gaps: Changing Inequality in U.S. College Entry and Completion" (NBER Working Paper 17633, December 2011) at http://www.nber.org/papers/w17633; and David Brooks, "The Opportunity Gap," *New York Times*, July 10, 2012, A19.

56. Alesina and Glaeser, *Fighting Poverty.*

57. Thomas B. Edsall, "Hello, Heterogenity," *New York Times*, June 4, 2012, citing exit poll data for 1992–2008 and 2020 projections by Alan I. Abramowitz, "Beyond 2010: Demographic Change and the Future of the Republican Party," Center for Politics, University of Virginia, March 11, 2010.

58. Robert D. Putnam and David Campbell, *American Grace: How Religion Divides and Unites Us* (New York: Simon & Schuster, 2010), chap. 8; and Edsall, "Hello, Heterogeneity," citing Robert P. Jones and Daniel Cox, "The 2011 American Values Survey," Public Religion Research Institute.

59. See Chetty et al., "The Fading American Dream," on absolute income mobility falling among successive cohorts of baby boomers; and Piketty, Saez, and Zucman, "Distributional National Accounts" on taxable labor income remaining flat since 1980 for 90 percent of earners. See Barry Bosworth, Gary Burtless, and Kan Zhang, "Later Retirement, Inequality in Old Age, and the Growing Gap in Longevity between Rich and Poor," Brookings Institution, 2016, https://www.brookings.edu/wpcontent/uploads/2016/02/BosworthBurtlessZhang_retirementinequalitylongevity_012815.pdf, estimating top-decile male earners born in 1920 can expect to live an average of 79.3 years, 5 years more than bottom-decile earners, increasing to 8 years more for men born 20 years later, in 1940; Raj Chetty et al., "The Association Between Income and Life Expectancy in the United States, 2001–2014, *Journal of the American Medical Association* 315, no. 16 (2016): 1750–66, reporting life expectancy in the top 1 percent of earners now exceeds those in the bottom 1 percent by 15 years for men and 10 years for women; Henry J. Aaron, "Demographic Effects on the Equity of Social Security Benefits," in *The Economics of Public Services*, ed. Martin S. Feldstein and Robert P. Inman (New York: Macmillan, 1977), 151–73; and U.S. Government Accountability Office, "Retirement Security: Shorter Life Expectancy Reduces Projected Lifetime Benefits for Lower Earners," GAO-16-354, March 2016, https://www.gao.gov/assets/680/676086.pdf, reporting that life expectancy for the bottom decile of male wage earners turning 66 in 2016 has risen 0.7 of a year over the past 30 years, compared to 8.1 years for the top decile of male wage earners.

60. Earning enough to save for a secure retirement, and reversing more than 70 percent of the decline in absolute income mobility for cohorts born since 1940, requires more equal distribution of income from economic growth, not just greater GDP growth, conclude Chetty et al., "The Fading American Dream." Cf. Tipton, "Social Differentiation and Moral Pluralism," 15–40, 278–81 (see preface, n. 5); and Roger Friedland and Robert P. Alford, "Bringing Society Back In: Symbols, Practices, and Institutional Contradictions," in Walter W. Powell and Paul J. DiMaggio, eds., *The New Institutionalism in Organizational Analysis* (Chicago: University of Chicago Press, 1991), 204–31.

# CHAPTER 2

1. Hospital for Special Surgery advertisement, *New York Times*, November 15, 2010, A11. HSS was ranked #1 in the nation for orthopedics and #5 for geriatrics by *U.S. News & World Report* in its 2013–14 "Best Hospitals" survey.

2. Taylor, *Sources of the Self* (Cambridge, MA: Harvard University Press, 1989), 355–521; and Colin Campbell, *The Romantic Ethic and the Spirit of Consumerism* (Oxford: Basil Blackwell, 1987).

3. Wallace Stevens, "Peter Quince at the Clavier," *The Collected Poems of Wallace Stevens* (New York: Knopf, 1965), 91.

4. See Michel Foucault, "On the Genealogy of Ethics," in Paul Rabinow, ed., *The Foucault Reader* (New York: Pantheon Books, 1984), 340–72, on "taking care of oneself" in classical, Christian, and modern cultural contexts.

5. Prudential Insurance Company, "Day One Stories Presented by Prudential," originally at http://www.dayonestories.com. See "Real-Life Retirement Stories—#DayOne," https://www.youtube.com/playlist?list=PLCD12E008DA3AF671.

6. AARP, "What's Next in Your Life," at http://www.aarp.org/. Videos no longer accessible.

7. Raymond James Financial Services, Inc., "Life Well Planned," at www.lifewellplanned.com. Site content has changed since this writing.

8. Here and below, see Benjamin Franklin, *The Way to Wealth* (1757; Princeton, NJ: Princeton Cambridge, 2010); and Franklin, *The Autobiography of Benjamin Franklin, including Poor Richard's Almanack, and Familiar Letters* (1791; New York: Cosimo, 2011), 224, 239. See also *Wikiquote*, s.v. "Benjamin Franklin," https://en.wikiquote.org/wiki/Benjamin_Franklin; and Bartleby.com, http://www.bartleby.com/349/authors/77.html.

9. See Max Weber, *The Protestant Ethic and the Spirit of Capitalism* (New York: Scribner, 1958), chap. 2, esp. 52–54, on the duty and virtue of "proficiency in a calling" rooted in a Calvinist soteriology at odds with eudaemonism, translated into an entrepreneurial ethic of success by Benjamin Franklin, and imposed as an institutional necessity by the "iron cage" of industrial capitalism.

10. Franklin, *The Way to Wealth*, 17–18 (see note 8, above).

11. Ibid.

12. Benjamin Franklin, *Autobiography. Poor Richard. Letters* (New York: D. Appleton, 1902), 232.

13. Raymond James, Inc., "Life Well Planned."

14. Interview, San Francisco, June 2011.

15. Interview, Palo Alto, September 2011.

16. Quoted from Thich Nhat Hanh, *The Art of Power* (New York: HarperOne, 2007): "Love is critical to our happiness. . . . What is the use of having more money if you suffer more? You become a victim of your own success. . . . To me a civilized society is one where people have the time to live their daily lives deeply, to love and take care of their family and community," 14–15.

17. Interview, San Francisco, September 2011.

18. "There are 47 percent of the people who will vote for the president no matter what. There are 47 percent who are with him, who are dependent upon government, who believe that they are victims, who believe the government has a responsibility to care for them," Mitt Romney explained to donors to his 2012 bid to unseat an incumbent president wed to welfare-state support of the poor claiming entitlements in exchange for their votes, recorded at a Florida fundraising dinner in a video released by *Mother Jones* magazine. See David Corn, "SECRET VIDEO: Romney Tells Millionaire Donors What He REALLY Thinks of Obama Voters," *Mother Jones*, September 17, 2012, http://www .motherjones.com/politics/2012/09/secret-video-romney-private-fundraiser/.

19. Interview, Atlanta, June 2011.

20. Interview, Berkeley, September 2012.

21. Interview, Palo Alto, September 2012.

22. See David C. Korten, *When Corporations Rule the World* (Bloomfield, CT: Kumarian, 1995); and Alan Trachtenberg, *The Incorporation of America* (New York: Hill and Wang, 1982).

23. Compare, for example, Duane Elgin, *Voluntary Simplicity: Toward a Way of Life That Is Outwardly Simple, Inwardly Rich* (New York: Harper, 2010), and Karl Marx on a truly communist society, "where nobody has one exclusive sphere of activity but each can become accomplished in any branch he wishes, society regulates the general production and thus makes it possible for me to do one thing today and another tomorrow, to hunt in the morning, fish in the afternoon, rear cattle in the evening, criticize after dinner, just as I have a mind, without ever becoming hunter, fisherman, shepherd or critic," in "The German Ideology" in *The Marx-Engels Reader*, ed. Robert C. Tucker (New York: Norton, 1978), 160; and Amy Zipkin, "Choosing the College Town Lifestyle in Retired Life," *New York Times*, November 26, 2016.

24. Erik H. Erikson, "Life Cycle," 286–92 in *International Encyclopedia of the Social Sciences*, ed. David L. Sills (New York: Free Press and Macmillan, 1968), esp. 286, 292.

25. Ibid., 291–92.

26. Here and below see Marc Freedman, *Encore: Finding Work that Matters Most in the Second Half of Life* (New York: PublicAffairs, 2007), 1–4ff.

27. Ibid., back cover.

28. Ibid., 4–6.

29. Ibid., 8–11.

30. Interview, Palo Alto, June 2011.

31. See Coleman Barks, *Rumi: The Book of Love* (New York: HarperCollins, 2003), 124; and biblical calls to die and be reborn, including Romans 6:3 and John 5:24.

32. Laura B. Shrestha, "Life Expectancy in the United States," Congressional Research Service, updated August 16, 2006, http://www.menshealthnetwork.org/Library/CRSlife

expectRL32792.pdf; Claude S. Fischer and Michael Hout, *Century of Difference* (New York: Russell Sage Foundation, 2006), 97, 302n4.

33. See Bureau of Labor Statistics, "Labor Force Participation and Work Status of People 65 Years and Older," January 2013, and *Monthly Labor Review*, December 2015 and December 2016; Paul Taylor et al., "America's Changing Workforce: Recession Turns a Graying Office Grayer," Pew Research Center, September 3, 2009, http://www.pew research.org/2009/09/03/recession-turns-a-graying-office-grayer/; and Rich Morin, "The Threshold Generation," Pew Research Center, May 28, 2009, on labor participation rates rising for cohorts turning sixty-five or older in 2005 and 2000, compared to the 1995 cohort.

34. Tatjana Meschede, Laura Sullivan, and Thomas Shapiro, "From Bad to Worse: Senior Economic Insecurity on the Rise," Institute on Assets and Social Policy, Brandeis University, July 2011, https://iasp.brandeis.edu/pdfs/2011/LLOL4.pdf.

35. Interview, Silicon Valley, 2012.

36. Interview, Atlanta, 2013.

37. Romans 8:38-39: "For I am convinced that neither death, nor life, nor angels, nor rulers, nor things present, nor things to come, nor powers, nor height, nor depth, nor anything else in all creation, will be able to separate us from the love of God in Christ Jesus our Lord."

38. See Ecclesiastes, esp. chaps. 1; 2:24; 3:1-22; 4:9-12; 5:15-20; 9:7-9; 12:5-14, with its echoes of Greek philosophy in reflecting on the limits of reason, questioning Hebrew tradition, and affirming that life with its limits is still worth living, before adding an orthodox postscript (12:9-14) to fear God and keep his commandments in order to grasp the sayings of the wise, for of "making many books there is no end, and much study is a weariness of the flesh."

39. See Mary Oliver, "When Death Comes," *New and Selected Poems* (Boston: Beacon Press, 2005), 1:10–11: "When it's over, I want to say: all my life/I was a bride married to amazement. / I was a bridegroom, taking the world into my arms. / . . . I don't want to end up simply having visited this world."

40. Interview, Silicon Valley, 2013. See the 1928 Book of Common Prayer of the Episcopal Church of the United States, "The Order for the Burial of the Dead," 324.

41. See Shunryu Suzuki, "Nirvana, the Waterfall," in *Zen Mind, Beginner's Mind* (New York and Tokyo: Walker/Weatherhill, 1970), 88–91.

42. Interview, Atlanta, 2011.

43. See Frederick Buechner, "The End Is Life," *The Magnificent Defeat* (New York: Seabury Press, 1966), 85–86, professing that Jesus just "somehow got up, with life in him, and the glory upon him."

44. Interview, Atlanta, 2011.

45. See Marla F. Frederick, *Between Sundays: Black Women and Everyday Struggles of Faith* (Berkeley and Los Angeles: University of California Press, 2003), 10–18, on the moral agency of "spirituality" lived out among faithful friends, citizens, and community

activists—many of them retirees—every day of the week, by contrast to "religiosity" confined to churchly rites and routines on Sunday.

46. Taylor et al., "Twenty to One: Wealth Gaps Rise to Record Highs between Whites, Blacks and Hispanics," Pew Research Center, July 2011, at http://www.pewsocialtrends .org/2011/07/26/wealth-gaps-rise-to-record-highs-between-whites-blacks-hispanics/, citing Census Bureau data to show that the median wealth of African-American households fell by 53 percent from 2005 to 2009, Hispanics by 66 percent, and Asians by 54 percent, compared to 16 percent for whites, yielding median wealth for whites twenty times that of Black households in 2009, at their lowest point in net worth since 1984. Blacks with no net worth rose from 29 percent in 2005 to 35 percent in 2009, Hispanics from 23 to 33 percent, and whites from 11 to 15 percent.

47. Mary Pattillo, "The Black Middle Class as Employees and Consumers," *New York Times*, July 25, 2011, argues that partisan "war on big government" wounds middle-class black families most of all as both public-sector workers and citizens who depend on public schooling, public hospitals, and public safety, since the public sector is the leading employer of black men and the second-largest employer of black women, totaling more than one in five employed blacks, compared to one in seven whites.

48. See Barbara Dafoe Whitehead, "The Changing Pathway to Marriage," in *Family Transformed* (Washington, DC: Georgetown Press, 2005), ed. Steven M. Tipton and John Witte Jr., 168–84; and D'Vera Cohn, "Love and Marriage," Pew Research Center, February 2013, http://www.pewsocialtrends.org/2013/02/13/love-and-marriage/.

# CHAPTER 3

1. The Bible has little to say about age-graded retirement as an institutional practice beyond specifying that Levite men at the age of fifty years "must retire from their regular service and work no longer," as God told Moses (Numbers 8:23-26 NIV), although they may still assist their younger brothers in performing their duties at the tent of meeting.

2. On the importance of human work before the fall, its transformation to toil afterwards, and the intellectual and physical tasks given to the man in Genesis 2 to make him co-creator with Yahweh, given the gift of human life formed from the dust of the ground and animated by God breathing into it to make a mortal union of earth and breath, by contrast to a tripartite mortal body, mind, and immortal soul, see Gene M. Tucker, "The Good Life: Human Existence in the Old Testament," unpublished lecture, 2010–2012.

3. Louis Dumont, "A Modified View of Our Origins: The Christian Beginnings of Modern Individualism," *Religion* 12 (1982): 1–27. On obedience to God as the appropriate response to God's saving act in the Exodus, before the law is given, see Gene M. Tucker, "Reading and Preaching the Old Testament," in *Listening to the Word*, ed. Thomas G. Long and Gail O'Day (Nashville: Abingdon Press, 1993), 33–51. God chose and constituted Israel as God's people out of love, Deuteronomy emphasizes (4:37-40), and Israel's obedience to God should therefore be motivated by a responding love (6:4-5), even if keeping God's statutes and commandments will bring blessings of long life and prosperity to the people and their posterity in the promised land (4:40), and disobedience will bring curses unto death, including fire and brimstone, like the rain that destroyed

Sodom and Gomorrah (29:22-23). Cf. modern debates over divine command and deontological ethics, including G. E. M. Anscombe, "Modern Moral Philosophy," *Philosophy* 33 (1958): 1–19; Alan Donagan, *The Theory of Morality* (Chicago: University of Chicago Press, 1977); and Edward Wierenga, *The Nature of God* (Ithaca, NY: Cornell University Press, 1989), in light of Kant's formulation in *The Groundwork of the Metaphysics of Morals* of the categorical imperative as an objective, rationally necessary, and unconditional principle authored by an autonomous rational will, and the claim in his *Critique of Practical Reason* that meeting the demands of the moral law requires belief in God and an afterlife to provide just rewards of happiness proportionate to good conduct and character in this life.

4. Robert N. Bellah, *Religion in Human Evolution* (Cambridge, MA: Harvard University Press, 2011), 316–23; Stephen A. Geller, "God of the Covenant," in *One God or Many? Concepts of Divinity in the Ancient World*, ed. Barbara Nevling Porter, *Transactions of the Casco Bay Assyriological Institute* 1 (2000): 290–96.

5. Robert L. Calhoun, "Work and Vocation in Christian History," in John Oliver Nelson, ed., *Work and Vocation* (New York: Harper and Brothers, 1954), 82–115; Robert A. Markus, "Work and Worker in Early Christianity," in John Todd, *Work* (London: Darton, Longman and Todd, 1960), 13–26; and Wayne Meeks, *The Origins of Christian Morality: The First Two Centuries* (New Haven, CT: Yale University Press, 1995).

6. Calhoun, "Work and Vocation in Christian History," 91–94. Pachomius, a former Roman soldier, organized an early monastic community in upper Egypt according to a common rule joining rites of prayer with military regimen to provide for adequate rest and food, apprenticeship for novices, and a discipline shared for all monks, who must work at skilled trades. Basil, a graduate of the Platonic academy in Athens, built a monastery in the East with a hospital, guest house, and workshops designed to follow the maxim "Zealous work is as necessary as daily bread," and to fulfill the law of neighbor-love through diligent and devoted labor. Benedict's rule in the West followed Basil in rejecting solitary asceticism, while ordering labor, study, and rest in monastic communities of prayer; and calling for work in the library and copying room for those too frail or old for heavy labor.

7. See Bellah, *Religion in Human Evolution*, 8–11, here and below; Max Joseph, "Sabbath," in Isaac Landman, ed., *The Universal Jewish Encyclopedia* (New York: Universal Jewish Encyclopedia Co., Inc., 1943), 295; "Jewish Religious Year: The Sabbath," *Encyclopedia Britannica* (Encyclopedia Britannica Online, 2009); Isaac Klein, *A Guide to Jewish Religious Practice* (New York: Jewish Theological Seminary of America, 1979); Judith Shulevitz, "How the Sabbath Keeps the Jewish People," *Haaretz*, April 2, 2010, quoting Ahad Ha'am.

8. "Sabbath" and "Sunday," in F. L. Cross, ed., *The Oxford Dictionary of the Christian Church* (Oxford: Oxford University Press, 2005); Everett Ferguson, "Sabbath," *Encyclopedia of Early Christianity* (Abingdon, UK: Routledge, 2013), 1007–8; R. J. Bauckham, "Sabbath and Sunday in the Post-Apostolic Church," "Sabbath and Sunday in the Medieval Church in the West," and "Sabbath and Sunday in the Protestant Tradition," in Don A. Carson, ed., *From Sabbath to Lord's Day: A Biblical, Historical and Theological Investigation* (Grand Rapids, MI: Zondervan, 1982; repr., Eugene, OR: Wipf & Stock, 1999), 252–98, 299–310, 311–42.

9. Westminster Confession of Faith (1646), chap. 21, "Of Religious Worship and the Sabbath Day," sec. 7, Center for Reformed Theology and Apologetics (CRTA), at http://www.reformed.org/documents/wcf_with_proofs/index.html?body=/documents/wcf_with_proofs/ch_XXI.html. See Augustine, *De Civitate Dei*, Bk. 10, chap. 6: "This is the Christian's sacrifice. We are one body with Christ, as the Church celebrates in the sacrament of the altar . . . wherein is shown that in that oblation the Church is offered." Cf. *Augsburg Confession* (1530), Article XXIV; and the Thirty-Nine Articles of Religion (1563), Article XXXI.

10. See Bellah, *Religion in Human Evolution*, 10–11, on rites of Sabbath observance by reference to ethics of prayerful work and prayer as the work of God among Benedictine monks, work as meditative practice among Zen Buddhist monks, and diligent Puritans as monks in the world of everyday work and family life.

11. A. W. H. Adkins, *Moral Values and Political Behaviour in Ancient Greece* (New York: Norton, 1972), 25–26, citing Hesiod, *Works and Days,* and Phocylides (fragment 10). Adkins, 32–57, interprets moral excellence and virtue (*arête*) as a matter of competitive success in tension with cooperative forms of moral excellence in the historical shift of Greek society from the stability of a landed aristocracy farming small family plots across generations to more individual and risky forms of commercial and artisanal enterprise in a money economy that expands economic inequality and sparks civic strife. Obedience to law by citizens who can rule and be ruled with equal justice ranks first among the virtues for Plato in the *Laws*, (922a, 667a), by contrast to the warrior-like courage of oligarchs, who compete in public affairs to help their own households and friends, and harm their enemies within the city, in the name of defending the freedom or self-sufficiency of an individual, clan, or faction.

12. Ibid., 36. *The Laws of Plato*, translated by Thomas L. Pangle (New York: Basic Books, 1980).

13. Adkins, *Moral Values*, 40.

14. Aristotle, *Politics*, 1986–2129, and *Nicomachean Ethics*, 1729–1867, in Barnes, ed., *The Complete Works of Aristotle*, vol. 2 (see chap. 1, n. 41).

15. A. W. H. Adkins, *Merit and Responsibility* (Oxford: Oxford University Press, 1960), 346–51, 354nn18–25, criticizes Aristotle in book 10 of the *Nicomachean Ethics* for declaring "theorizing" or abstract speculation as the most perfect *arête*, and so subordinating practical and moral forms of excellence essential to civic merit and responsibility, contra Plato and Aristotle's own account in the *Politics*. By appealing to ideals of self-sufficiency and completeness in favor of philosophy as the most excellent human activity, charges Adkins, Aristotle rehearses to a new elite class of philosophizing intellectuals the cardinal virtue of the self-reliant aristocrat of earlier Greek society centered on households and clans led by elite warriors, and he fails to integrate such autonomy and independence with the moral claims of both family and city-state.

16. On the merger of moral transformation, religious piety, and civic duty by Epictetus on human purpose, see Luke Timothy Johnson, *Among the Gentiles: Greco-Roman Religion and Christianity,* (New Haven, CT: Yale University Press, 2009) chap. 5, esp. pp. 69–77, including its translation of Epictetus, "On Providence," 76–77. On care of the self at the center of ancient ethics of moral agency in counterpoint to Christianity and modernity, see Michel Foucault, "The Genealogy of Ethics: An Overview of Work in Progress" and

"The Ethics of the Concern for Self as a Practice of Freedom," in Paul Rabinow, ed., *The Essential Works of Michel Foucault*, vol. 1: *Ethics: Subjectivity and Truth* (New York: New Press, 1997), 253–80, 281–307

17. Calhoun, "Work and Vocation in Christian History," 94–111. By the end of the sixth century, church life led by Gregory I (590–604) comes to center on ideals embodied by a spreading network of monastic settlements, with fixed hours of work and sleep set within a daily round of prayer and praise devoted to God, which in turn become moral models for a newly civilized way of life in society at large. Monastic norms of constructive labor for all who can prayerfully pursue it counterpoint feudal forms of a contemplative quest for perfection as a higher order of Christian virtue that echoes Aristotle's highest good. Sacraments discipline the whole of daily life in the church governed by clerical hierarchies in dioceses and orders religious. Laymen organize quasi-monastic military orders for nobles, and guilds order the ranks of merchants and artisans growing in the middle classes of late medieval cities. Lay reform movements and quasi-monastic brotherhoods seek to simplify, localize, and democratize church life in vernacular languages, while Christian universities arise as guilds of scholars that rehearse old orders of work and rest as they create new ones in terms Aquinas sums up in the thirteenth century: God grants spiritual and civil authority to church and state through their respective ranks as members of organic bodies politic. Work as rationally ordered by God's providence serves the common life of humankind as a whole. Spiritual works of prayer, preaching, and contemplation rank higher than material "manual works" in the moral and social hierarchy of work, but all are necessary for human survival and civilization.

18. Cf. Weber, *The Protestant Ethic and the Spirit of Capitalism* (New York: Scribner, 1958), esp. chaps. 3–5 (see chap. 2, n. 9); and Robert N. Bellah, "Religious Evolution," especially pages 36–39 in his *Beyond Belief: Essays on Religion in a Post-Traditionalist World* (Berkeley and Los Angeles: University of California Press, 1991); and Martin Brecht, *Martin Luther: His Road to Reformation 1483–1521* (Minneapolis: Fortress Press, 1985), 62.

19. Bellah, "Religious Evolution," 37–39.

20. Weber, *The Protestant Ethic*, 85–88.

21. John Milton, *Paradise Lost*, XII, 581–87ff, in *Paradise Lost and Other Poems*, annotated by Edward Le Comte (New York: Penguin, 2000).

22. Calvin, *Commentaries* (Philadelphia: Westminster, 1958), 283.

23. Cf. Cotton Mather, *Essays to Do Good* (Boston, 1701), 21; J. I. Packer, "Doctrine of Justification in Development and Decline among the Puritans," *Westminster Conference Report 1969* (London, 1970); and Robert Michaelson, "Changes in the Puritan Concept of Calling or Vocation," in *New England Quarterly* 26 (September 1953), 331–56.

24. Richard M. Douglas, "Talent and Vocation in Humanist and Protestant Thought," in T. K. Rabb and Jerrold E. Siegel, eds., *Action and Conviction in Early Modern Europe* (Princeton, NJ: Princeton University Press, 1969), 261–98; and Douglas, "*Genus Vitae and Vocatio*: Ideas of Work and Vocation in Humanist and Protestant Usage," Publication No. 71, Department of Humanities, MIT, 1965.

25. K. A. Becker, "History of the Stanford–Binet Intelligence Scales: Content and Psychometrics," *Stanford-Binet Intelligence Scales, Fifth Edition Assessment Service Bulletin*, no. 1, 2003.

26. Cf. Weber, *Protestant Ethic*, 181–83, and Campbell, *The Romantic Ethic and the Spirit of Consumerism*, esp. 1–14, 202–27 (see chap. 2, n. 2); Ernst Troeltsch, *The Social Teaching of the Christian Churches* (New York: Harper and Row, 1960), esp. 729–802; Robert N. Bellah et al., *Habits of the Heart* (Berkeley and Los Angeles: University of California Press, 1985), chaps. 2, 3, 5, 9.

27. Cf. Thomas Hobbes, *Leviathan: Or the Matter, Forme, and Power of a Commonwealth Ecclesiasticall and Civil*, ed. Michael Oakeshott (New York: Collier Books, 1962); and Adam Smith, *The Theory of Moral Sentiments* (Oxford: Oxford University Press, 1976).

28. Smith, *Theory of Moral Sentiments*, I.ii.4.1–3, 39–40.

29. William Wordsworth, "The World Is Too Much with Us," *Poems in Two Volumes* (London: Longman, 1807).

30. Ralph Waldo Emerson, *Nature* (Boston: James Munroe and Company, 1836), esp. introduction, chaps. 1, 6–8.

31. Immanuel Kant, *Kritik der reinen Vernunft*, ed. R. Schmidt (Leipzig, 1944), 95, quoted in Josef Pieper, *Leisure: The Basis of Culture* (San Francisco: Ignatius, 2009), 26–27.

32. Immanuel Kant, *Von einem neuerdings erhobenen vornehmen Ton in der Philosophie* (Hamburg: Meiner, 1920), 387–406, esp. 390. Cf. Ancient Greek and medieval praise of receptive, contemplative modes of intellectual knowledge as well as sensuous perception, for example, Heraclitus in behalf of "listening to the essence of things" in Fragment 112 (Diels); and Aquinas in *Quaestiones disputate de veritate*, 15, 1, in behalf of the non-discursive "faculty of spiritual vision," exercising the capacity of *simplex intuitis* in understanding as *intellectus*, by medieval contrast to understanding as *ratio*. "The essence of virtue consists in the good rather than in the difficult," judges Aquinas, so virtue enables us to follow our natural bent—as given by God, springing from divine love, and joining in the play of divine wisdom—instead of laboring to master our natural inclinations at Kantian odds with the moral law. Cf. Kant's *Kritik* and Aquinas, *Summa Theologica* II–II, 123, 12 ad 2, as quoted in Pieper, *Leisure*, 28–29, 33–34. Romantic expressivism since Rousseau rises to challenge Lockean deism and Kantian rationalism in defining selfhood in the modern West alongside cultural currents of scientized naturalism and Judeo-Christian theism, argues *Sources of the Self* (Cambridge, MA: Harvard University Press, 1989), 428ff.

33. Cf. Alfred Lord Tennyson, "In Memoriam A. H. H.," 1849, or "The Way of the Soul": "I hold it true, whate'er befall; / I feel it when I sorrow most: / 'Tis better to have loved and lost / Than never to have loved at all." Canto 27; Hoagie Carmichael and Mitchell Parish, "Stardust" (Warner/ Chappell Music, PeerMusic, EMI, 1929); Pharrell Williams, "Happy" (EMI/April Music, 2014); George and Ira Gershwin, "Our Love Is Here to Stay" (Gershwin/ Chappell Music, 1938); and Foucault, "Technologies of the Self," in his *Ethics: Subjectivity and Truth*, 249.

34. Alexis de Tocqueville, *Democracy in America*, ed. J. P. Mayer (Garden City, NY: Doubleday Anchor, 1969), 535–37.

35. Ibid., 530.

36. Franklin, *The Way to Wealth* (1757; Princeton, NJ: Princeton Cambridge Publishing Group, 2010), 6–7, 11.

37. Thomas Bender, *Community and Social Change in America* (Baltimore and London: Johns Hopkins University Press, 1982).

38. John W. Meyer, "Self and Life Course: Institutionalization and Its Effects," in Thomas et al., *Institutional Structure* (Newbury Park, CA: SAGE Publications, 1987), 242–47ff (see chap. 1, n. 5).

39. Cf. Meyer, "Self and Life Course"; and Taylor, *Modern Social Imaginaries* (Durham and London: Duke University Press, 2004), esp. 1–30.

40. Across party lines, 76 percent of Americans are worried about insecurity in retirement, 88 percent agree that "the nation faces a retirement crisis," and more than two in three favor secure defined-benefit pensions over 401(k) plans, support public-sector pensions, and oppose reducing Social Security benefits for both current and future retirees, according to Diane Oakley and Kelly Kenneally, "Retirement Security 2017," National Institute on Retirement Security, February 2017, http://www.nirsonline.org/storage/nirs /documents/2017%20Conference/2017_opinion_nirs_final_web.pdf.

41. Social Security Administration, "FDR's Statements on Social Security," available at https://www.ssa.gov/history/fdrstmts.html, as quoted here and below. Also see Social Security Administration, "Historical Background and Development of Social Security," esp. 28–37, https://www.ssa.gov/history/briefhistory3.html.

42. Senator Bernie Sanders, "Text of Bernie's Announcement," May 26, 2015, https://bernie sanders.com/news/bernies-announcement.

43. President Franklin Roosevelt, "Presidential Statement," August 14, 1935, American Presidency Project, http://www.presidency.ucsb.edu/ws/?pid=14916.

44. President Franklin Roosevelt, "Message to Congress," June 8, 1934, American Presidency Project, http://www.presidency.ucsb.edu/ws/index.php?pid=14690.

45. President Franklin Roosevelt, "Message to Congress on Social Security," January 17, 1935, https://www.ssa.gov/history/fdrstmts.html#message2.

46. Senator Bernie Sanders, "Dear Colleague Letter on the So-Called 'Fiscal Cliff,'" November 28, 2012, at http://www.democraticunderground.com/10021904482.

47. Bernard Sanders et al., letter to colleagues, 2012, 1, https://www.sanders.senate.gov/imo /media/doc/092012-DearColleague.pdf.

48. President Franklin Roosevelt, "Fireside Chat," September 30, 1934, American Presidency Project, http://www.presidency.ucsb.edu/ws/?pid=14759, here and below.

49. President Franklin Roosevelt, "Radio Address on the Third Anniversary of Social Security," August 15, 1938, American Presidency Project, http://www.presidency.ucsb.edu/ws/index .php?pid=15523.

50. President Franklin Roosevelt, "Campaign Address on the 'Economic Bill of Rights,'" October 28, 1944, https://www.ssa.gov/history/fdrstmts.html#bill of rights, here and below.

51. See Saez, "Striking It Richer: The Evolution of Top Incomes in the United States," University of California, Berkeley, updated June 2016 from *Pathways* magazine, Winter 2008; and Piketty, Saez, and Zucman, "Distributional National Accounts" (see chap. 1, n. 59). From 1947 to 1979 median family income more than doubled to $58,573 in 2013 dollars, at a pace that would have topped $124,000 by 2013 instead of reaching only $63,815, reported John Harwood, "For Solution to Income Stagnation, Republicans and Democrats Revise their Playbooks," *New York Times*, December 29, 2014, A10. Also see Eileen Patten and Jens Manuel Krogstad, "Black Child Poverty Rate Holds Steady, Even as Other Groups See Declines," Pew Research Center, July 14, 2015, http://www.pewresearch.org/fact-tank/2015/07/14/black-child-poverty-rate-holds-steady-even-as-other-groups-see-declines/; and chap. 1, n. 18.

52. "President Barack Obama's Inaugural Address," January 21, 2009, posted by Mason Phillips, White House: Archives, https://obamawhitehouse.archives.gov/blog/2009/01/21/president-barack-obamas-inaugural-address, as quoted here and below.

53. "Inaugural Address by President Barack Obama," The White House, Office of the Press Secretary, January 21, 2013, at https://obamawhitehouse.archives.gov/the-press-office/2013/01/21/inaugural-address-president-barack-obama.

54. Cf. Obama, "Inaugural Address," 2013, and *Mother Jones*, "Romney Tells Millionaire Donors what he REALLY Thinks of Obama Voters," September 17, 2012, transcribed from a video recording of Mitt Romney speaking at a campaign fundraiser in Boca Raton, Florida, May 17, 2012 (see chap. 2, n. 18). In 2011, 46.4 percent of American households paid no federal income tax, according to IRS data analyzed by the Tax Policy Center, but two-thirds of these households did pay payroll taxes, and most paid some combination of state, local, property, sales, and gasoline taxes. More than half of all households paying no federal income taxes earn less than $16,812 per year, below the poverty line, with 44 percent moved off tax rolls by elderly tax benefits, and another 30 percent by credits for children and the working poor. Of the 18.1 percent of American households paying neither federal income taxes nor payroll taxes in 2011, 10.3 percent were elderly and 6.9 percent were non-elderly households earning under $20,000 per year. Voters over sixty-five favored Romney over Obama by 53 to 38 percent in 2012 polls, as did voters in eight of the top ten states with the lowest income tax liability. See Molly Moorhead, "Mitt Romney Says 47 Percent of Americans Pay no Income Tax," PolitiFact, September 18, 2012, http://www.politifact.com/truth-o-meter/statements/2012/sep/18/mitt-romney/romney-says-47-percent-americans-pay-no-income-tax/.

55. Rep. Steve Scalise, Chairman, Republican Study Committee, "RSC Release FY 2014 Budget: Back to Basics," March 18, 2013, press release; and "Back to Basics: A Fiscal Year 2014 Budget," at http://flores.house.gov/solutions/rsc-back-basics-fy2014-budget.htm. No longer accessible.

56. Ibid.

57. Judson Phillips, "A Cause to Rally to; a Battle to Fight," *Tea Party Nation Forum*, March 19, 2013, 4, at http://www.teapartynation.com/forum/topics/a-cause-to-rally-to-a-battle-to-fight. No longer accessible.

58. Jonathan Tasini, "Playboy Interview: Bernie Sanders," *Playboy*, October 17, 2013, 130.

59. Sanders, "Text of Bernie's Announcement."

60. Cf. Patrick Healy, "Bernie Sanders's Message Resonates with a Certain Age Group: His Own," *New York Times*, May 28, 2015; Bernie Sanders, quoted in W. Gardner Selby, "Half of All Americans Have Less than $10,000 in their Savings Accounts," April 9, 2015, PolitiFact, http://www.politifact.com/texas/statements/2015/apr/09/bernie-s/bernie-sanders-says -half-americans-have-less-10000/; U.S. Government Accountability Office, "Retirement Security: Most Households Approaching Retirement Have Low Savings," GAO-15-419, May 12, 2015, at https://www.gao.gov/products/GAO-15-419.

61. "Clinton and Trump: Their Plans for Social Security," *AARP Bulletin* 57, no. 56, July–August, 2016, 10.

62. Adam Nagourney and Jeff Zeleny, "Clinton Uses Sharp Tactics in Tense Debate," *New York Times*, April 17, 2008, A16; and Jonathan Easley, "Sanders Presses Clinton on Social Security Plan," *The Hill*, April 14, 2016.

63. Democratic Platform Committee, 2016 Democratic Party Platform, July 21, 2016, http://www.presidency.ucsb.edu/papers_pdf/117717.pdf, 6–7. Democratic policy initiatives to expand Social Security, fueled by grass-roots progressive coalitions since 2013, led to more than twenty bills introduced by lawmakers, including Bernie Sanders and Elizabeth Warren in 2015, advanced Sanders's presidential campaign, and moved Hillary Clinton to support higher benefits in the 2016 primary campaign, reported Mark Miller, "Social Security Expansion Gaining Support in Washington," *New York Times*, July 16, 2016, B4.

64. See National Committee to Preserve Social Security and Medicare, "Trump 2.0 on Social Security," February, 2016, http://www.ncpssm.org/EntitledtoKnow/entryid/2189/trump -2-0-on-social-security; and "Clinton and Trump," *AARP Bulletin*, 10.

65. See "Clinton and Trump," 10; and Jon Perr, "GOP Platform Breaks Trump's 'No Cuts' Promise on Social Security and Medicare," *Daily Kos*, July 24, 2016, https://www.dailykos .com/stories/2016/7/24/1550423/-GOP-platform-breaks-Trump-s-no-cuts-promise-on -Social-Security-and-Medicare.

66. Committee on Arrangements for the 2016 Republican National Convention, Republican Platform 2016, 23–25. Private accounts for Social Security dropped from Paul Ryan's budget plans after GOP House resistance in 2010 to their estimated cost of $2 trillion, but efforts to privatize Medicare persisted in the House. Despite Trump's campaign pledges to the contrary, the 2016 Republican Platform vowed to transform Medicare to a "premium support model" of capped vouchers to purchase private insurance and shift health care costs onto seniors themselves, according to Jon Perr, "GOP Platform Breaks Trump's 'No Cuts' Promise." In December 2016, Sam Johnson (R-TX), chairman of the House Social Security subcommittee, introduced a bill backed by the House Freedom Caucus to slash Social Security benefits for all but the poorest beneficiaries, raise the retirement age to 69, reduce annual cost-of-living adjustments, and cut taxes that high earners pay on a portion of their benefits. Tom Price (R-GA), incoming Health and Human Services secretary, proposed automatic spending cuts on most federal programs in the event of rising debt levels, if Congress passed Trump's proposed tax cuts, including a projected $1.7 trillion cut to Social Security over ten years, equivalent to a cut of $168 in the average monthly benefit of $1,240, based on budget analysis by the Center for American Progress, cited in "Will Mr. Trump Cave on Social Security?" *New York Times*

editorial, December 18, 2016, SR10. Trump and Ryan agreed to support tax cuts for top earners, trim Medicaid for the poor, protect Social Security and Medicare for today's seniors, and prune them for tomorrow's seniors, while Trump added $3 trillion in middle-class tax cuts, $115–500 billion for child care and $137 billion in deficit-financed tax breaks for infrastructure, reports Matt O'Brien, "Donald Trump Is Just Another Republican When It Comes to the Budget," *Washington Post*, March 2, 2017.

67. Rakesh Kochhar, et al., "Attitudes about Aging: A Global Perspective," Pew Research Center, January 2014, at http://www.pewglobal.org/2014/01/30/attitudes-about-aging-a-global-perspective/, chap. 1, p. 10, 2013 survey, Q130.

68. See David Madland and Keith Miller, "Polling Shows Americans Want Retirement Policy Reform," Center for American Progress Action Fund, January 2014, 1–12, at https://www.americanprogressaction.org/issues/economy/reports/2014/01/30/83193/polling-shows-americans-want-retirement-policy-reform/; Robert J. Shiller, "How Wage Insurance Could Spur Innovation," *New York Times,* March 13, 2016, BU5; Robert J. Shiller, *The New Financial Order: Risk in the 21st Century* (Princeton, NJ: Princeton University Press, 2003); and Oakley and Kenneally, "Retirement Security 2017."

69. Edmund L. Andrews, "Federal Government Faces Balloon in Debt Payments," *New York Times*, November 23, 2009, A1, 4. On manifold moral goods, including the virtues of institutions as well as persons, see Tipton "Social Differentiation and Moral Pluralism," in *Meaning and Modernity: Religion, Polity, and Self*, ed. Richard Madsen et al. (Berkeley and Los Angeles: University of California Press, 2002), 15–40; and Roger Friedland and Robert R. Alford, "Bringing Society Back In: Symbols, Practices, and Institutional Contradictions," in Walter W. Powell and Paul J. DiMaggio, eds., *The New Institutionalism in Organizational Analysis* (Chicago: University of Chicago Press, 1991), 232–63. On the manifold languages and social spheres of justice, see Jennifer Hochschild, *What's Fair?* (Cambridge, MA: Harvard University Press, 1991); and Michael Walzer, *Spheres of Justice: A Defense of Pluralism and Equality* (New York: Basic Books, 1983), and Walzer, *Thick and Thin: Moral Argument at Home and Abroad* (Notre Dame, IN: University of Notre Dame Press, 1993).

# CHAPTER 4

1. Social Security Administration, "Annual Performance Plan for FY 2012," page 36: "Nearly 80 million baby boomers will file for retirement benefits over the next 20 years—an average of 10,000 per day." In 2011 the oldest baby boomers began turning sixty-five, and the cohort will continue to do so over a period of nineteen years, amounting to some 4 million people per year retiring at a rate of almost eleven thousand per day, with some retiring before or after turning sixty-five, yielding estimates of 80 million retiring over twenty years at ten thousand per day. See preface, n. 1.

2. Steven M. Tipton, *Getting Saved from the Sixties* (Berkeley and Los Angeles: University of California Press, 1982); Madsen, "The Archipelago of Faith, 1263–1301 (see preface, n. 2); Wilhelm, Rooney, and Tempel, "Changes in Religious Giving Reflect Changes in Involvement," 217–32 (see preface, n. 2).

3. Weber, "The Social Psychology of the World Religions," 267–301 (see preface, n. 3); and Bellah, "Religious Evolution," 358–74 (see ibid.).

4. Mark Chaves, *Congregations in America* (Cambridge, MA: Harvard University Press, 2004); Mark Chaves and Shawna Anderson, "Changing American Congregations," *Journal for the Scientific Study of Religion* 53, no. 4 (2014): 676–86; Mark Chaves, Helen M. Giesel, and William Tsitsos, "Religious Variations in Public Presence," in Robert Wuthnow and John H. Evans, eds., *The Quiet Hand of God* (Berkeley and Los Angeles: University of California Press, 2002), chap. 4; Omri Elisha, *Moral Ambition* (Berkeley and Los Angeles: University of California Press, 2011).

5. See, for example, Marla Frederick, *Between Sundays* (Berkeley and Los Angeles: University of California Press, 2003); Mary Pattillo-McCoy, *Black Picket Fences* (Chicago: University of Chicago Press, 2013); Richard L. Wood, *Faith in Action* (Chicago: University of Chicago Press, 2002); and Omar McRoberts, *Streets of Glory* (Chicago: University of Chicago Press, 2005).

6. Michael Hout and Claude S. Fischer, "Explaining Why More Americans Have No Religious Preference: Political Backlash and Generational Succession, 1987–2012," *Sociological Science* 1 (October 2014): 423–47; Cary Funk et al., "'Nones on the Rise: One-In-Five Adults Have No Religious Affiliation," Pew Research Center, October 9, 2012, http://www.pewforum.org/2012/10/09/nones-on-the-rise/; Gregory Smith et al, "U.S. Public Becoming Less Religious," Pew Research Center, November 3, 2015, http://www.pewforum.org/2015/11/03/u-s-public-becoming-less-religious/.

7. All material quoted and paraphrased here and below is drawn from repeated rounds of participant observation in these congregations in Silicon Valley and Atlanta in 2012–2015, including taped interviews with their members, leaders, and partners in selected service projects. I am grateful for their hospitality, honesty, and insight.

8. See Perry Miller, *The Life of the Mind in America: From the Revolution to the Civil War* (New York: Harcourt, Brace & World, 1965), pt. 1; Timothy L. Smith, *Revivalism and Social Reform* (Nashville: Abingdon Press, 1957); George Marsden, *Fundamentalism and American Culture* (Oxford: Oxford University Press, 2006); John Howard Yoder, *Body Politics: Five Practices of the Christian Community Before the Watching World* (Harrisonburg, VA: Herald Press, 1992); Rick Warren, *The Purpose Driven Church* (Grand Rapids, MI: Zondervan, 1995).

9. Cf. James Davison Hunter, *American Evangelicalism: Conservative Religion and the Quandary of Modernity* (New Brunswick, NJ: Rutgers University Press, 1983), chap. 3; Christian Smith, *American Evangelicalism: Embattled and Thriving* (Chicago: University of Chicago Press, 1998), chaps. 1–4; and George Marsden, "Preachers of Paradox," in Mary Douglas and Steven Tipton, eds., *Religion and America* (Boston: Beacon Press, 1983), 150–68.

10. "Divorce and Relationship Rescue" weekly meetings feature small-group discussion following psychologists, therapists, attorneys, and other expert speakers discussing "ways to heal and begin putting your life together," along with "Christian psychology video seminars," including series based on Henry Cloud and John Townsend, *Boundaries* (Grand Rapids, MI: Zondervan, 1992) and *Safe People* (Grand Rapids, MI: Zondervan, 1995).

11. Stephen Ministries is a national nonprofit Christian education organization that has trained more than six hundred thousand lay people "to provide high-quality, confidential, Christ-centered care" in one-to-one counseling relationships since 1975 in twelve thousand congregations in the United States and overseas to serve 1.5 million "people struggling through a difficult time in their life—experiencing grief, divorce, job loss, chronic or terminal illness, or some other life crisis," at http://www.stephen ministries.org.

12. See, for example, Menlo Church, "The Main Thing—Lessons from a Thousand Funerals," May 24, 2015, video interview and transcript, at http://menlo.church/sermon/the-main -thing-lessons-from-a-thousand-funerals/.

13. Ernst Troeltsch, *The Social Teaching of the Christian Churches* [1911] (London: Allen and Unwin, 1931); H. Richard Niebuhr, *The Social Sources of Denominationalism* (New York: Henry Holt, 1929) and *The Kingdom of God in America* (New York: Harper and Row, 1937); Martin Marty, *The Public Church* (New York: Crossroad, 1981); and David A. Roozen, William McKinney, and Jackson W. Carroll, *Varieties of Religious Presence: Mission in Public Life* (Cleveland: Pilgrim Press, 1983), chap. 2.

14. Cf. Tocqueville, *Democracy in America*, ed. J. P. Mayer (Garden City, NJ: Doubleday Anchor, 1969), 292ff; H. Richard Niebuhr, *Christ and Culture* (New York: Harper and Row, 1951); Stanley Hauerwas, *A Community of Character* (Notre Dame, IN: University of Notre Dame Press, 1981); David Hollenbach, "Justice as Participation," in *Justice, Peace, and Human Rights: American Catholic Social Ethics in a Pluralistic World* (New York: Crossroad, 1988), 72–83; and Steven M. Tipton, *Public Pulpits* (Chicago: University of Chicago Press, 2007), 425–42.

# Conclusion

1. Cf. Wallace Stevens, "The Good Man Has No Shape," *The Collected Poems of Wallace Stevens* (New York: Knopf, 1954), 364, considering Christ crucified by contrast to worldly ideals of the good life; and Aristotle, *Nicomachean Ethics* 1.10–11, weighing Solon's advice that no one be called happy while he still lives by contrast to happiness seen as inherently excellent activity of soul and the happy man as one who "will do and contemplate what is excellent, and he will bear the chances of life most nobly and altogether decorously, if he is 'truly good' and 'foursquare beyond reproach.'"(1100b, 18–21). See Kurt Pritzl, "Aristotle and Happiness after Death: Nicomachean Ethics 10–11," *Classical Philology* 78, no. 2 (April 1983): 101–11.

2. See, for example, "83 Things Every Man Should Do Before He Dies: Experiences, Endeavors, Opportunities, Journeys . . . ," *Esquire*, April 4, 2014, in light of Thomas Hobbes, "Life it selfe is but Motion, and can never be without Desire, nor without Feare, no more than without Sense." *Leviathan* [1651], ed. Michael Oakeshott (New York: Macmillan, 1962), pt. 1, chap. 6, p. 55. On market exchange and double-entry bookkeeping as models of moral meaning see Louis Dumont, *From Mandeville to Marx* (Chicago: University of Chicago Press, 1977), chap. 6; and Albert O. Hirschman, *The Passions and the Interests* (Princeton, NJ: Princeton University Press, 1977), pt. 1. On pain and pleasure alone governing what humankind should and shall do, see Jeremy Bentham, *An Introduction*

*to the Principles of Morals and Legislation* [1789] (London: Methuen, 1982), chaps. 1–2, 31–32, including the utilitarian logic of asceticism authorized by divine revelation, since God does not "either speak or write to us. How then are we to know what is his pleasure? By observing what is our own pleasure, and pronouncing it to be his."

3. On Romantic ideals of selfhood expressed here and now in the moment, see Taylor, *Sources of the Self* (Cambridge, MA: Harvard University Press, 1989), pts. 4–5; César Graña, *Bohemian versus Bourgeois* (New York: Basic Books, 1964); Campbell, *The Romantic Ethic and the Spirit of Consumerism* (see chap. 2, n. 2); and Tipton, *Getting Saved from the Sixties* (Berkeley and Los Angeles: University of California Press, 1982), chap. 1.

4. For criticism of utilitarian and expressive traditions of individualism in American culture, see Bellah et al., *Habits of the Heart* (Berkeley and Los Angeles: University of California Press, 1985), chaps 2, 3, 6, 11.

5. On social membership see Michael Walzer, *Spheres of Justice* (New York: Basic Books, 1983), chap. 2, and his *Thick and Thin* (Notre Dame, IN: University of Notre Dame Press, 1994), chap. 4; Bellah et al., *Habits of the Heart*, chaps. 4, 7–11; and Clifford Geertz, "Thick Description: Toward an Interpretive Theory of Culture," in his *The Interpretation of Cultures* (New York: Basic Books, 1973), 5, on cultural webs of significance humans spin through social relationships.

6. James Stockinger, "Locke and Rousseau: Human Nature, Human Citizenship, and Human Work," PhD diss., Department of Sociology, University of California, Berkeley, 1990, so depicts social interdependence enacted through "the hands of other people that supply the needs of our bodies, both in our infancy and beyond."

7. See Bellah, *Religion in Human Evolution* (Cambridge, MA: Harvard University Press, 2011), 8–43, on the ubiquity of rites of interaction and rites of passage; Walzer, *Spheres of Justice*, pt. 1, esp. pages 6–10, on diverse social goods distributed in distinct institutional spheres; and Steven M. Tipton, "Moral Languages and the Good Society," *Soundings* 69, nos. 1–2 (1986): 165–80, on the common pursuit of goods diverse enough to debate and share.

8. To compare forms of religious and philosophical conversion as modes of moral transformation, reform, and restoration from vice to virtue in early Christianity and diasporic Judaism within the Greco-Roman world, see Wayne Meeks, *The Origins of Christian Morality* (New Haven, CT: Yale University Press, 1993), esp. chaps. 2, 3, 6, 7, 9; and Luke Timothy Johnson, *Among the Gentiles* (New Haven, CT: Yale University Press, 2009), esp. chaps. 3, 5, 8, 11, 13, 16.

9. See Erik Erikson on the virtues of generativity in adulthood and wisdom in old age in accepting finitude as well as responsibility in his "Life Cycle," *International Encyclopedia of the Social Sciences* (New York: Macmillan, 1968), 4:286–92; Michael Walzer, "The Divided Self," 85–104 in his *Thick and Thin: Moral Argument at Home and Abroad* (Notre Dame, IN: University of Notre Dame Press, 1994) on the diverse moral perspectives of multiple selves tied to definite institutional roles and settings interrelated through both internal and public forms of moral dialogue and argument; and Wayne Meeks, "Senses of an Ending," 174–88, 192–95ff, in his *The Origins of Christian Morality*, on apocalyptic and eschatological visions of a single, universal final judgment by God of each person and the whole world.

10. On the cultural roots of modern common sense see Taylor, *Sources of the Self* and *A Secular Age* (Cambridge, MA: Harvard University Press, 2007); Hirschman, *The Passions and the Interests*; and Jean-Christophe Agnew, *Worlds Apart* (Cambridge, MA: Cambridge University Press, 1986). See Jürgen Habermas, *Religion and Rationality* (Cambridge, MA: MIT Press, 2002), 62–63, 130–33, 148–49, on the universalistic, egalitarian spirit of modern democracy, human rights, and the sovereignty of individual conscience as the legacy of the Judaic ethic of justice, the Christian ethic of love, and the Socratic ethic of reciprocity in unforced dialogue between autonomous human beings in a *polis*. For an institutionalist account of the modern world polity devolving from the dominant universalistic historical culture of Western religion and the global Christian church, circa 1500, see John W. Meyer, John Boli, and George M. Thomas, "Ontology and Rationalization in the Western Cultural Account," 28, in Thomas et al., *Institutional Structure* (Newbury Park, CA: SAGE Publications, 1987). For a history of the Western legal tradition developing from Greco-Roman and Judaic roots through the twelfth-century papal revolution, the Protestant revolutions of Lutheran Germany and Anglo-Calvinist England, then the French, American, and Russian revolutions, see Harold Berman, "The Western Legal Tradition in a Millennial Perspective: Past and Future," *Louisiana Law Review* 60, no. 3 (2000): 739–63, and his *Law and Revolution* (Cambridge, MA: Harvard University Press, 1983).

11. "There is an innumerable multitude of sects in the United States. They are all different in the worship they offer the Creator, but all agree concerning the duties of men to one another," observed Alexis de Tocqueville, *Democracy in America* [1835, 1840], trans. George Lawrence, ed. J. P. Mayer (New York: Harper Perennial Modern Classics, 2006), 290.

12. Cf. Deuteronomy 6:4-5, as interpreted by Stephen Geller and Robert Bellah; and Plato, *Laws*, I, 643–45, 650, as interpreted by A. W. H. Adkins, quoted and cited in chapter 3.

13. See Smith, *Theory of Moral Sentiments* (Oxford: Oxford University Press, 1976), pts. 1–6, on opposing interests, improper affections, selfish passions, corrupted moral sentiments, and the need of individuals to discipline their sense of propriety, merit, duty, and utility through heeding the authority of conscience as an impartial spectator and God's sovereign viceroy in each breast.

14. See, for example, Sigmund Freud, *Group Psychology and the Analysis of the Ego* [1922] (New York: W. W. Norton, 1959); David Riesman, *The Lonely Crowd* (New Haven, CT: Yale University Press, 1950); Abraham Maslow, *Motivation and Personality* (New York: Harper, 1954); Philip Rieff, *The Triumph of the Therapeutic* (New York: Harper, 1966); Bellah et al., *Habits of the Heart*, chaps. 3, 5; and Gregory Berns, *Satisfaction: Sensation, Novelty, and the Science of Finding True Fulfillment* (New York: Henry Holt, 2005).

15. Taylor, *Modern Social Imaginaries* (Durham and London: Duke University Press, 2004), 23–32, sums up this interplay of social imaginaries, moral practices, and institutions. Through images and stories, people share ways of imagining and understanding their social existence, how they fit together and interact, which underlie their mutual expectations and moral norms of how things usually go and ought to go. Such common understandings make shared practices possible, and these practices in turn largely carry these understandings implicitly, without explicit analysis or theorizing. This interplay yields the repertory of collective actions a given social group can learn and undertake at a given

time, for example, to take part in a general election, a pop concert, or a cocktail-party conversation. See Clifford Geertz, "Ethos, World View, and the Analysis of Sacred Symbols," in his *The Interpretation of Cultures*, 126–41, for a related dramaturgical account of symbolic meaning enacted in rites and scripted in myths that span social practices and institutions; and Wayne Meeks in *The Origins of Christian Morality* (New Haven, CT: Yale University Press, 1995) on the dramaturgical formation of a moral order through a set of Christian moral practices centered on baptism and the eucharistic supper, to show how "making morals means making community."

16. Cf. Aristotle, *Nicomachean Ethics*, bks. II–III; Plato, *Laws*, I, 643–45, 650ff; Alasdair MacIntyre, *After Virtue* (Notre Dame, IN: University of Notre Dame Press, 1981, 2007); and Tipton, "Social Differentiation and Moral Pluralism," in *Meaning and Modernity, Religion, and Self*, ed. Richard Madsen et al. (Berkeley and Los Angeles: University of California Press, 2002), 15–40, esp. 34, 280n40.

17. Here and below I draw on Carol Newsom, "Understanding and Hope in a Time of Climate Change: A Conversation with the Bible," 131–45 in Rex D. Matthews, ed., *The Vocation of Theology: Inquiry, Dialogue, Adoration* (Nashville: Wesley's Foundery Books, 2017) for its fresh reading and profound interpretation of Genesis to reframe covenantal human responsibility for the crisis of climate change within the encompassing story of biblical creation and eschatology. See Bellah, *Religion in Human Evolution*, ix–xxiv, 576–606, on play, ritual, and theory in axial-age utopias to reframe practical wisdom and responsibility in the face of ecological crisis today. On humans as cultural animals who must communicate to cooperate, see Clifford Geertz, "The Impact of the Concept of Culture on the Concept of Man," 33–54 in his *The Interpretation of Cultures*; and Jürgen Habermas, "Toward a Reconstruction of Historical Materialism," *Communication and the Evolution of Society* (Boston: Beacon Press, 1979), 130–77.

18. Newsom, "Understanding and Hope," 138–41, citing Genesis 1:26-30 on God giving humans earthly dominion; Genesis 2:17, Deuteronomy 4:26, 11:26, 30:19 on biblical blessing and curse; and Ecclesiastes 3:15, Isaiah 65:17, and Revelation 21:1 on cosmogonic and eschatological time. Warming by more than a half degree Fahrenheit since 2013, the earth reached its highest temperature on record in 2016 for the third year in a row to register since 2000 a total of sixteen of the seventeen hottest years recorded since 1880, according to NASA data, with Arctic heat extremes increasing the likelihood of an eventual rise of fifteen to twenty feet in sea level, reports Justin Gillis, "For Third Year the Earth in 2016 Hit Record Heat," *New York Times*, January 19, 2017, A1, 8.

19. Cf. Newsom, "Understanding and Hope," 142–45, citing Ezekiel 40–48 and Revelation 21–22, on eschatological urban visions of a New Eden and a New Jerusalem; Plato, *Laws*, 665c, on the good city perpetually singing to itself in moral harmony, with everyone sharing in hymns that continually change and vary in every way to give singers unsatiated pleasure in their performance; and Augustine, *Confessions*, (i.1,1) on humans joining angels in the eternal chorus of the City of God. See Anastasia-Erasmia Peponi, "Choral Anti-Aesthetics," in Peponi, ed., *Performance and Culture in Plato's Laws* (Cambridge: Cambridge University Press, 2013), 222.

# INDEX

Sweden, 77

Tax Policy Center, 209n54

taxes, 10, 13, 209n54

Taylor, Charles, 207n32, 208n39, 214n3, 214n10, 215n15

Tea Party movement, 13, 127, 129

Thoreau, Henry David, 112

Tillich, Paul, 22

Tocqueville, Alexis de, 40, 64, 113–14, 215n11

Trump, Donald, 13, 15; election of, 194n31, 196n36; on entitlements, 129–30; popularity of, 196n37

tutors. See mentoring programs

"Tyler, Kelsey," 2, 33–41, 45, 183

unemployment rates, 192n20

unions, 45, 121

Unitarians, 146

utopian communities, 71, 74, 78, 101–5

virtue, 152–53, 205n11, 205n15; Aquinas on, 207n32

volunteering, 3, 59, 63–65; in Atlanta, 136–37, 154–73; as "drive-by do-gooding," 147; for home care, 136, 165–66; in hospitals, 150; international opportunities for, 151, 161, 170; in Silicon Valley, 136–37, 144–54. See also civic organizations

voting patterns: in 2012 election, 126; in 2016 election, 13–15, 129, 194n31, 196n36

wages, 6–11, 45, 188n1; African Americans', 13, 192n20; living, 21, 27–30, 41, 45, 70, 131, 180; women's, 189n4, 190n7. See also income inequality

Walzer, Michael, 214

Warren, Elizabeth, 69, 210n63

"Weaver, Del," 184

Weber, Max, 103, 107, 109, 200n9

Wesley, John, 86

Westminster Confession of Faith, 100, 205n9

Whitman, Walt, 113

"Williams, Greg," 160–63, 173

Wordsworth, William, 111

work ethic, 88, 108–9

World Economic Forum, 11

Zen Buddhism. See Buddhism

CPSIA information can be obtained
at www.ICGtesting.com
Printed in the USA
FSHW04n1327020418
46455FS